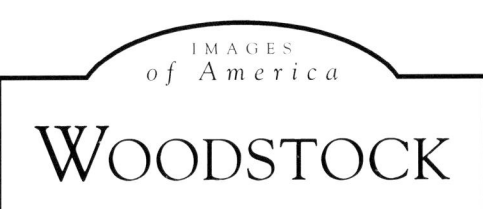

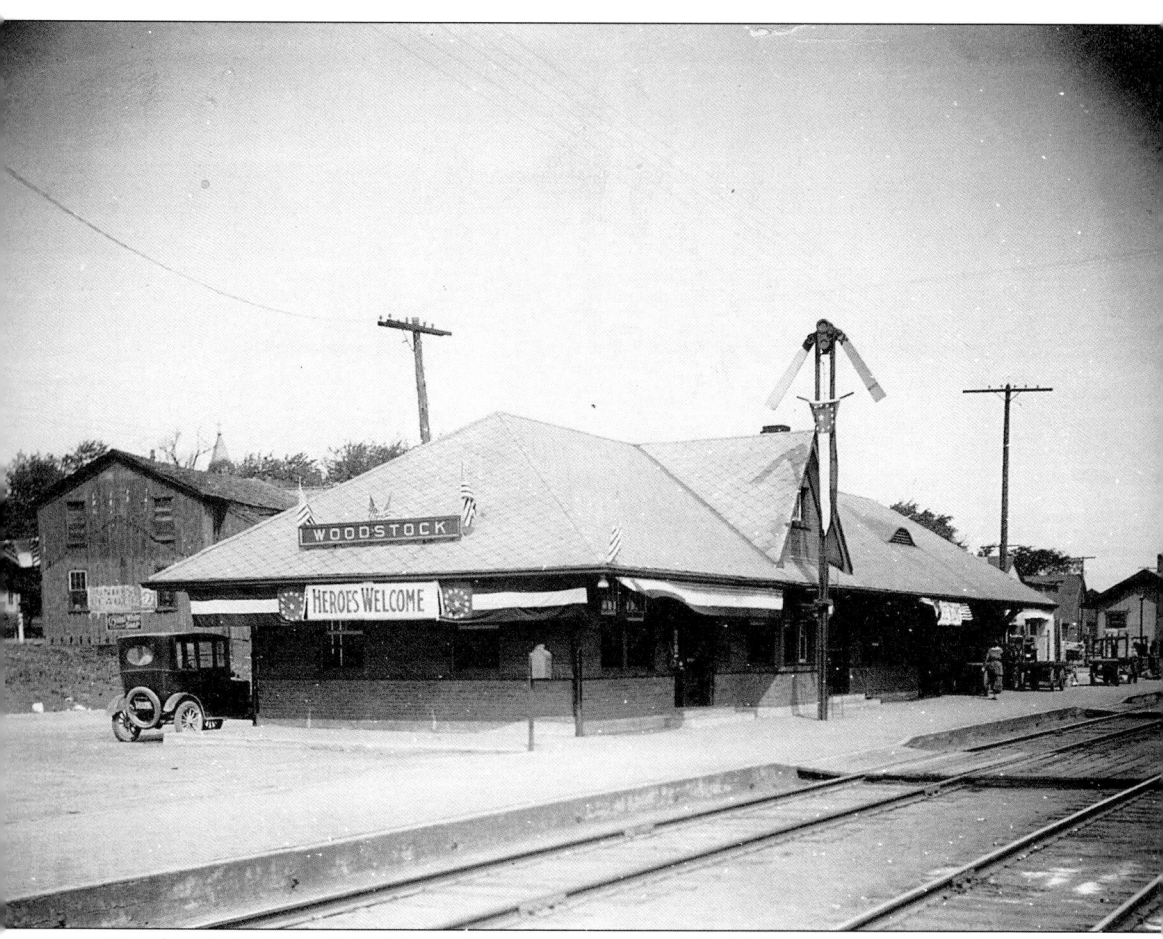

Woodstock invited all McHenry County veterans of World War I to a huge welcome home celebration in June 1919. The town was decked out in patriotic bunting. Guests arriving by train were greeted by these banners at the Chicago and Northwestern station, built in 1912.

On the cover: The ever-present patriotic spirit of the Oliver Typewriter Company is captured here. The image comes from a collection of photographs and documents chronicling the various industries that occupied the Oliver building for almost a century. The collection was donated to the McHenry County Historical Society when the last company to occupy the building, Woodstock Die Cast Corporation, closed the factory in 1990. (Courtesy of McHenry County Historical Society.)

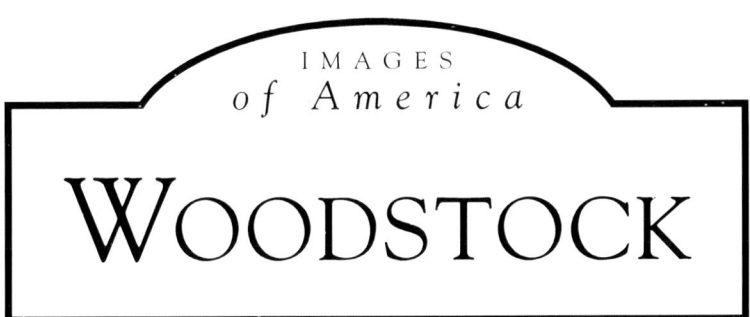

IMAGES of America

WOODSTOCK

Nancy L. Baker

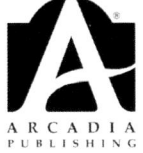

Copyright © 2006 by Nancy L. Baker
ISBN 978-0-7385-4080-1

Published by Arcadia Publishing
Charleston, South Carolina

Printed in the United States of America

Library of Congress Catalog Card Number: 2006924326

For all general information contact Arcadia Publishing at:
Telephone 843-853-2070
Fax 843-853-0044
E-mail sales@arcadiapublishing.com
For customer service and orders:
Toll-Free 1-888-313-2665

Visit us on the Internet at www.arcadiapublishing.com

Contents

Acknowledgments 6

Introduction 7

1. Centerville 9
2. On and off the Square 15
3. Typewriter City: An Industrial Town 33
4. An Extraordinary School 53
5. Crime and Crime-fighters 61
6. Welcome Home 71
7. Be It Ever So Humble 79
8. Old-fashioned Fun 91
9. Some Signs of the Times 109
10. Caring for Young and Old 117

Acknowledgments

The McHenry County Historical Society staff and volunteers are an amazing group of people. The museum library is a tribute to their dedication. Working with staff members Nancy Fike, Grace Moline, and Nancy Irwin is not only educational, but fun. Museum volunteers are full of information on quite an interesting variety of local history topics. McHenry County residents should feel confident that their photographic history is well preserved.

Woodstock resident and photojournalist Don Peasley donated a significant photograph collection to the McHenry County Historical Society. Since 1947, he has chronicled thousands of events in Woodstock and McHenry County. Several photographs from the Peasley collection are reproduced in this book and many more would have been used if space permitted.

Since the day I first walked into the Woodstock Public Library to research local history (which was more years ago than I care to recall), library director Maggie Field Crane has pointed me in the right direction. In her unofficial role as Woodstock archivist and champion of local history, Maggie has compiled a very comprehensive photographic record of the town.

The chapter about the Woodstock Children's Home and the Old People's Rest Home would not have been possible without the help of Woodstock Christian Life Services marketing director LeeAnn Atwood, who graciously provided the photographs of these facilities.

One of the places everyone should visit in Woodstock is the Dick Tracy Museum, located in the 1857 McHenry County Courthouse. I appreciate the assistance museum director James Johnson gave me in securing the use of the Dick Tracy images and in providing introductions to Chester Gould's daughter Jean O'Connell and her daughter-in-law Cynthia O'Connell, who both shared information about the properties Chester Gould owned in Woodstock.

I have truly enjoyed discovering more about the unique history of my community. There are many intriguing people and places that I was unable to include in the book because of the lack of reproducible photographs, and I hope readers will be inspired to visit local museums and use the public library to learn more.

INTRODUCTION

Woodstock had a unique beginning. Unlike most towns of the 1840s, Woodstock, or Centerville as it was originally called, started as a plat recorded on the books of McHenry County and was selected as the new county seat. A few enterprising citizens laid out streets and built a courthouse; then people moved to Woodstock. Many of the early residents came from New England and had settled elsewhere in McHenry County. No doubt they felt at home with the New England town square design.

As the county seat, Woodstock was home to many judges, attorneys, and other politicians. These citizens were active not only in county affairs but also in city government. They owned businesses in town, belonged to fraternal organizations and churches, and raised children who attended Woodstock schools.

Woodstock citizens have always been a patriotic lot, and they welcomed people from neighboring towns to join them for parades, festivals, and fairs. Residents have been quick to answer the call to duty to serve in the military and quick to celebrate their safe return.

Woodstock has suffered far more than its fair share of fires, and blazes have claimed many buildings. The new buildings that were constructed afterward were almost always far more substantial than those that preceded them. One of the fires occurred on the same day as the great Chicago fire, and although most of the town was spared, the west portion of the south side of the square, where the Woodstock Opera House now stands, was destroyed.

In the 1890s, Woodstock business leaders formed a public improvement committee to raise funds and bring industry to town. Its success led to the location of the Oliver Typewriter Company, just north of the square. Oliver, and the companies that succeeded it, employed hundreds of Woodstock residents, as well as residents from surrounding towns. The firm created a boom in the housing industry and influenced the decision of other industries to locate in the area as well.

The extraordinary Todd School for Boys provided a unique education for those lucky enough to attend. The range of educational experiences and activities was virtually limitless. Just a bit up the road was the Woodstock Children's Home, which offered a kind and caring environment, but certainly with none of the luxury experienced by the Todd School students.

Famous and infamous people have left their mark on Woodstock. Actors, artists, politicians, mobsters, social reformers, journalists, and scientists have mixed the citizenry and collectively made Woodstock a unique and interesting place.

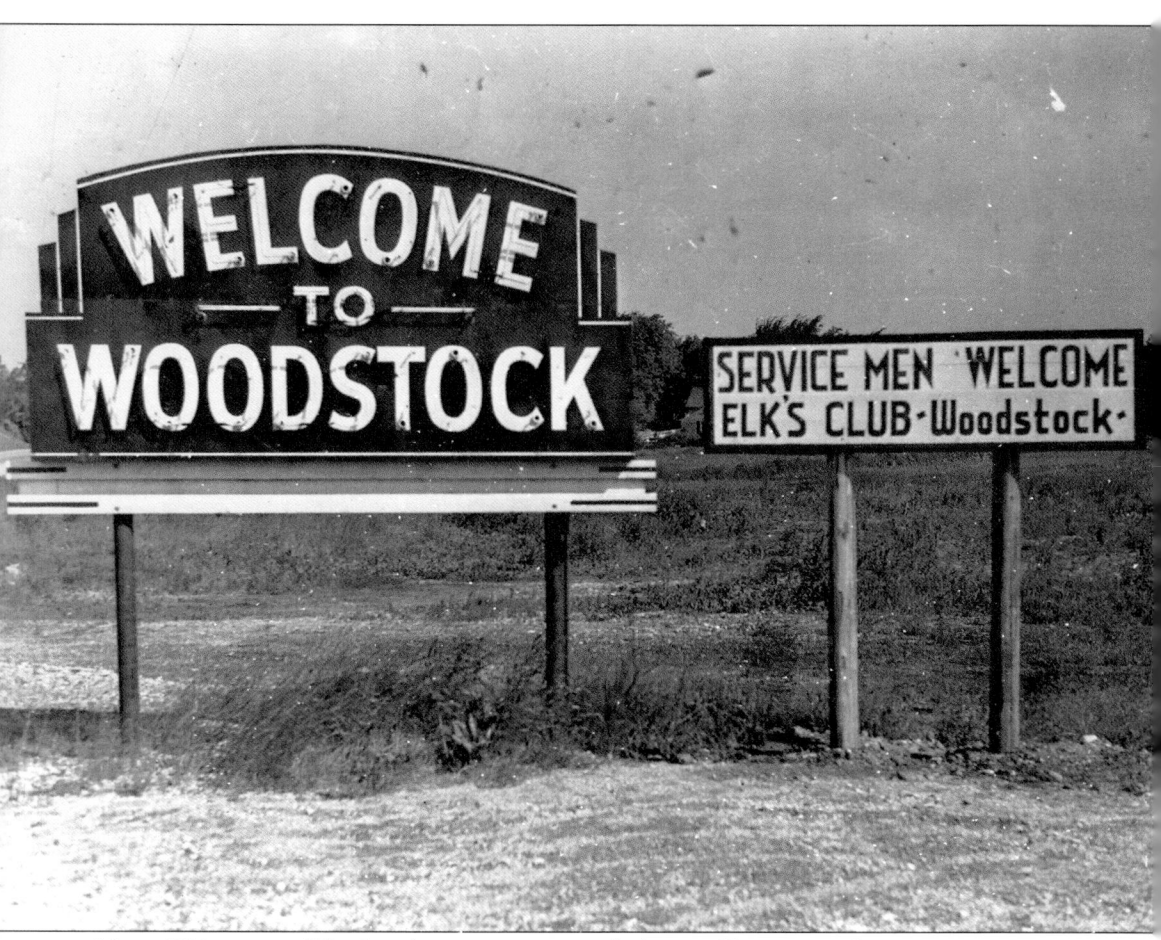

Neon Welcome to Woodstock signs were installed in 1955 as part of a campaign to entice Carthage College to select the town as the site of its new campus. Though Carthage ultimately selected another location, the neon signs continued to greet visitors both day and night.

One

CENTERVILLE

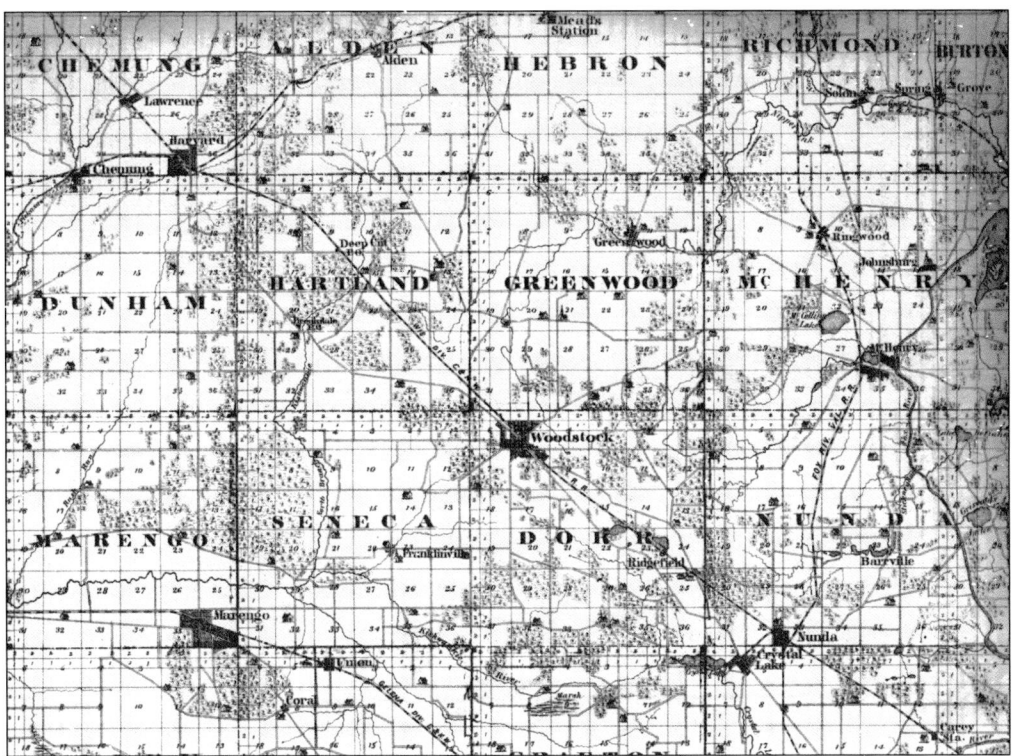

In 1844, a special election was held to select a new county seat. A site was chosen in the geographic center of McHenry County. Alvin Judd prepared a plat, which created a two-acre public square with streets surrounding it, and the new town was labeled Centerville. A plain, two-story frame building 33 by 40 feet in size was constructed for a courthouse. The sheriff's office, living quarters, and jail were on the first floor, while the courtroom occupied the second floor. This room was used for everything from political meetings to religious services to school classes. Early the following the year, the new community felt that the name Centerville should be changed, and settler Joel Johnson was given the distinction of selecting a new name. Johnson chose Woodstock, the name of his old home in Vermont. In 1852, the state legislature passed a bill allowing the incorporation of Woodstock as a village.

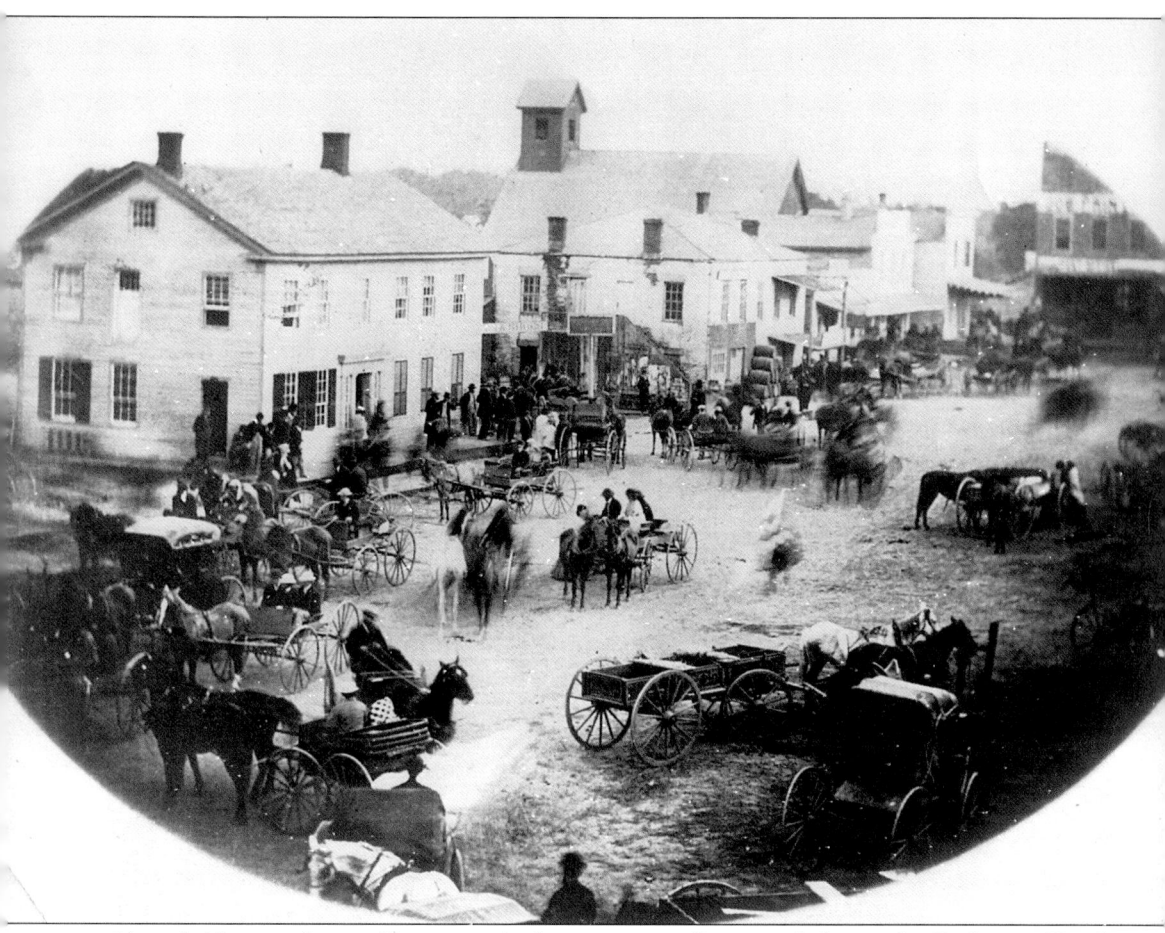

Alvin Judd erected a small tavern, which was eventually expanded into the Exchange Hotel, shown on the left. To its right is the building known as the Rat Hole. The first church in Woodstock was erected by the Presbyterians in 1847. It was later dismantled and moved to Greenwood Township. More and more people were drawn to the growing settlement. A newspaper was established, additional churches were built, and in 1851, the first three-story brick building was constructed by Neill Donnelly on the west side of the square. (Courtesy of Woodstock Public Library.)

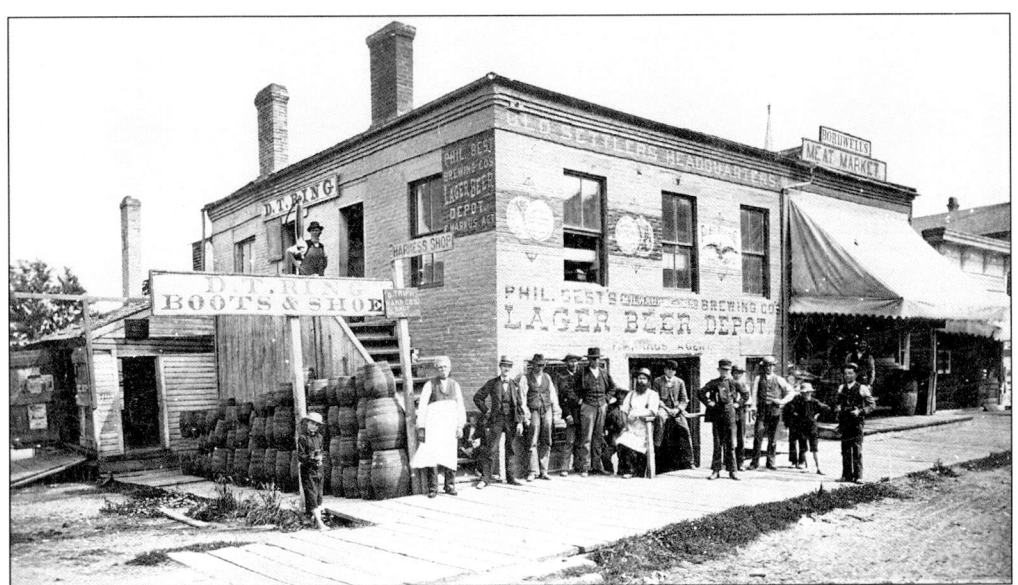

The Rat Hole was constructed in 1846 to provide room for county offices and records. It was a two-story brick building with thick walls and a tin roof. The story goes that in the winter of 1847, a strong wind lifted the roof off of the building. County officers were frightened and rushed out. Merchant Henry Petrie greeted them with laughter and exclaimed, "See the damned rats crawl out of their hole." When the new courthouse was constructed, the Rat Hole was sold to lawyer Lindsey Joslyn. This photograph was taken in the 1880s, just a few years before the building was destroyed by fire. (Courtesy of McHenry County Historical Society.)

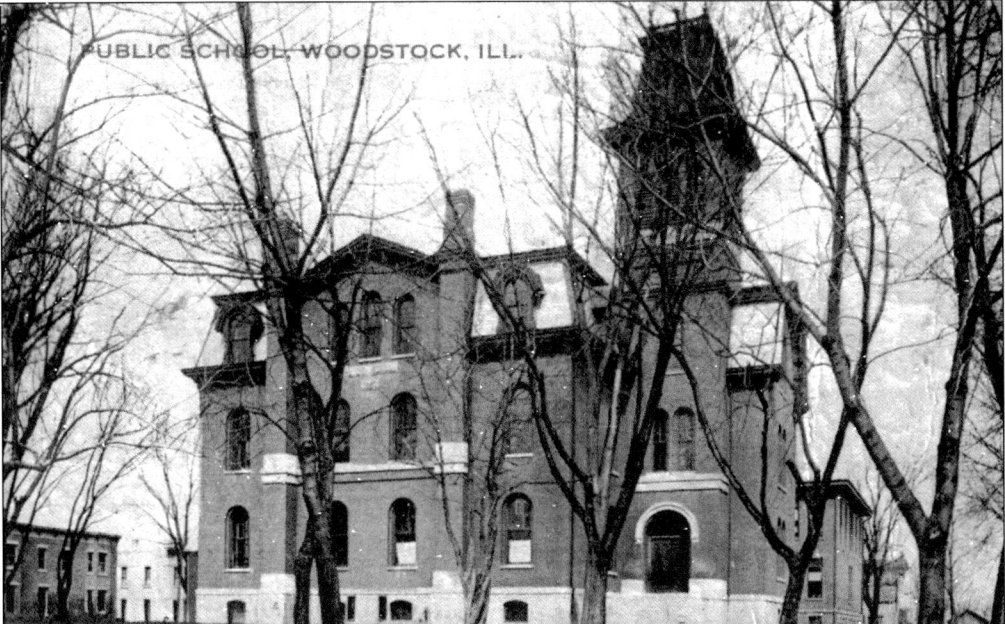

The first school was built on this lot in 1847, and in 1867, the school in the foreground replaced it. Facing South Street, the school had two entrances and two outhouses—one for girls and one for boys. In 1906, Central School was constructed on the north side. The 1867 school burned in 1919, but Central School, now city hall, survived.

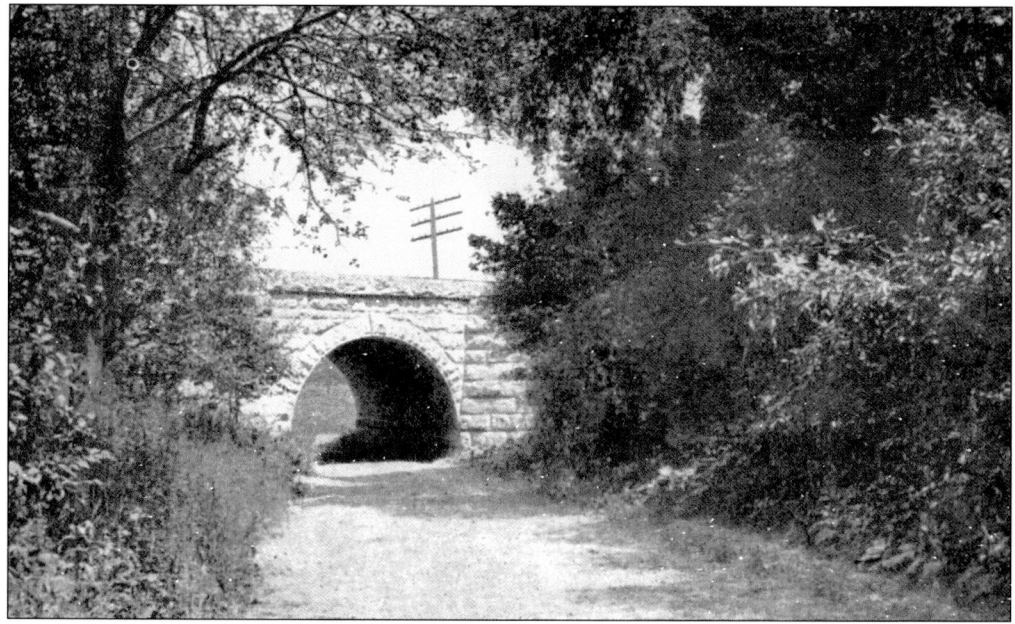

In 1855, the Chicago, St. Paul, and Fon du Lac Railroad reached Woodstock. The Chicago and Northwestern Railroad then acquired the line and extended it through Wisconsin. The South Street arch, shown here, was constructed for a single track in 1869 and was widened to accommodate a second track in 1897. The structure demonstrates a very unusual form of construction known as a helicoidal or spiral arch. Few examples of this technique are known to exist in this country.

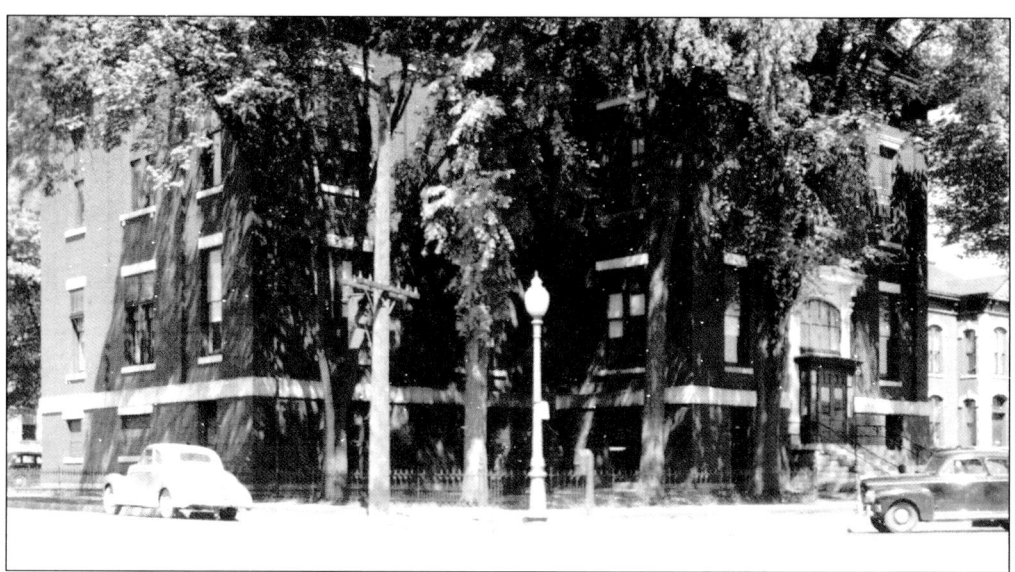

In 1855, county commissioners began planning a new courthouse. John Mills Van Osdel, "Chicago's first architect," was selected to design the building. Woodstock citizens purchased the ground owned by Mary McMahon and occupied by Hills Tavern. In exchange, the county donated the park in the square to the village of Woodstock. The sheriff's house and jail were constructed next door in 1887.

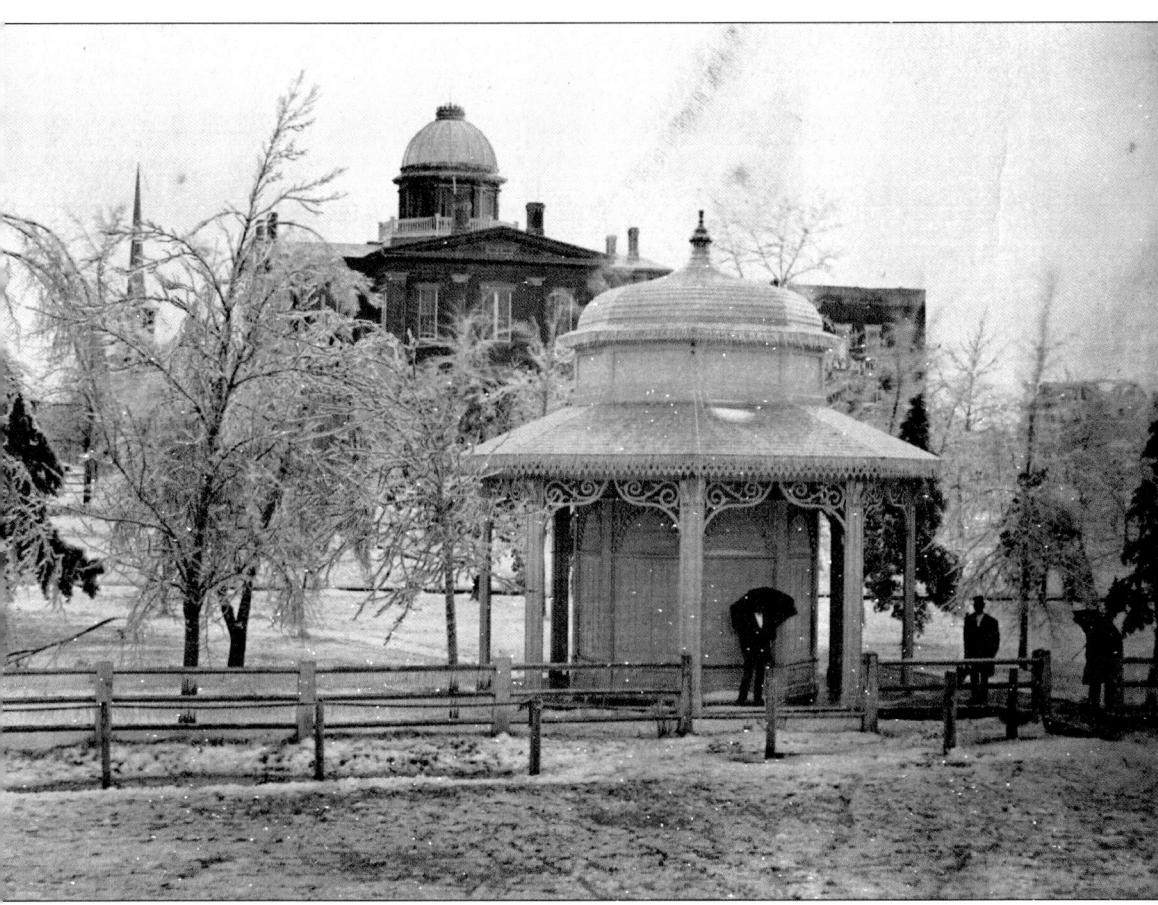

The park in the square remained bare and unplanted for several years. In 1858, a contract was reportedly let to grade and fence the park. In 1859, contractors indeed graded the public square and rounded the corners, while also spreading manure, seeding, and planting trees. Wood sidewalks were not replaced by concrete until 1905. The original springhouse was constructed in the 1870s over the site of a natural spring believed to have health benefits; however, a 19th-century chemical analysis determined that the water held no unique healing properties. The structure that stands today is a replica of the original. (Courtesy of McHenry County Historical Society.)

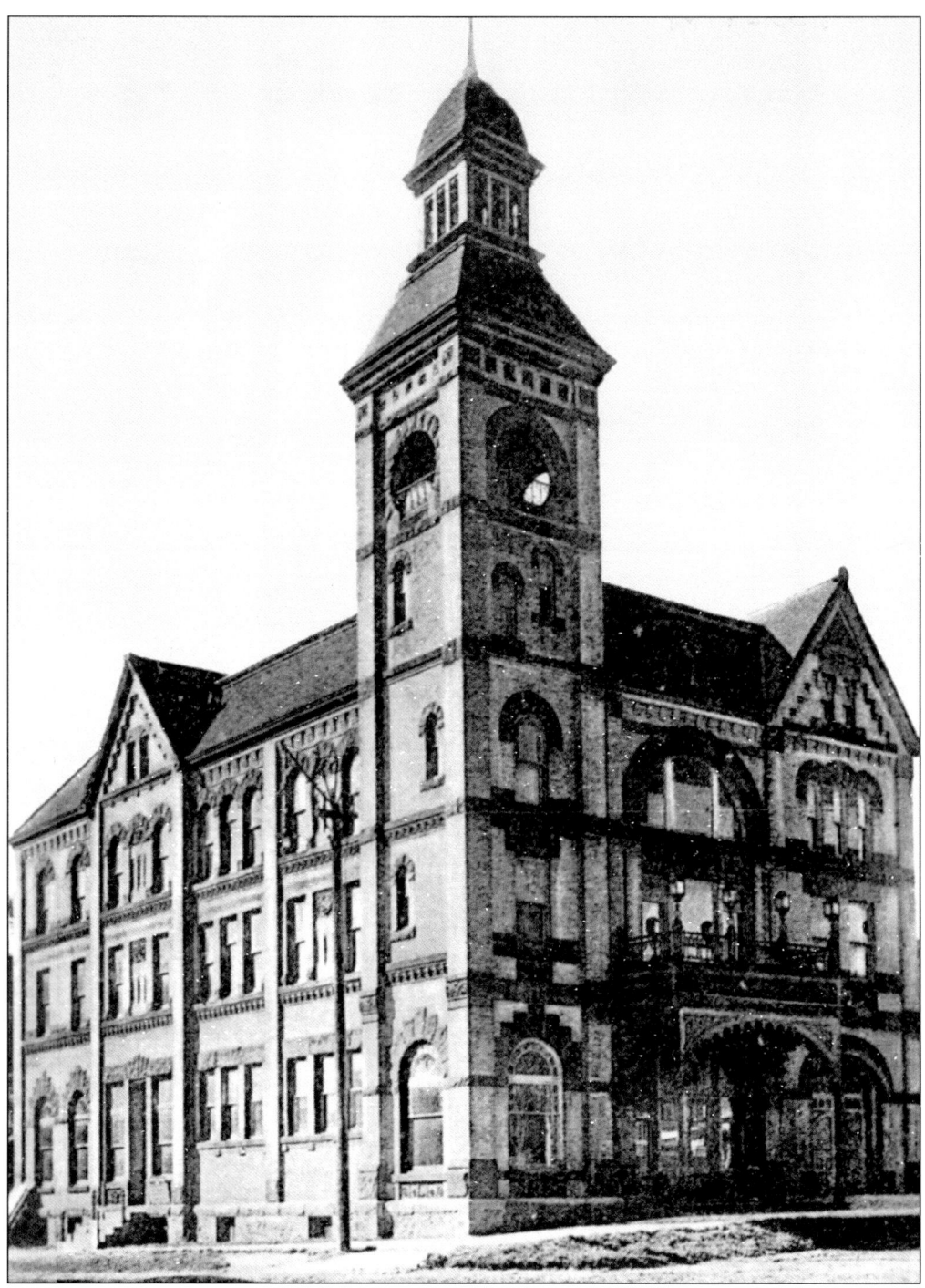

In 1873, citizens voted to incorporate as a city, although 17 more years passed before Woodstock had a city hall. The vacant site of the old Bunker Store was selected, and in 1889, the city hall was erected. Dedicated on September 2, 1890, it housed city offices, the public library, and the fire department for many years. The second-floor Woodstock Opera House brought many visitors.

Two
ON AND OFF THE SQUARE

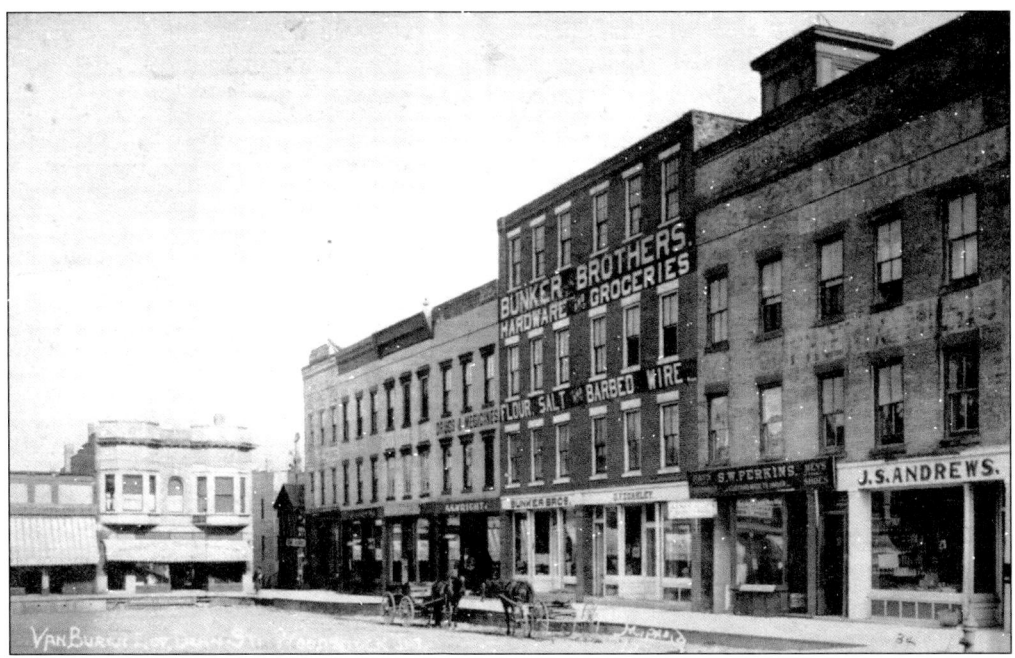

The name Phoenix Block referred to several buildings erected in a very similar style on the south side of the square, east of Dean Street, in the early 1850s. The building farthest to the right was constructed first. Among its tenants were the Park House Hotel on the second floor and Phoenix Hall on the third floor. Phoenix Hall served the young city as the meeting hall, concert hall, dance hall, and even roller-skating rink. John Kellogg purchased the corner building and, in 1903, added a three-story section to the back. In 1904, he installed equipment for public baths in the basement of the new addition. Special times were set aside for ladies. (Courtesy of McHenry County Historical Society.)

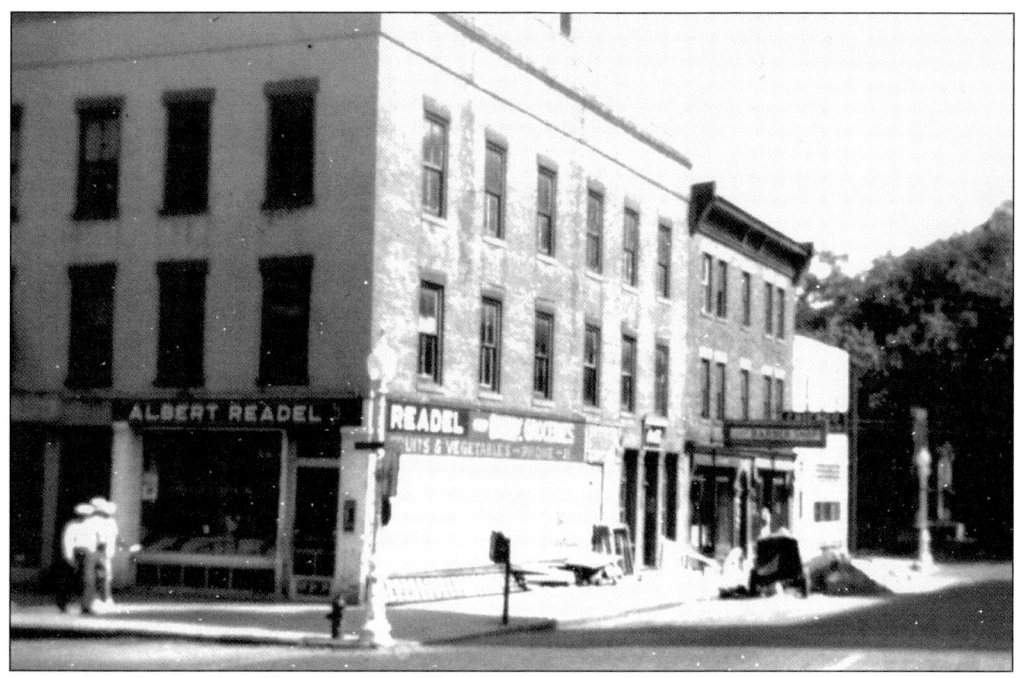

The original corner building was very deteriorated, possibly due to fire, when Chester Gould purchased it from John Kellogg's widow in 1940. (Courtesy of Jean O'Connell.)

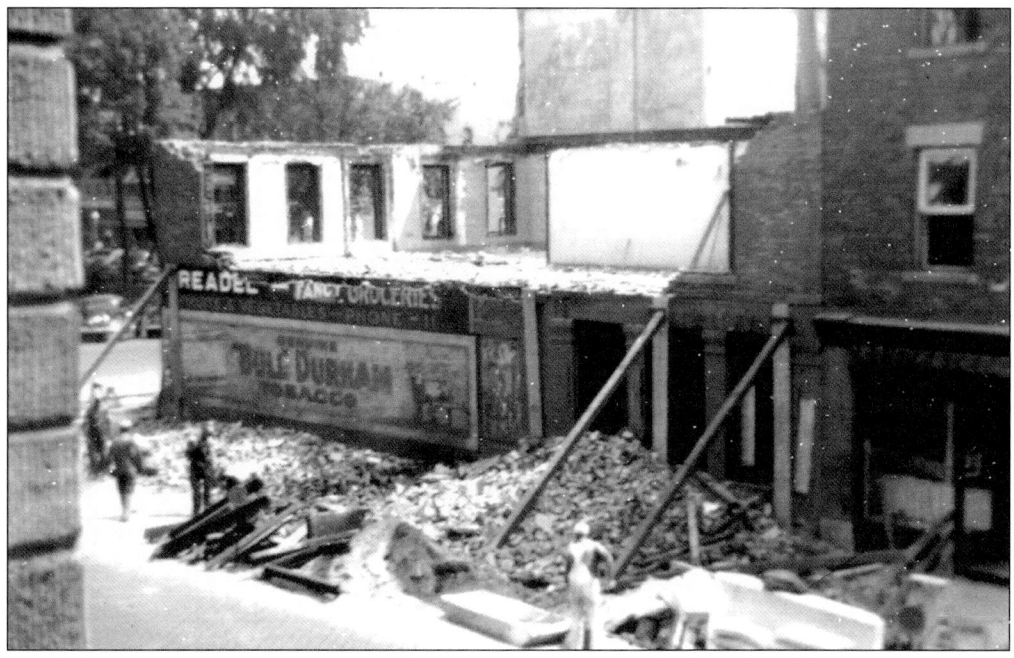

Gould hired contractors to demolish the entire structure in 1941 and build a new one on the site. Gould rented out second-story offices in the new two-story building. He retained a small office, which was also where his brother Ray lettered many *Dick Tracy* cartoons. (Courtesy of Jean O'Connell.)

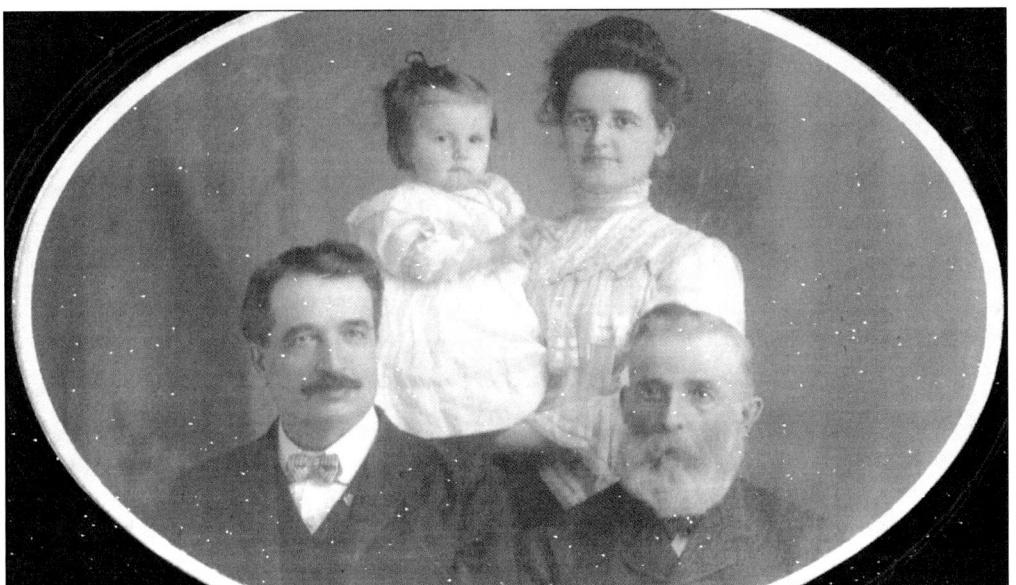

Henry Schneider, a barber for over 65 years, learned his trade at the age of 14 when he was an apprentice at the Pratt House. He was so small that a platform was built for him to stand on. In his shop was a set of shelves with 24 decorated shaving mugs, each bearing the name of its owner in large gold letters. By the time Schneider was 80, most of the mug owners had passed away. Henry is pictured in the lower left corner of this photograph showing four generations. (Courtesy of McHenry County Historical Society.)

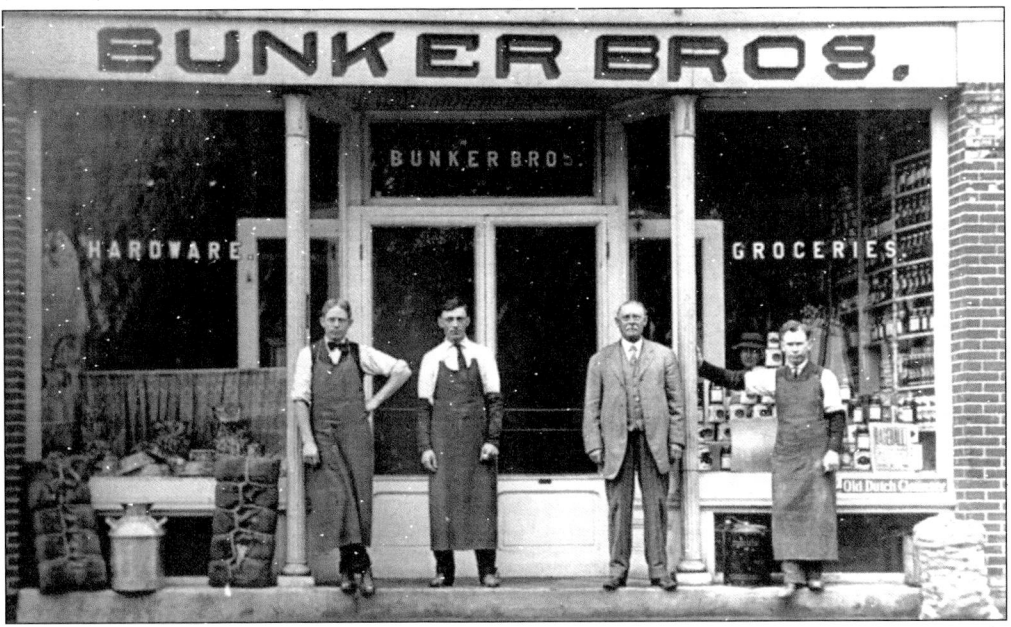

In 1871, Bunker Brothers bought the only four-story building in the Phoenix Block. Previously occupied by the Pratt House hotel, the structure was remodeled to accommodate the grocery, hardware, and crockery business. George K. and Amos K. Bunker operated the concern until sometime after 1912. The Bunkers were descendants of the family that owned the land on which the Battle of Bunker Hill was fought.

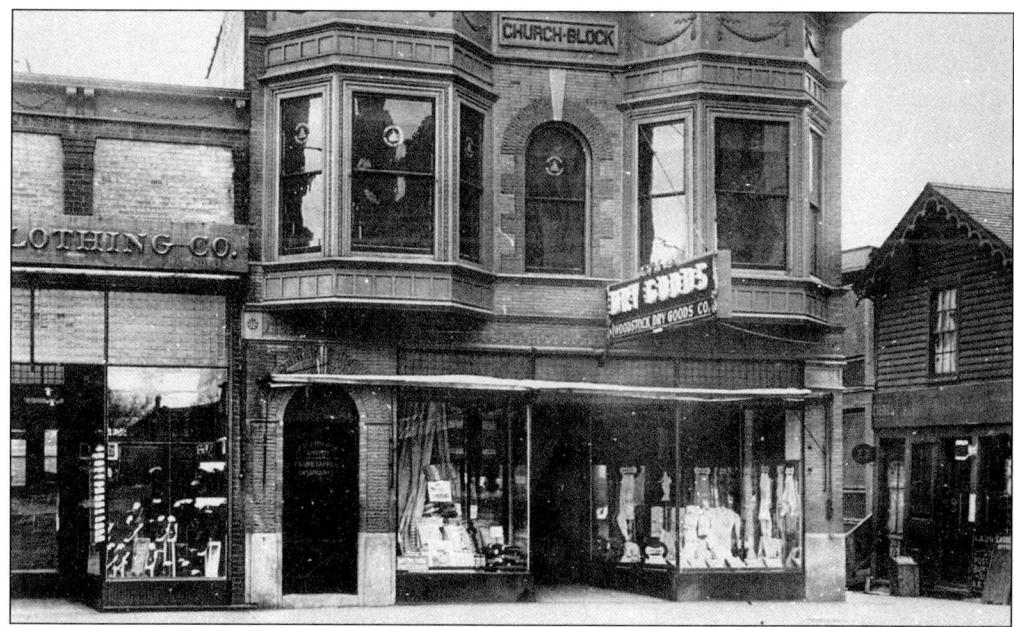

In 1893, a fire in Malachi "Mac" Church's livery stable destroyed all the structures between Van Buren and East Jackson Streets. In 1899, former county sheriff Church erected a new building, and although he died before he was able to occupy it, the stone bearing the name Church Block can still be seen there. For 76 years, the Woodstock Dry Goods store was located in this building. (Courtesy of McHenry County Historical Society.)

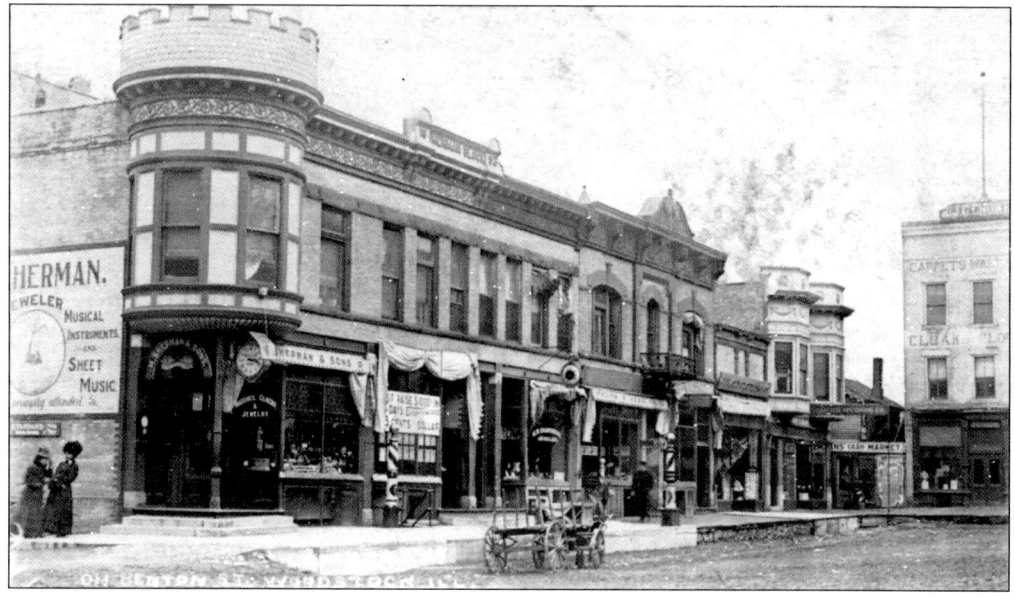

Marvin Sherman founded his jewelry business in Woodstock in 1866. Following the destruction of the old Rat Hole building by fire in 1893, Sherman bought the property and erected a new building with three storefronts. He kept the corner storefront for himself and leased the others. Sherman was an inventor and a collector of curios, which could also be found in his store. A clock projected over the sidewalk and continued to do so even after the State Bank of Woodstock purchased the property. (Courtesy of McHenry County Historical Society.)

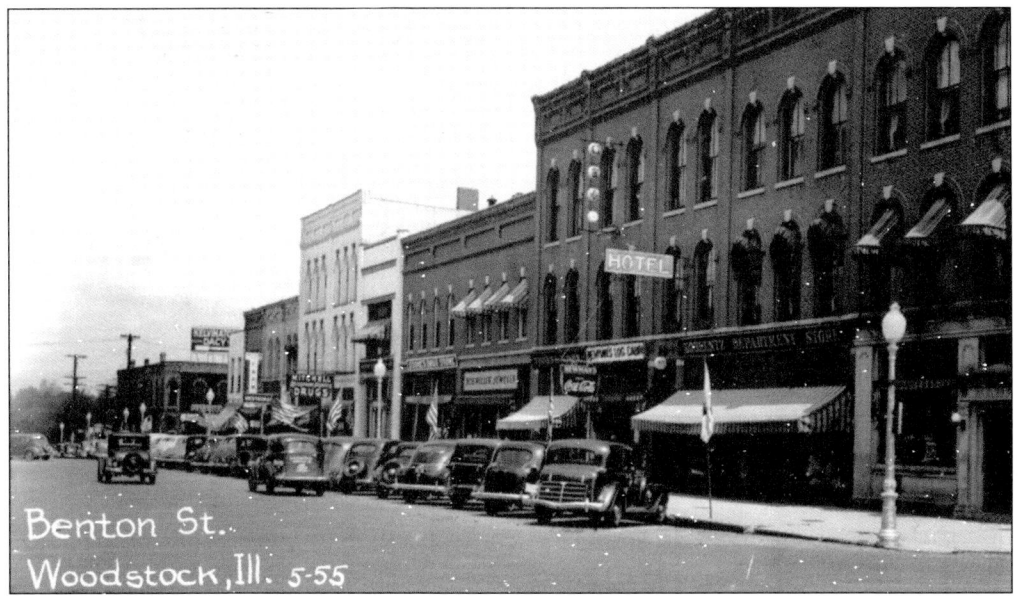

In 1872, fire consumed this entire block of Benton Street. The Murphy Block, on the right side of the photograph, was erected by John J. Murphy in 1875 on the site of the Exchange Hotel. Before it was even completed, the post office occupied a space on the first floor. The second floor was used as a hotel. The third floor was referred to variously as the National Hall, the Woodstock Opera House, and Murphy's Hall. Following the completion of city hall, which contained a new opera house, Murphy's Hall was best known as a dance hall.

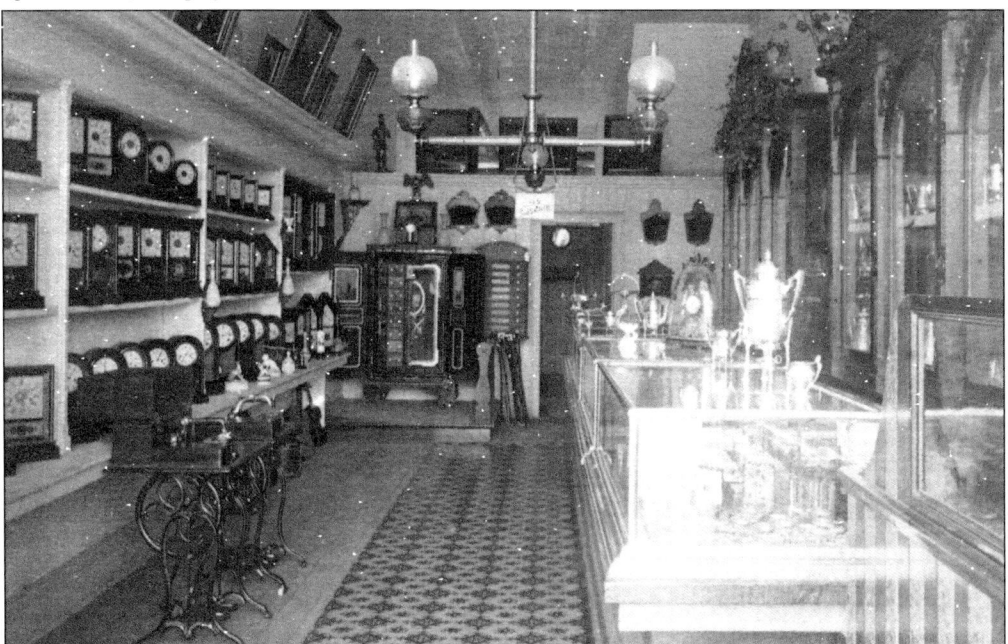

E. W. Blossom's jewelry store was an early tenant of the Phoenix Block on Van Buren Street. After construction of the Murphy Block on Benton Street, Blossom's moved to the space between the post office and Murphy's Dry Goods store. Blossom's was dubbed "the Opera House Jeweler." (Courtesy of McHenry County Historical Society.)

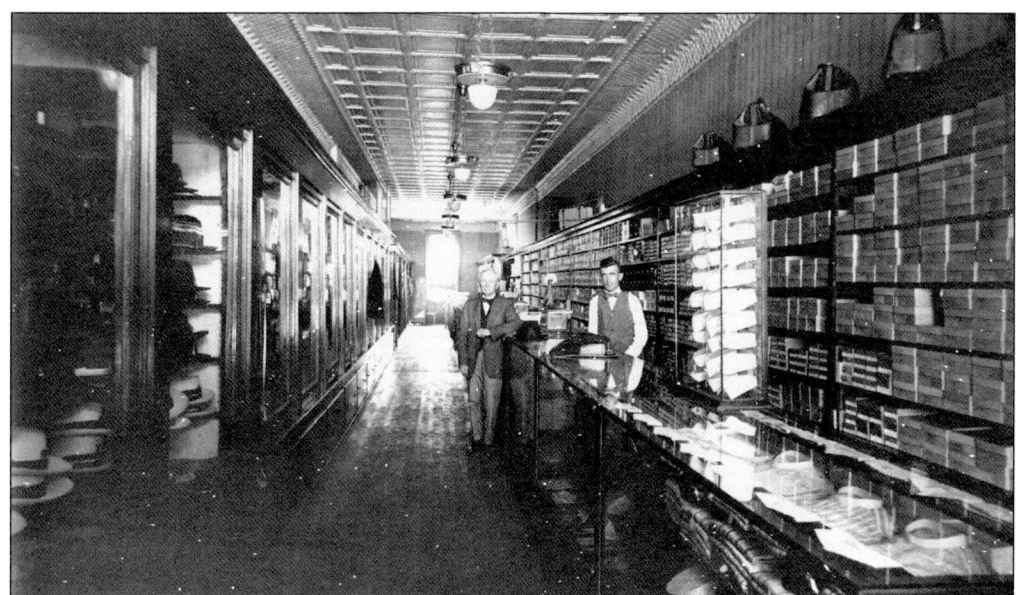

In 1886, Sam McNett and C. F. Thorne bought E. C. Jewett's boot and shoe business in the Murphy Block. Thorne bought out McNett's interest in 1888, thus marking the beginning of a menswear concern that spanned more than a century. Thorne's was considered the leading firm for men's furnishings and fashionable clothing. Thorne's son acquired an interest in the business in 1904. It was eventually purchased by Wienke and Beard. (Courtesy of McHenry County Historical Society.)

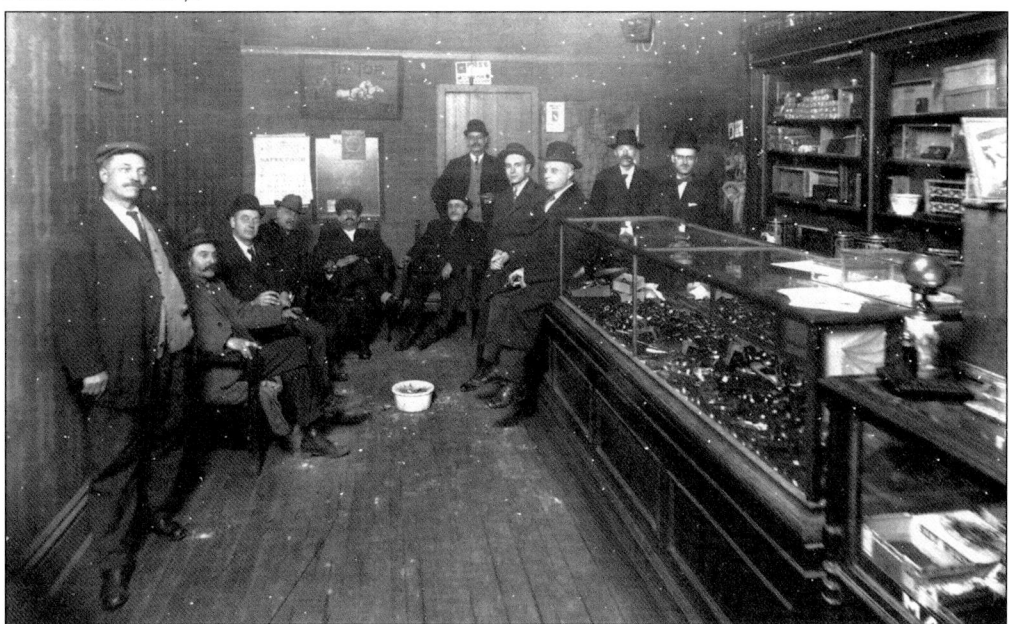

Thomas Jacobs spent 25 years in the cigar business before coming to Woodstock in 1899 to operate a cigar factory and tobacco store in the Murphy Block. He advertised that "tobacco is one of God's gifts to men when rightly used and when manufactured into high grade stock carries in its train none of the evil effects pessimists talk about." His motto was "smoke in this world, not in the next." (Courtesy of McHenry County Historical Society.)

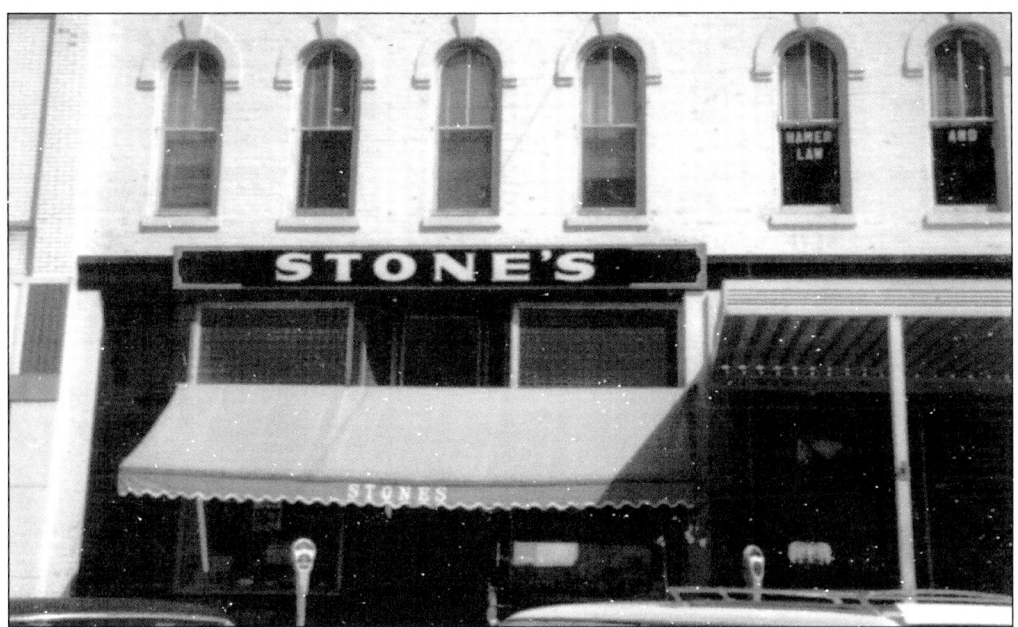

Dr. George F. Stone, in partnership with his son Edward, opened a drugstore in Woodstock in 1857. The original store was destroyed by the 1872 fire, but the two quickly rebuilt. Edward took over the business in 1887, following the death of his father. Like other drugstores of its time, Stone's sold drugs, patent medicines, books, stationery, school supplies, paints, and sundries. It remained a drugstore until 1966, when it became the Stone's on the Square Gift Shop.

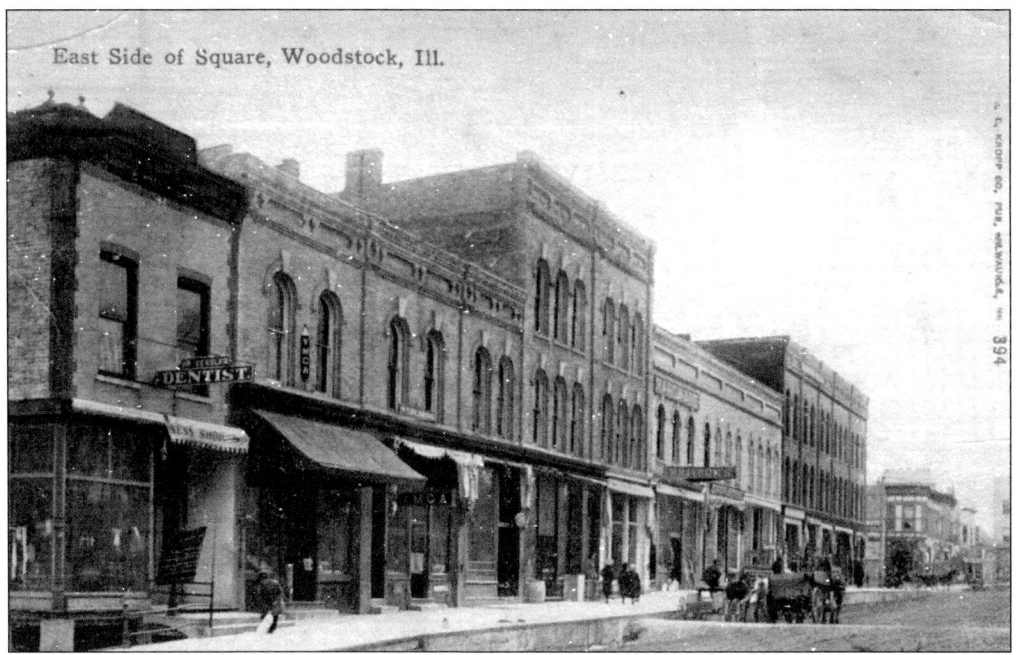

The three-story building in the center of this photograph was erected in 1873 by Merritt L. Joslyn. In 1886, Joslyn added a one-story section to the rear. The building consisted of two storefronts—one occupied by the Boston Store, then by Frank Bunker Dry Goods, and the other by a grocery store.

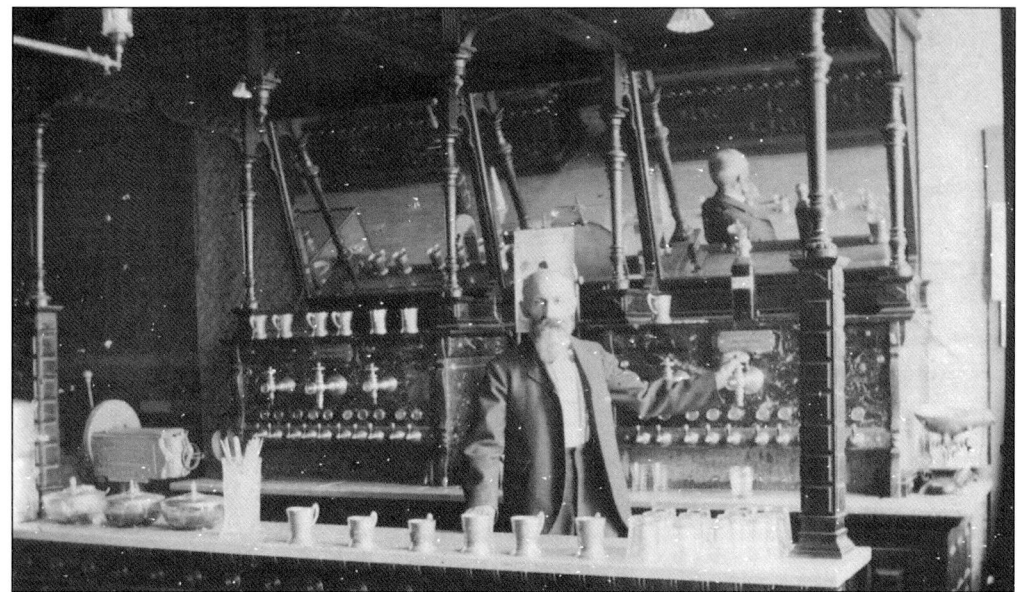

The Wittenburg and Bodenschatz Palace of Sweets was open for only a year, when it moved into the space vacated by Frank M. Bunker in the Joslyn Block. The store contained a soda fountain, candy counter, and seating area. The Palace of Sweets gave Woodstock its first regular taste of homemade ice cream, which was created in the building's basement. During the winter, it served all kinds of hot drinks and at all times carried a full line of cigars, tobacco, and confectioneries. (Courtesy of McHenry County Historical Society.)

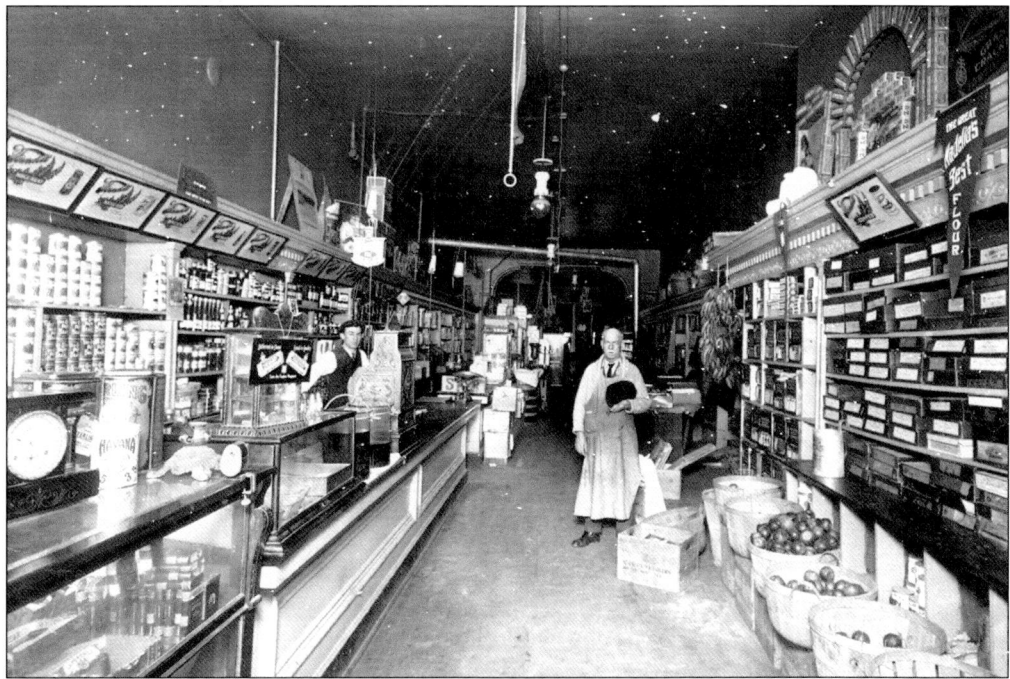

Kennedy Brothers Grocery sold groceries, crockery, glassware, shoes, and boots. Succeeding J. H. Higgins Grocery in December 1894, it was located in the other half of the Joslyn Block. (Courtesy of McHenry County Historical Society.)

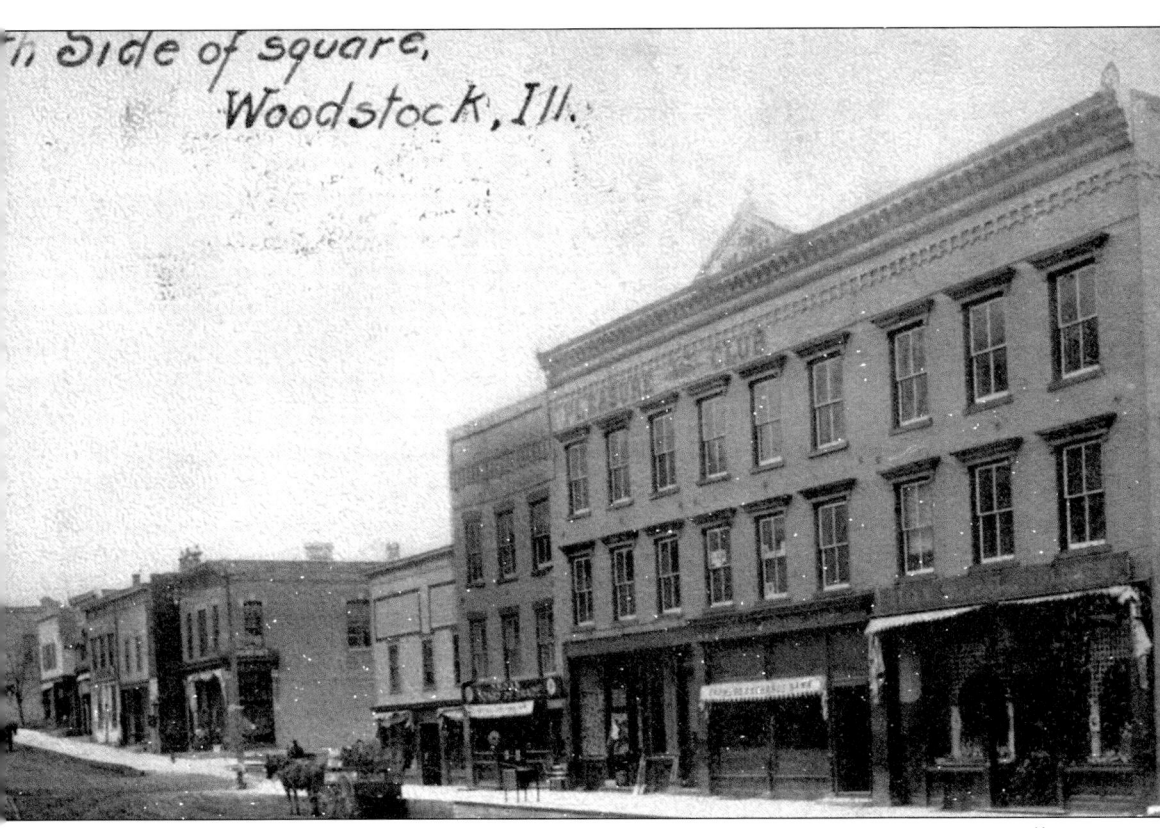

The four three-story buildings in this photograph, among the oldest in the square, were originally known as the Excelsior Block. The Woodstock Sentinel and the Medlar Photography Gallery occupied part of the third floor for many years. In the 1870s, Marmaduke Hoy acquired the three eastern blocks, and Luman T. Hoy ran the drugstore on the corner. Marmaduke owned the adjacent dry goods store and established a bank in the rear. The storefront to the west was a hardware store. The westernmost brick block contained a saloon called the Board of Trade and remained under different ownership. In 1886, workmen from Chicago raised the three Hoy structures four feet, to provide higher ceilings in the basement and on the first floor and to take care of the dampness problem in the basement. The first floors were lowered two feet. At the same time, a galvanized iron cornice with the inscription "Hoy Block 1886" was installed. (Courtesy of McHenry County Historical Society.)

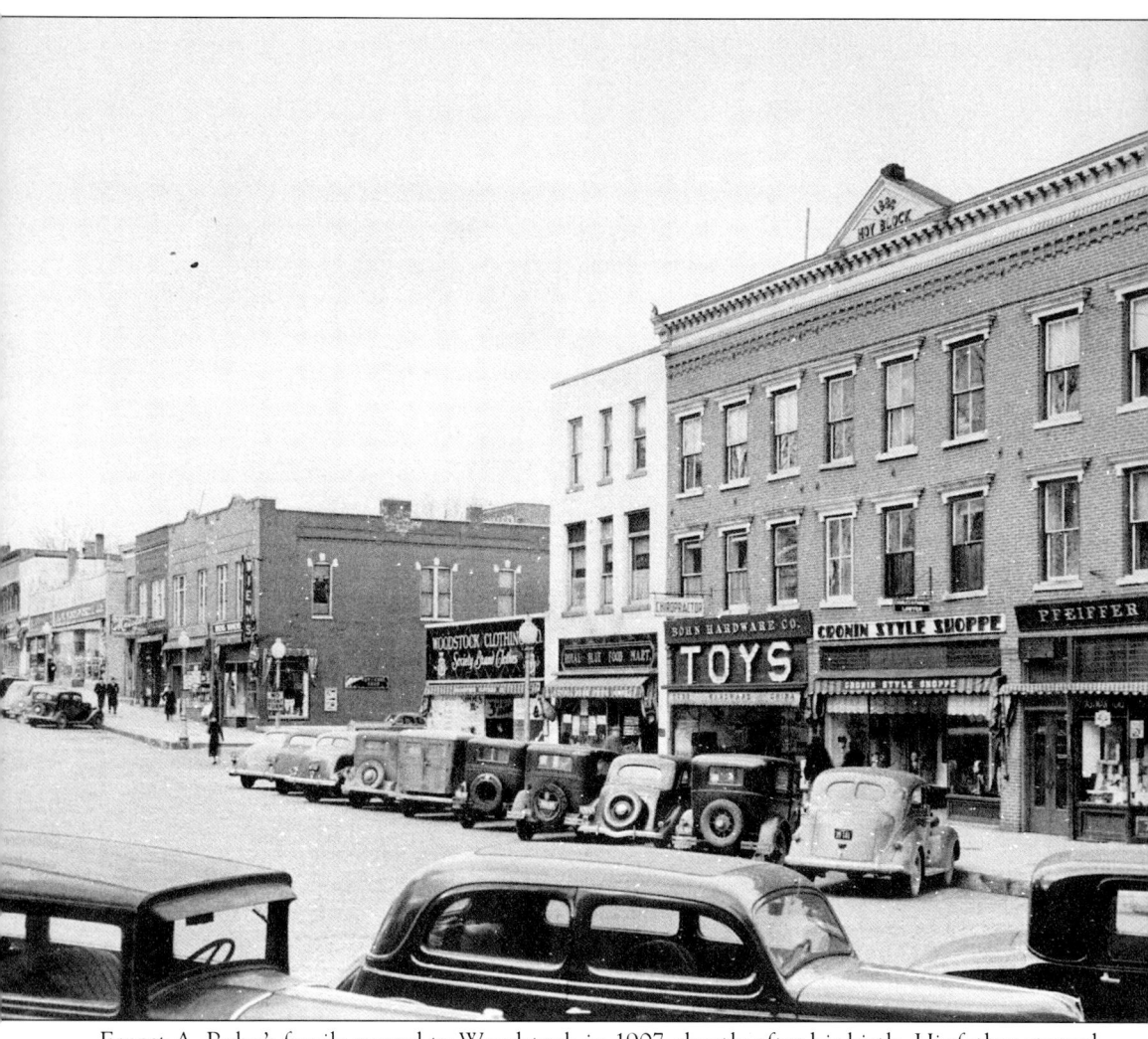

Ernest A. Bohn's family moved to Woodstock in 1907, shortly after his birth. His father started a Dean Street bakery business specializing in potato and cream bread. Ernest A. went to work in the A. O. Osborn Hardware Store in 1918 while still a student and graduated from Woodstock High School in 1925. In 1927, he moved to Madison, Wisconsin, and worked for a large hardware retailer. He returned to Woodstock in 1929, purchased the A. O. Osborn store on Cass Street, and opened his own hardware store in partnership with his sister Minnie. The store's Toys sign is visible near the center of this image. A second store, Bohn's Paint and Paper, opened on Van Buren Street in 1949. The Van Buren Street store underwent a major remodeling in 1951, and the two businesses were combined into three sales floors and a warehouse. (Courtesy of Woodstock Public Library.)

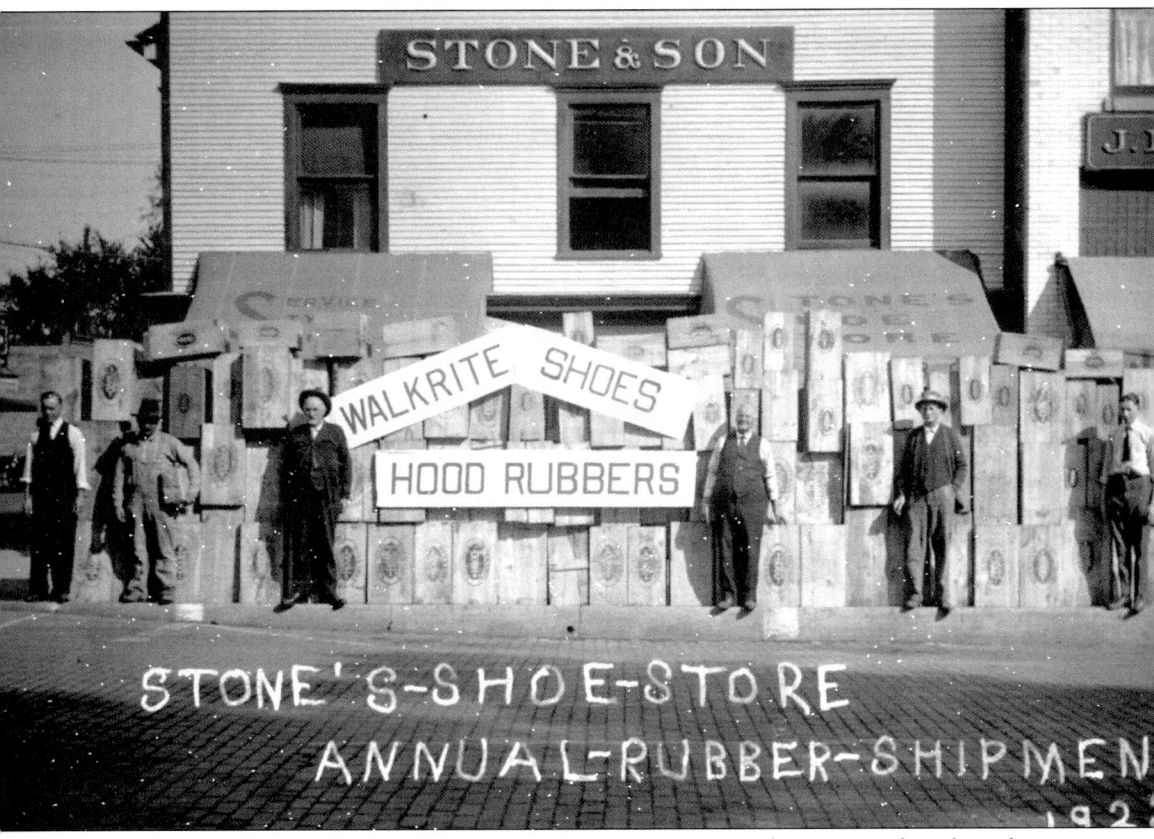

On January 28, 1936, fire destroyed the square's last remaining wood structure, thought to have been 80 to 90 years old at the time. It had been a shoe store for most of its history. Several other businesses in the building were also destroyed. The Bransby Photography Gallery, the fourth in line of photographers to occupy the second floor, was consumed along with the hundreds of negatives chronicling Woodstock's people, buildings, celebrations, and tragedies that had been taken by Bransby and previous occupants Mel Tripp, George Burbank, and M. Colton. At the time of the fire, the Stone and Son boot and shoe store had been in business for many years. Henry Stone, previously partnered with S. L. Hart, had purchased the business from W. H. Dwight, who had sold shoes and boots from the same location for 25 years. (Courtesy of McHenry County Historical Society.)

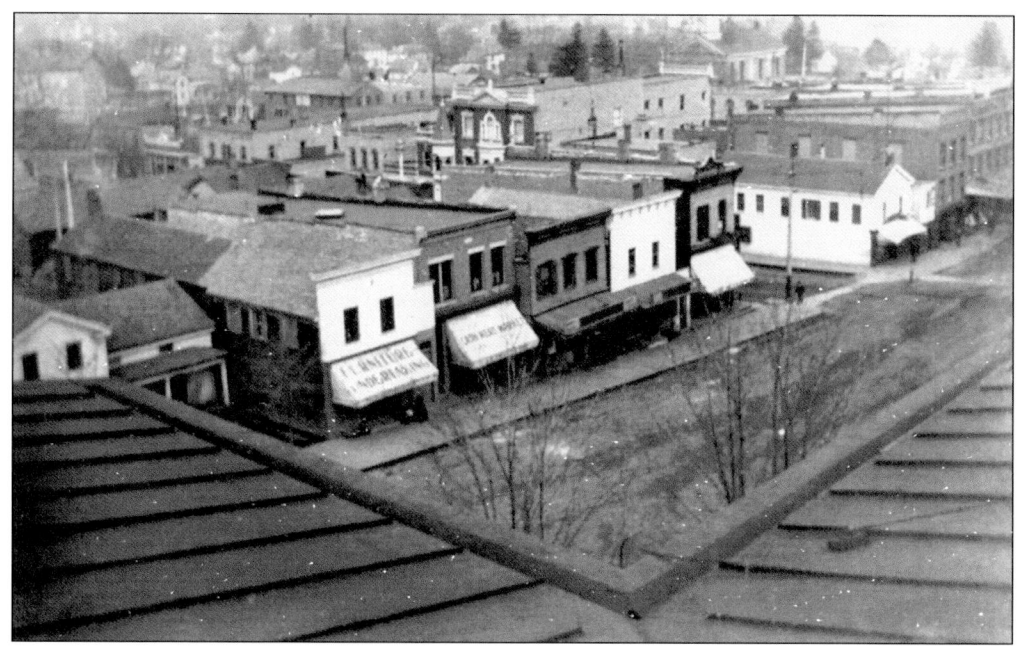

Cass Street still contained several wood frame structures in the early 1900s. The brick structure at the corner of Cass and Main Streets is the Kendall Block, erected in 1883. This image shows the newly constructed meat market in the middle of the block and the adjacent Rudolph Diesel undertaking and furniture business.

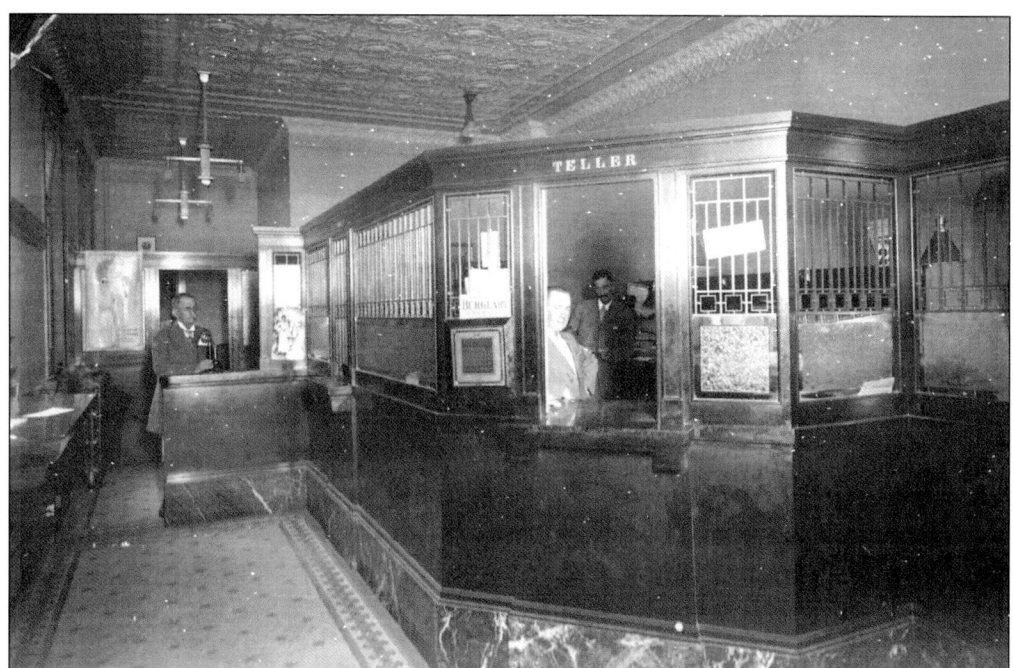

The State Bank of Woodstock, organized in 1889, occupied a two-story brick structure on Cass Street. Mayor E. C. Jewett served as cashier and E. E. Richards as bank president. The interior of the bank was considered very elaborate for its time. (Courtesy of McHenry County Historical Society.)

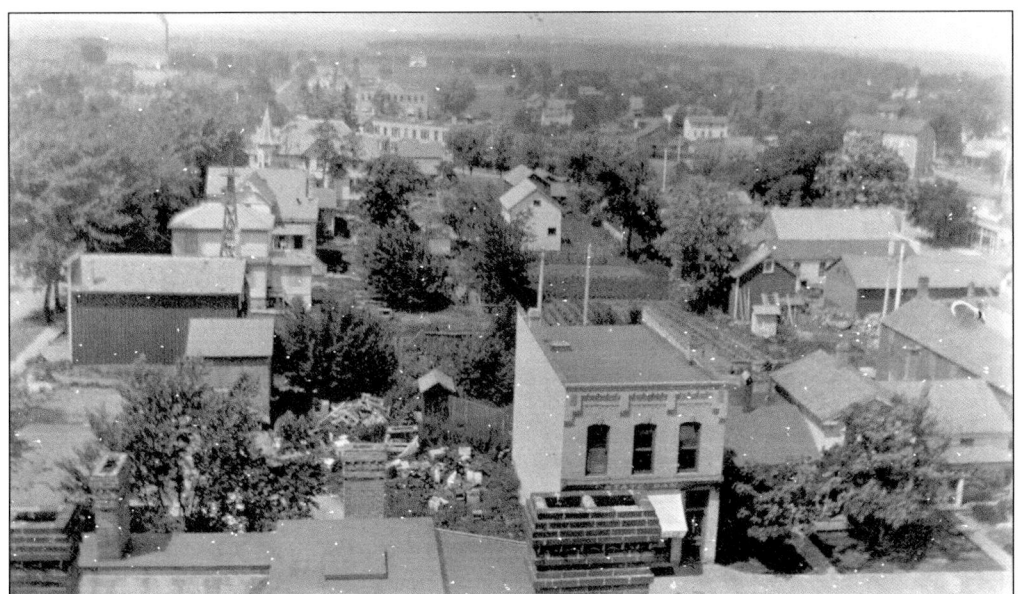

When the bank outgrew its Cass Street location in 1910, it moved to the Sherman building at the southeast corner of Benton and East Jackson Streets, and the Cass Street building became Moncur's Flower Shop. Moncur built a greenhouse behind the present-day movie theater on Main Street in 1912 and owned a truck farm outside of town. Among his customers were the Palmer House and the Cohen Company in Chicago, which received fresh vegetables. (Courtesy of McHenry County Historical Society.)

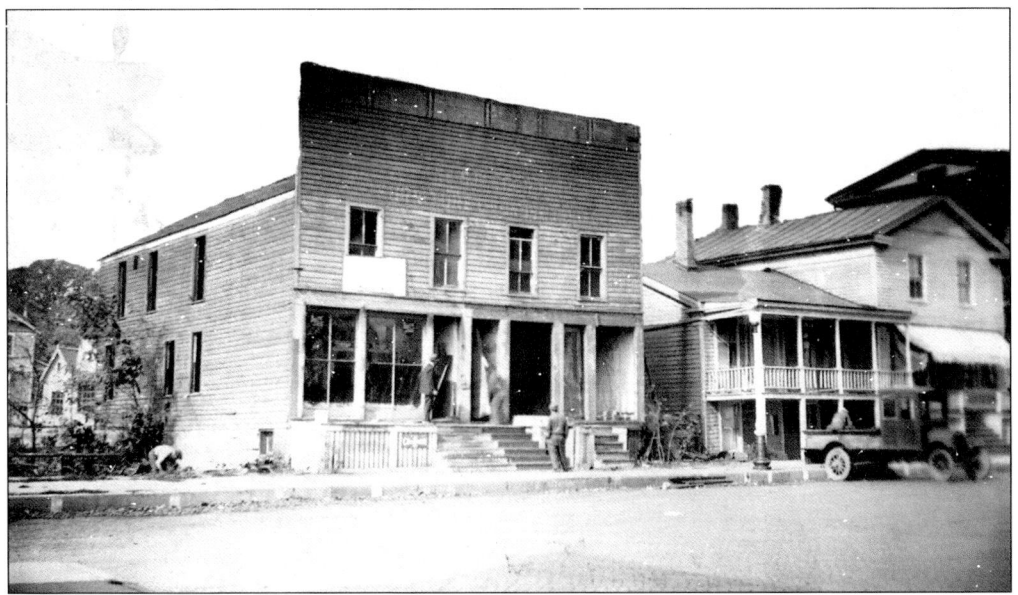

The structure on the right was the residence of John Donnelly, who had emigrated from Ireland in 1805. After marrying, he moved to property on the west side of the square. Donnelly died in 1884, but his daughters remained in the house where they were born. They lived in one half and ran a well-known millinery shop in the other. The building on the left was the Stafford Furniture and Undertaking establishment, which was demolished and replaced by a Montgomery Ward store in 1928. (Courtesy of Woodstock Public Library.)

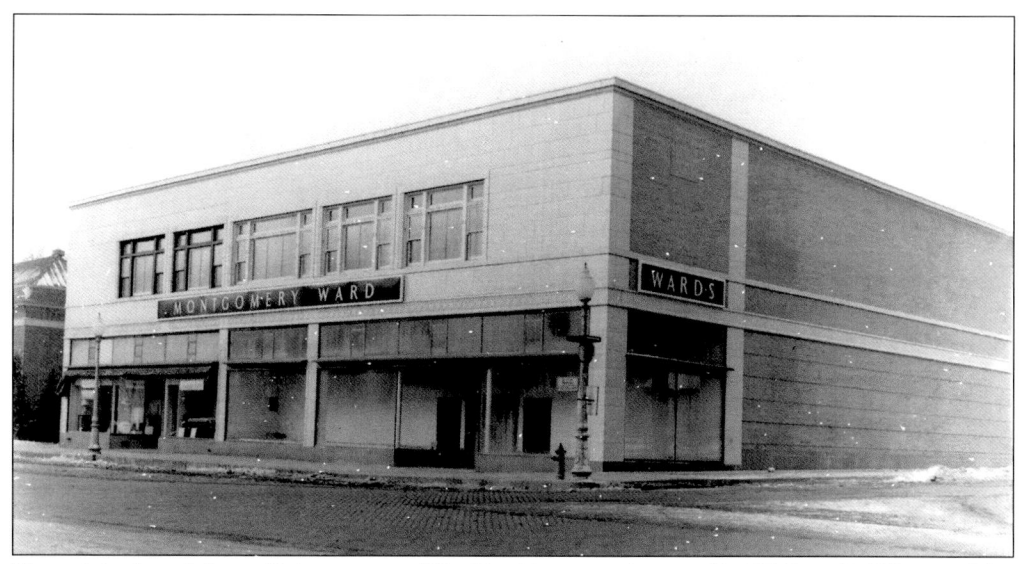

The original steel-framed Montgomery Ward building was designed by William P. Whitney. The terra-cotta walls came from the American Terra Cotta Company near Crystal Lake. An addition was constructed, and in 1934, the public was invited to visit the remodeled store. (Courtesy of McHenry County Historical Society.)

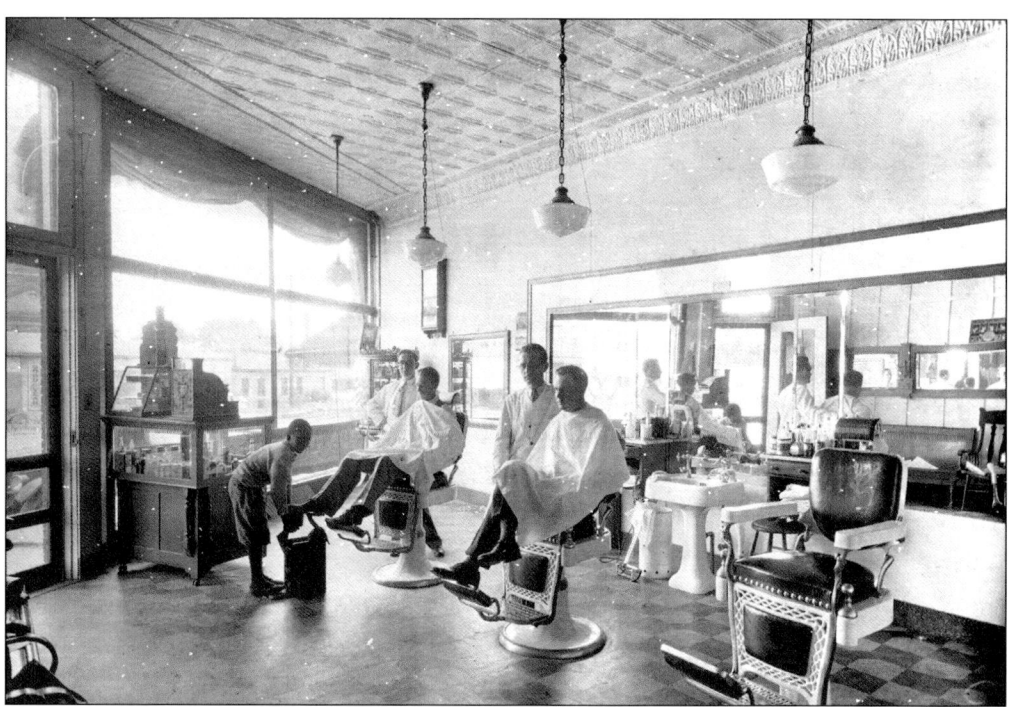

A veteran of both World Wars, Ray Heniken started a three-chair barbershop at the north end of Benton Street in the early 1920s. His son Edward later took over the business, and Ray went to work for Dan Quinlan at the Quinlan Land Office, selling real estate. During his 45 years in Woodstock, Ray was a barber, realtor, insurance agent, justice of the peace, and mayor.

Frank M. Bunker ran a grocery, crockery, and fruit business for 29 years, beginning in 1874. The business relocated from Benton Street to Main Street in 1898, to a building that had been damaged but not destroyed by the 1892 fire that had consumed all of the wood frame buildings on the east side of the street. A lunch counter was also part of the Main Street store. Upon Bunker's retirement in 1915, Alvin Heywood, who had first worked for him in 1898, bought the business and completely overhauled the building.

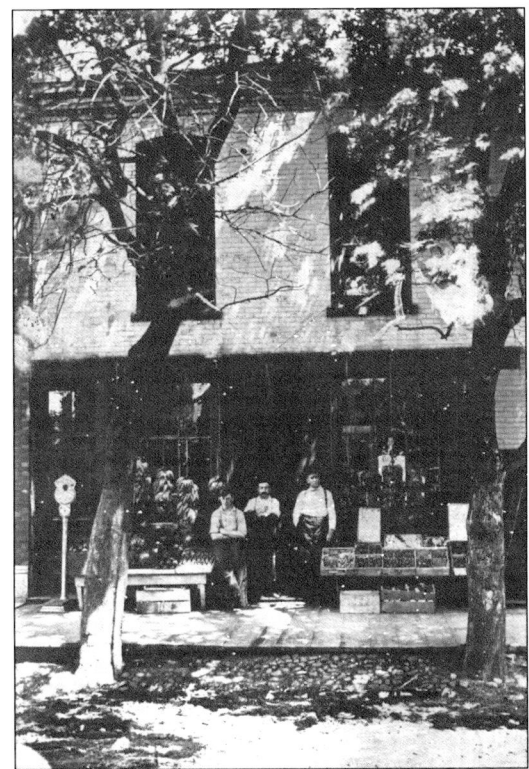

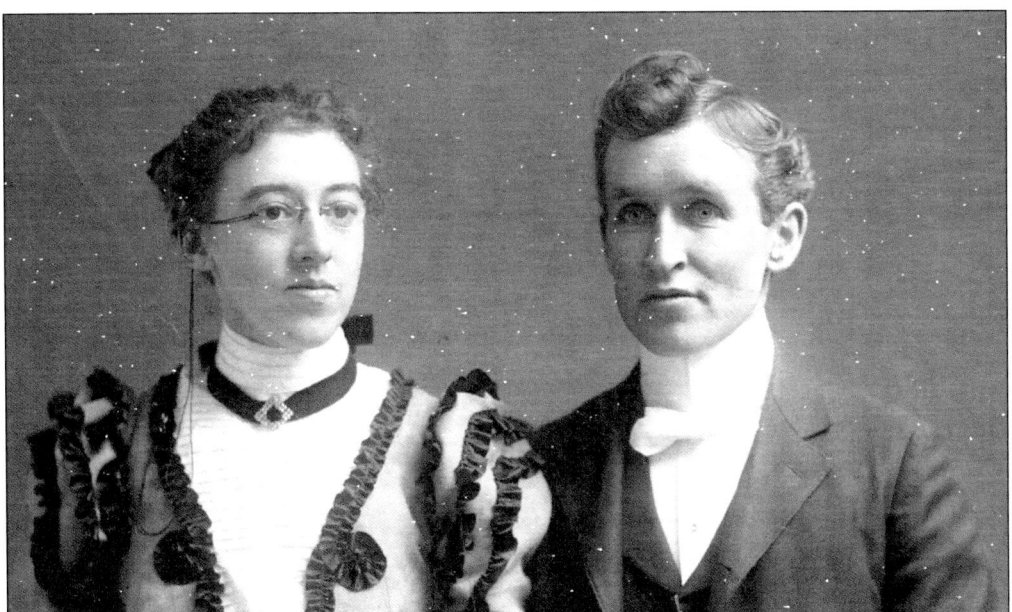

Alvin Heywood, born in Wisconsin in 1868, moved to McHenry County and worked for several years in businesses at Greenwood and Ringwood. Before being employed by Frank M. Bunker, he worked as a deputy sheriff and turnkey at the county jail. He left Bunker's employ to work at the Oliver Typewriter factory and at another grocery store but then returned to the Bunker establishment. Heywood married Lois Gertrude Sanford in 1898, and they had two children.

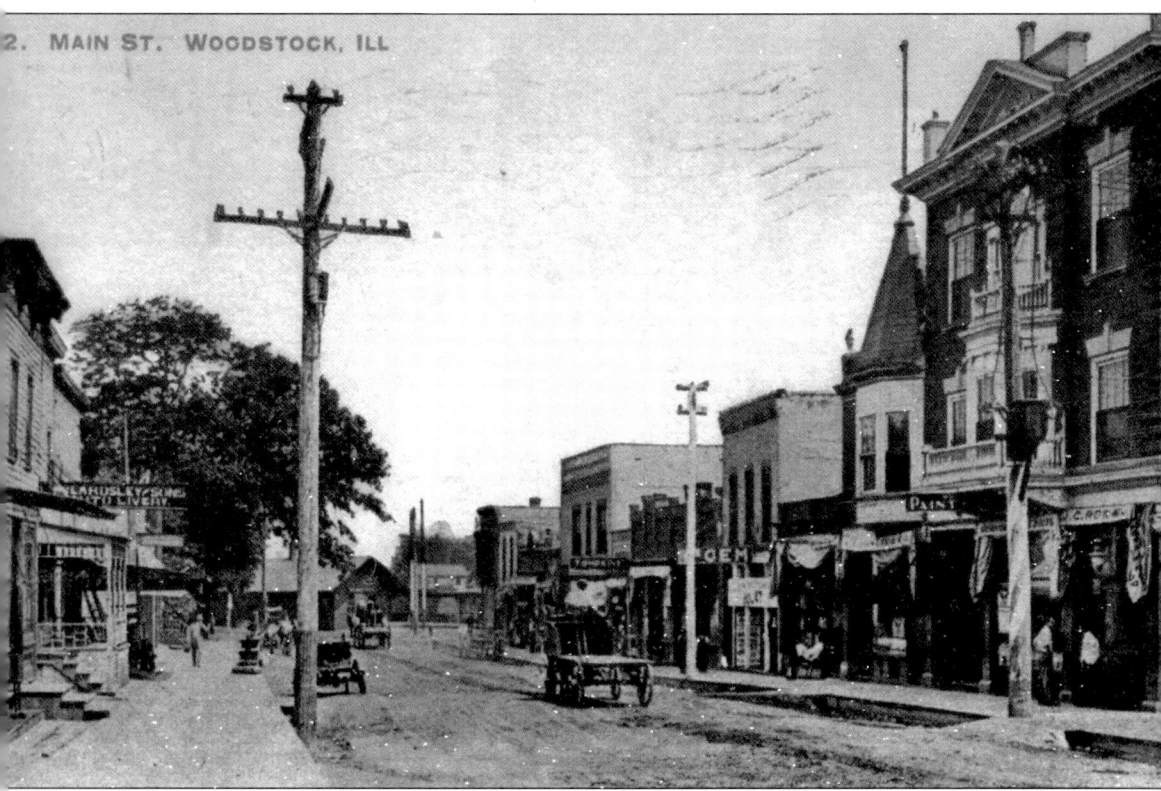

The three-story Waverly House is actually the second Waverly House on Main Street. It was erected for Marcellus Joslyn on the site of the original hotel, which had been destroyed by fire in 1892. The property was owned by the estate of his grandfather David Robinson. The first floor contained the office, kitchen, and dining room. The south side was used as the Rowe and Nails Barbershop and bath rooms. A bakery was located on the Benton Street side. Seventeen guest rooms, two bath rooms, a gentleman's toilet, washrooms, and a large linen closet were located on the second floor in 1900. The third floor was leased by the Odd Fellows as a lodge hall and also used by other fraternal organizations. The main part of the basement was occupied by bowling alleys, 124 feet in length, including the 8 feet extending under the public sidewalk. In the 1920s, Slavin, Eastman, and Pierce sold rugs, pictures, and stoves and ran an undertaking and ambulance business out of the building. It later became the Thomas B. Merwin Furniture Store and Funeral Home.

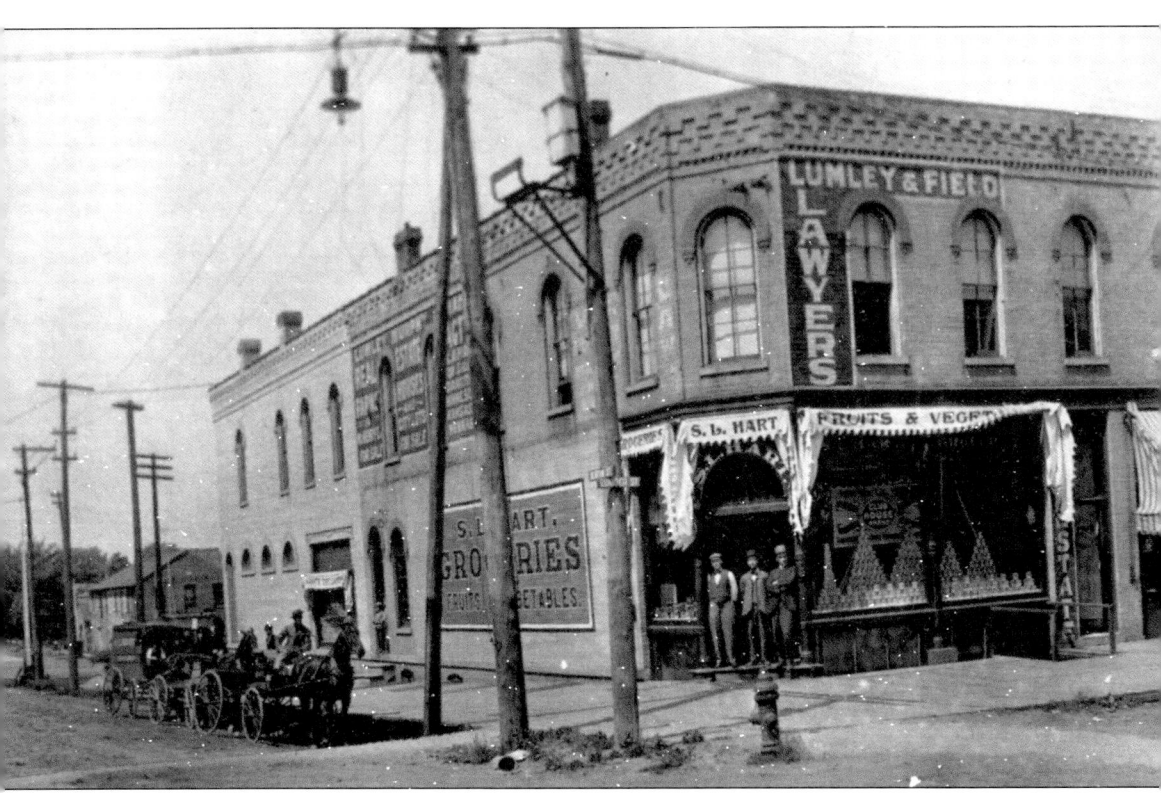

Timothy J. Dacy, described as an original and colorful character, erected the eastern half of this building in 1881, following a fire in March 1880 that destroyed his entire business. Dacy's son Charles recalled standing on the corner crying wildly and exclaiming, "The beautiful wagons, machines, and plows are burning up!" The fire started when thieves used dynamite to blow open two safes in the Express office, which was located in the Dacy building. An unlit fuse was also found on the railroad track. Dacy cleared the debris and auctioned off the damaged machinery and other goods. In 1886, he demolished a windmill and adjacent platform and constructed the building addition seen in this photograph. He continued in business until his death in 1886, when he was hit by a train while passing out cigars in celebration of the return of Company G from its training exercises in Springfield.

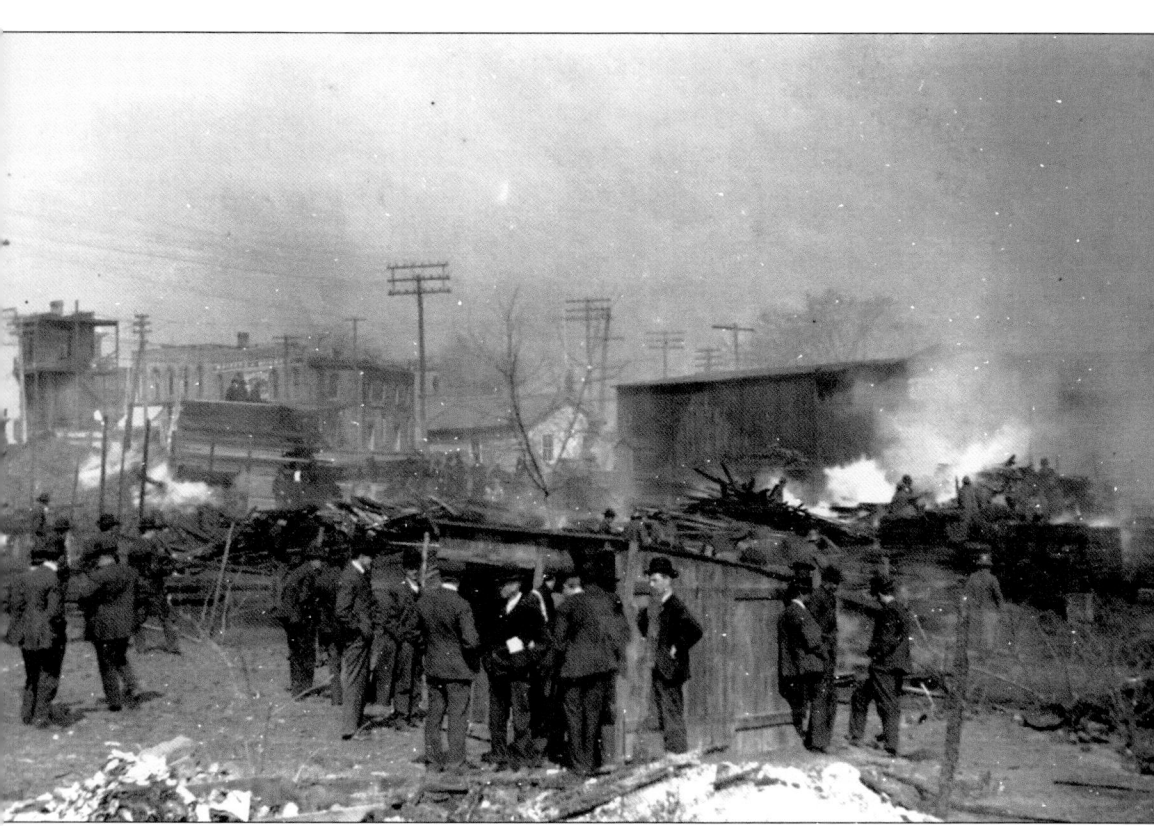

Fire consumed the Hall and Eckert Lumber Yard, located on East Judd Street east of the square, in April 1908. Around 3:00 a.m., a train crew noticed the blaze and sounded the engine's whistle. From Madison Street to the railroad tracks was a sea of flames; great clouds of cinders floated on the air for blocks. Erma Seiler Moote remembered waking to see the flames leaping in the air. Over the houses, high in the air, pieces of burning wood floated like paper. Her family did not yet have city water, so her brother Otto climbed on the roof and her brothers George and Rudi pumped water from the well, carrying it to the roof to pour over the burning pieces. It took firefighters about two hours to get it under control, but they worked all day to fully extinguish it. At the time of the fire, the city had only one well in operation, as workers were in the process of deepening the other one. Oliver Typewriter superintendent John Whitworth allowed the use of the Oliver reservoir, even though it would compromise Oliver's ability to fight its own fire if necessary. (Courtesy of McHenry County Historical Society.)

Three
TYPEWRITER CITY
AN INDUSTRIAL TOWN

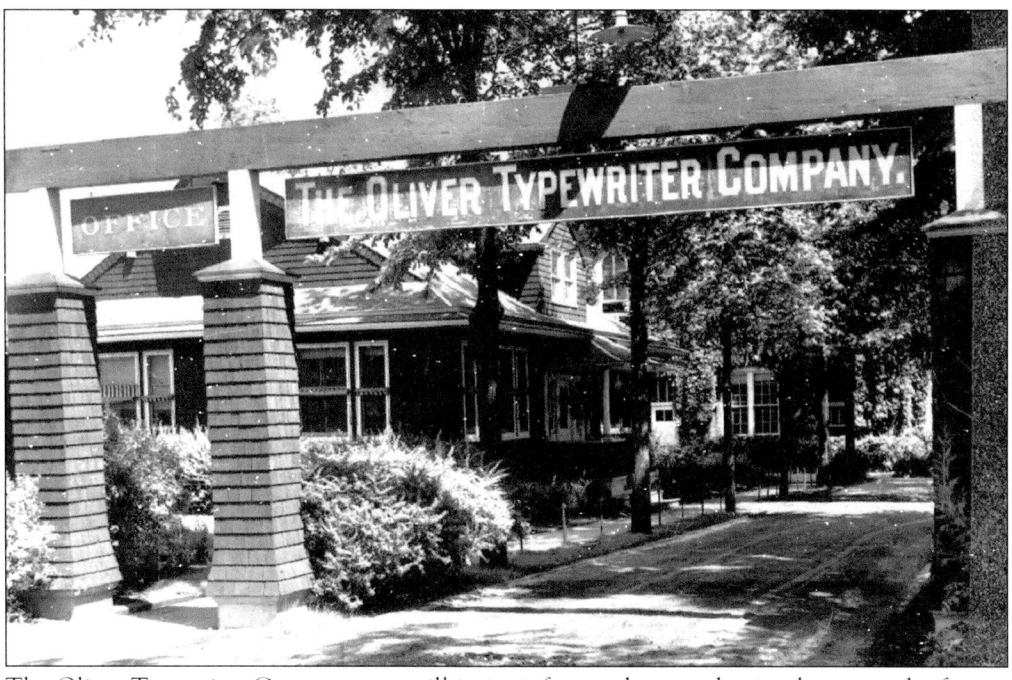

The Oliver Typewriter Company was still in its infancy when production began in the former Wheeler and Tappan Company factory in 1896. The Woodstock Public Improvement Committee had enticed Wheeler and Tappan to town by agreeing to erect a large building. Wheeler and Tappan manufactured and repaired pumping machines, including some especially large pumps for the Proctor and Gamble Company, Colgate, and other soap manufacturers, but its success was apparently short-lived. By 1896, the quarters were vacant, and the city donated the property to the Oliver Typewriter Company on the condition that it remain in town for five years. Oliver produced one of the first visible typewriters, as the carriage did not have to be raised to see the letters typed on the paper. Many large corporations used these typewriters, including most of the railroad companies, Carnegie, American Steel and Wire, Heinz Pickle, John Hancock Insurance, and Montgomery Ward, as well as the United States Treasury. To keep up with the demand, several additions were constructed. (Courtesy of McHenry County Historical Society.)

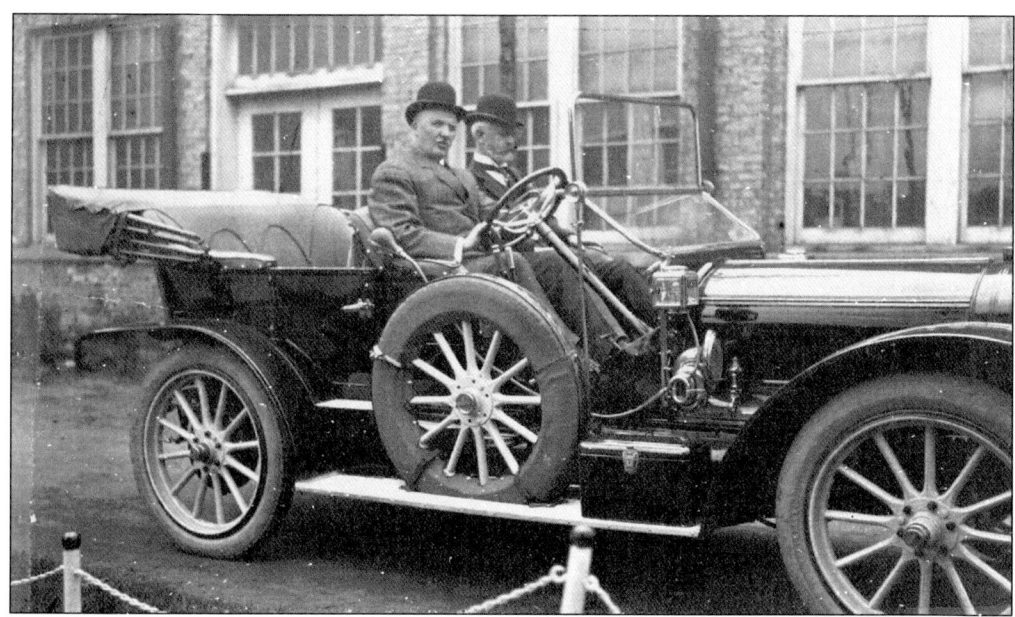

Oliver had its own fire brigade, its own wells, and a sprinkler system for emergencies. The company also supplied its own electricity. John Whitworth, the driver of this Jeffery automobile, served as the plant manager and company vice president. His passenger is company president Lawrence Williams. Whitworth was instrumental in both expanding the plant and keeping it in Woodstock. (Courtesy of McHenry County Historical Society.)

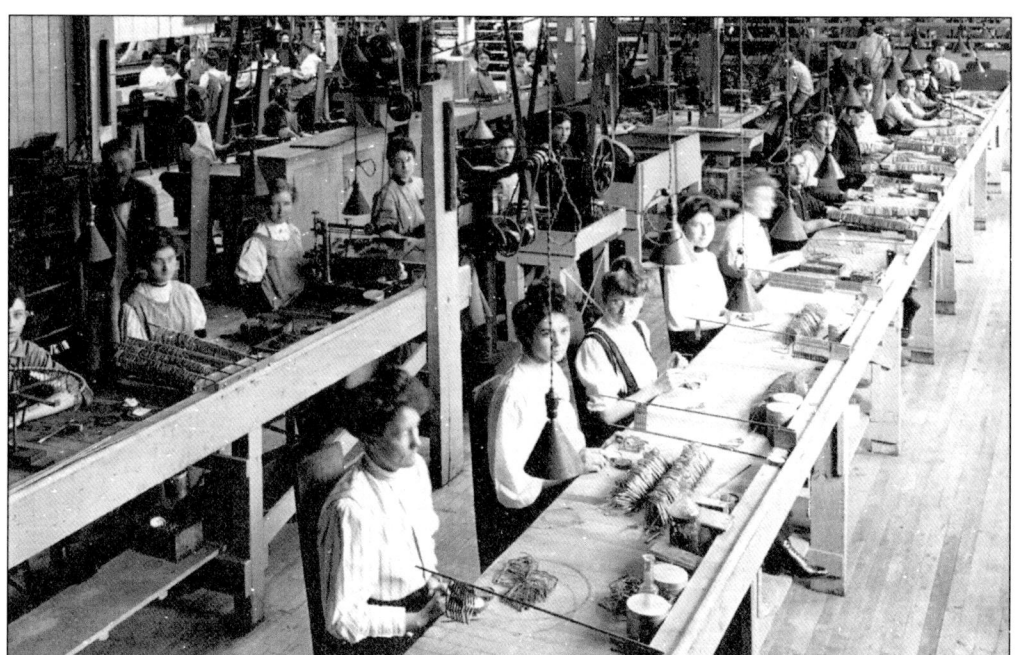

During World War I, Oliver had a large workforce that included many women, allowing the plant to operate around the clock. The company continued making typewriters, especially for use by the military, but also produced munitions for the British army. (Courtesy of McHenry County Historical Society.)

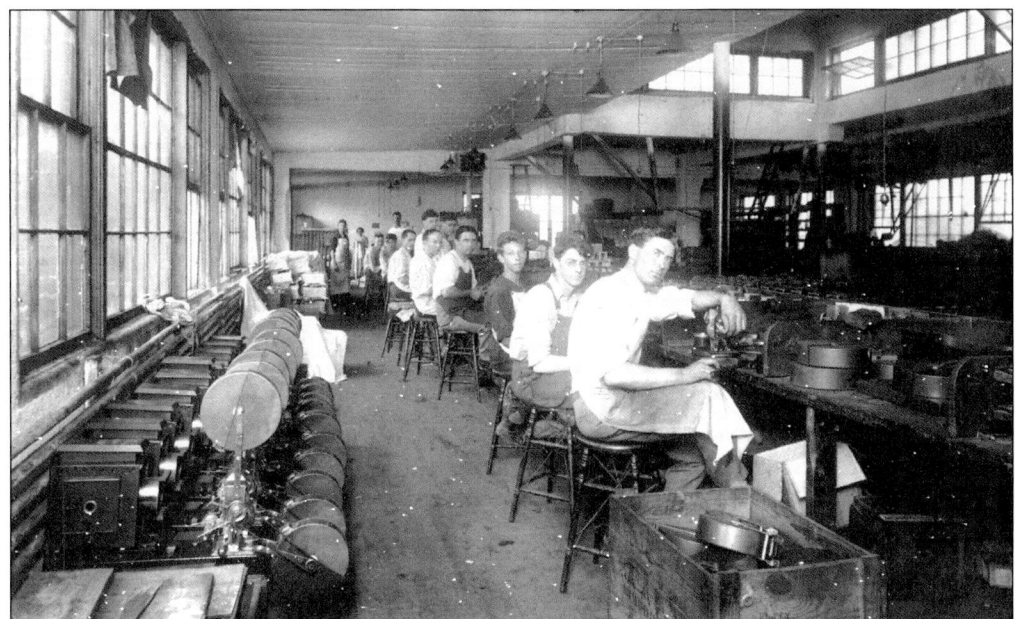

Following World War I, the company went into subcontract work to keep employees busy and make use of the several hundred machines, tools, and equipment left over from war production. Among the items produced were the computing sanitary scale, automobile parts, and two-piece motor valves. At some point in its history, Oliver also produced moving picture projectors like those shown here. (Courtesy of McHenry County Historical Society.)

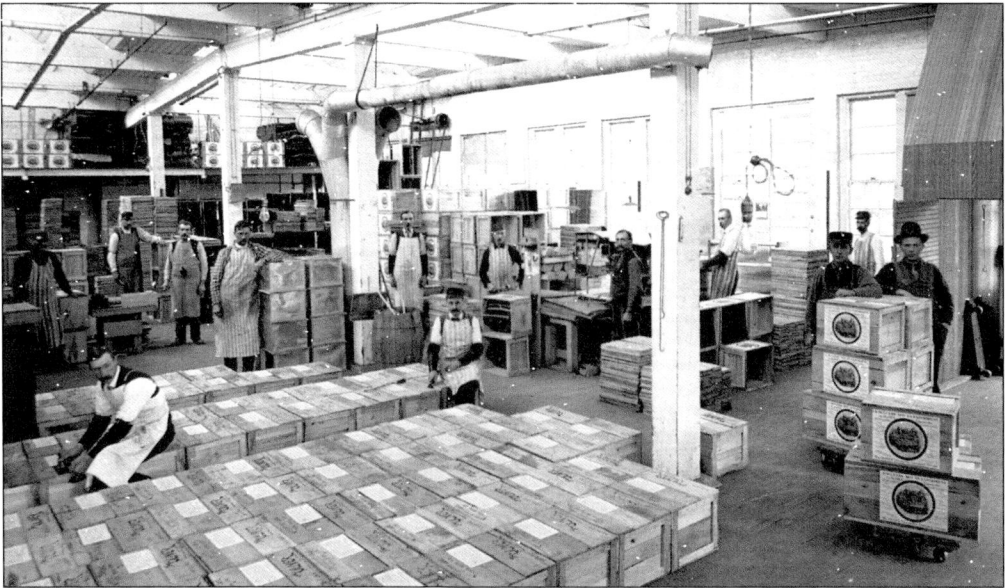

A complete change in marketing strategy occurred after World War I. Oliver closed its domestic and foreign sales offices and cut the price of the typewriters in half. Sales were made directly to customers who ordered their typewriters from coupons found in newspapers and magazines. Business increased rapidly until a minor depression in 1921–1922, when collections seriously hurt the company's financial well-being. The last typewriter was made in 1926, the plant was put up for sale, and assets were liquidated. (Courtesy of McHenry County Historical Society.)

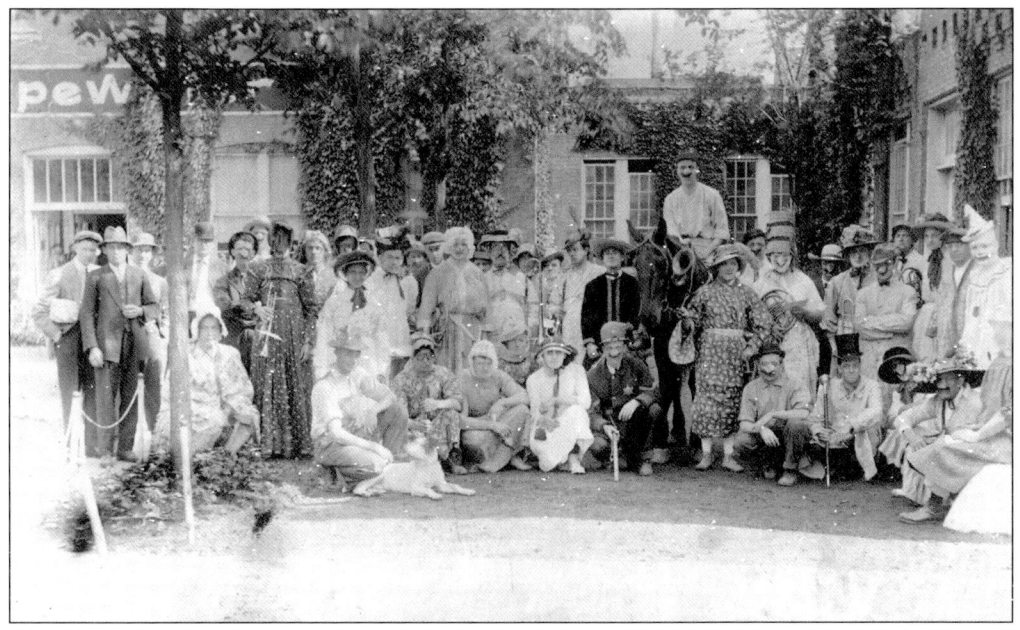

Oliver was more to Woodstock than a major employer. No matter what a person's position with the company, his or her activities, including marriages, births, deaths, promotions, transfers, accidents, and even hunting and fishing successes, were reported in "Oliver News" columns in the local newspapers. (Courtesy of McHenry County Historical Society.)

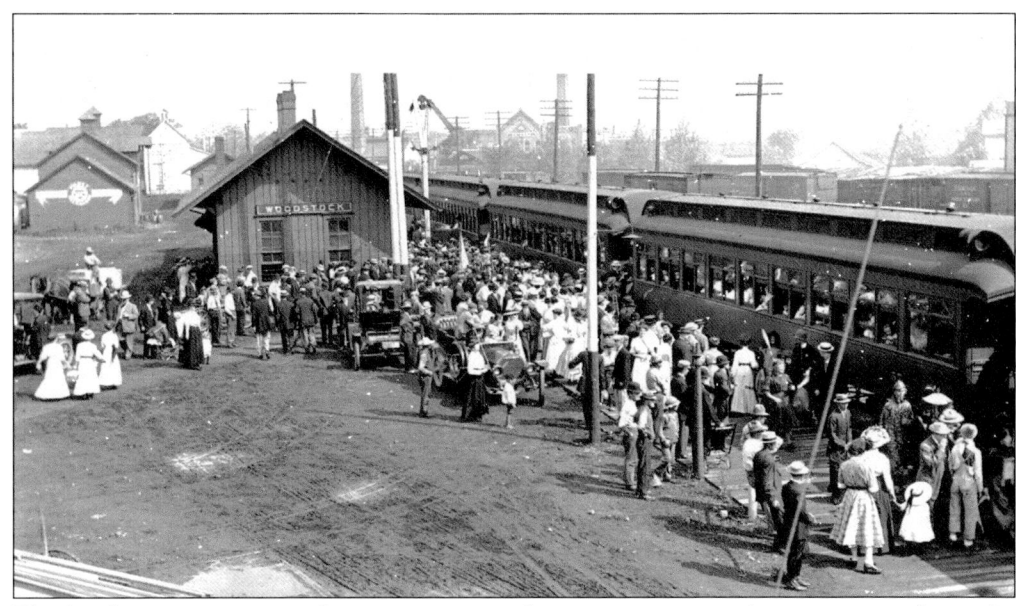

The local newspapers carried many accounts of picnics, parties, and programs involving the families of Oliver employees and anyone who wished to attend. Oliver provided the focus for many social activities. A special train was arranged to take employees and Woodstock residents to the annual picnic in Fox River Grove. (Courtesy of Woodstock Public Library.)

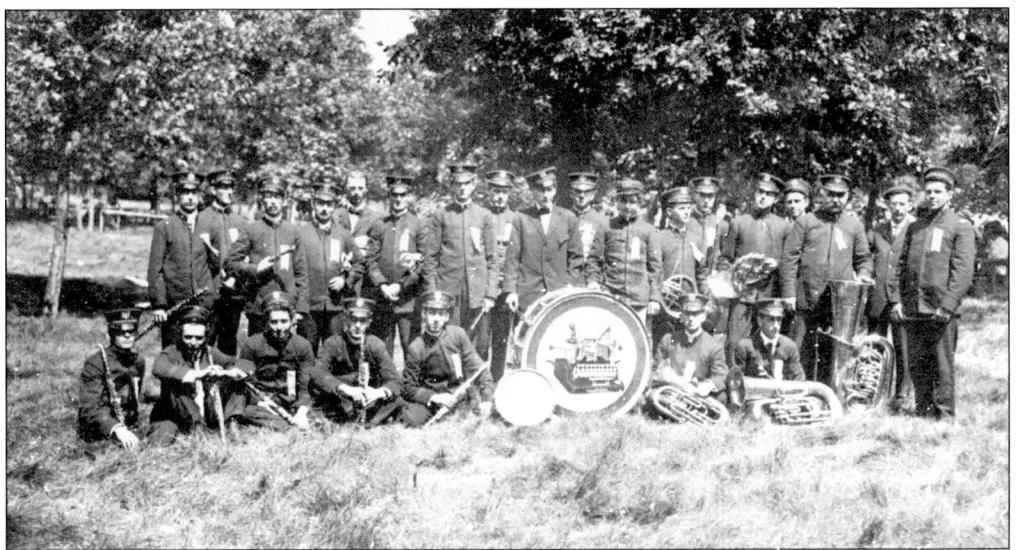

Oliver sponsored a band, which was a popular attraction throughout the county for many years. The group played at concerts, parades, and political rallies. When a special train brought the annual arrival of the Oliver sales force to Woodstock just before Christmas, the Oliver Typewriter Band met them at the station and marched to the factory. The band also played at the train station when companies of local men left for military service during World War I. (Courtesy of McHenry County Historical Society.)

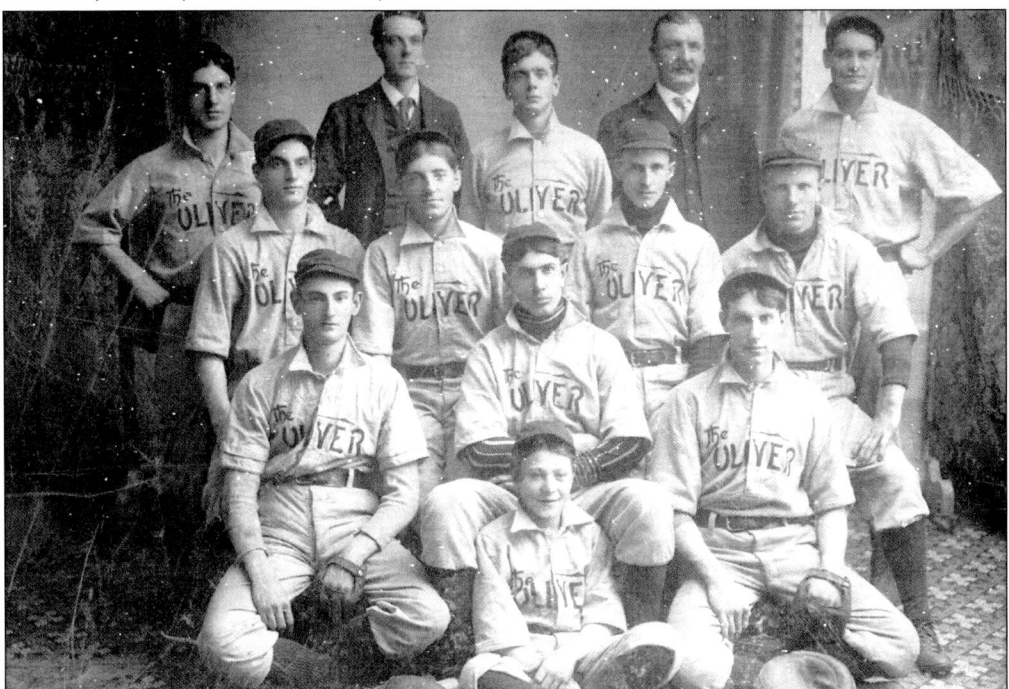

The Oliver baseball team was reportedly one of the best semiprofessional teams ever in the Chicago area. Three members of the 1902 Olivers went on to play in the major leagues, the most famous of which was George Moriarity. The company also fielded a women's baseball team, as well as other sports teams. (Courtesy of McHenry County Historical Society.)

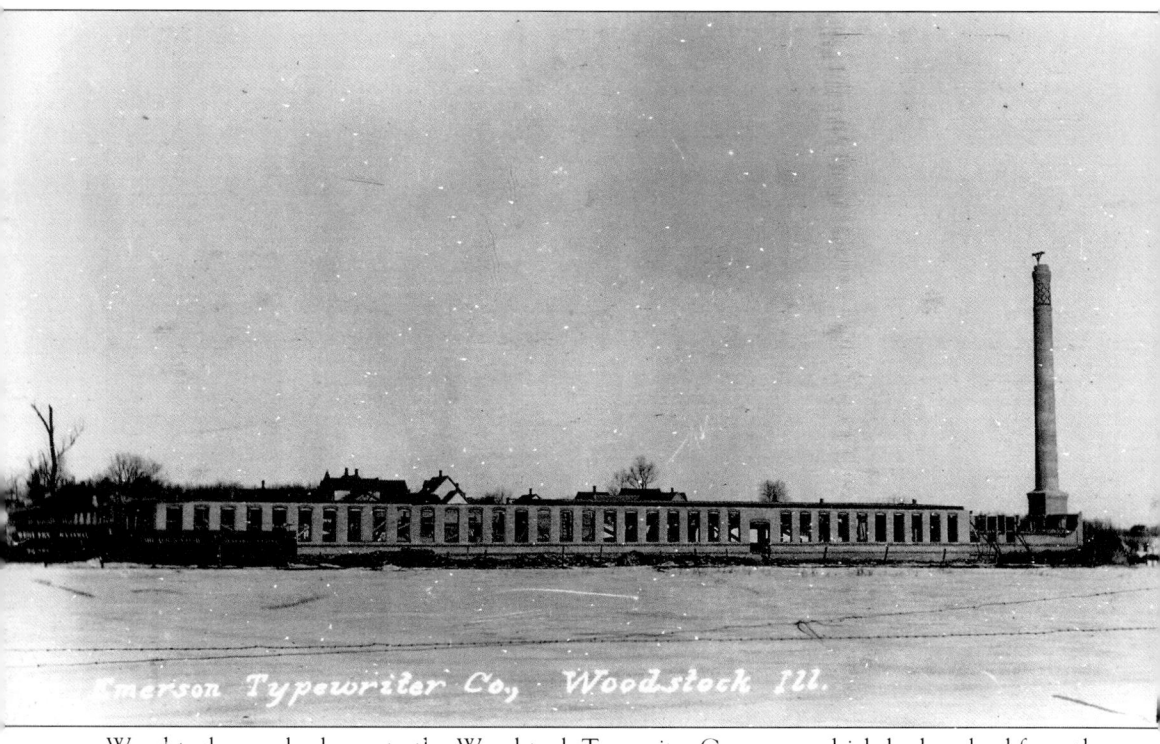

Woodstock was also home to the Woodstock Typewriter Company, which had evolved from the Emerson Typewriter Company. Organizing in 1907 on the East Coast, in 1908 Emerson moved to a plant at Momence, Illinois, where it employed about 70 men. Business grew and in 1909, Emerson representative George Fecke visited Woodstock. At a large gathering at city hall, he said that the company would relocate if Woodstock would subscribe at least $30,000 of Emerson capital stock. The funds were raised and the new factory constructed. Built entirely of brick with a substantial maple floor, it was supplied with an abundance of light from the many windows and skylights. The smokestack rose 90 feet. Before the factory was even completed, an addition on the north side was started. The factory could be reached by a side track from the main line of the Chicago and Northwestern Railroad. This allowed raw materials to be delivered to the doors of the factory and, likewise, finished typewriters to be shipped out. (Courtesy of Woodstock Public Library.)

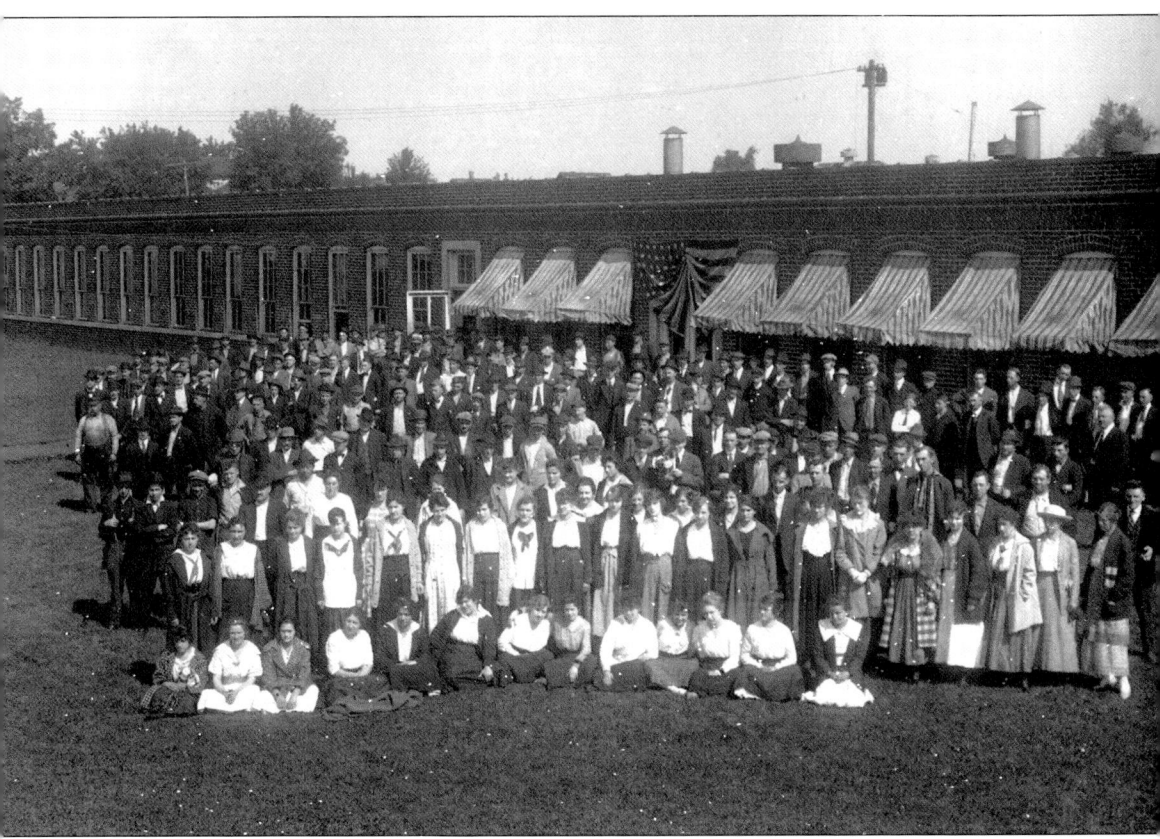

Woodstock began to call itself Typewriter City. Naturally, there was a good-natured rivalry between Emerson and Oliver employees. Emerson also formed its own company band and baseball team, and the Emerson Band even played at the Oliver annual picnic in Fox River Grove. With two typewriter factories running in town, housing was in short supply. In 1916, a dormitory was constructed in the old Stafford Furniture building on the west side of the public square, where about 20 beds were used nightly. Even the jail was pressed into service. In December 1910, Emerson laid off 35 to 40 employees indefinitely. The company discovered that the first machines had not held up as expected, and the factory suspended operations until a new model could be completed. It then became the Woodstock Typewriter Company, headed by Alva C. Roebuck, who was a one-third owner in Sears Roebuck Company. Emerson typewriter owners were given the first opportunity to purchase a Woodstock typewriter, and a liberal exchange policy was offered. (Courtesy of McHenry County Historical Society.)

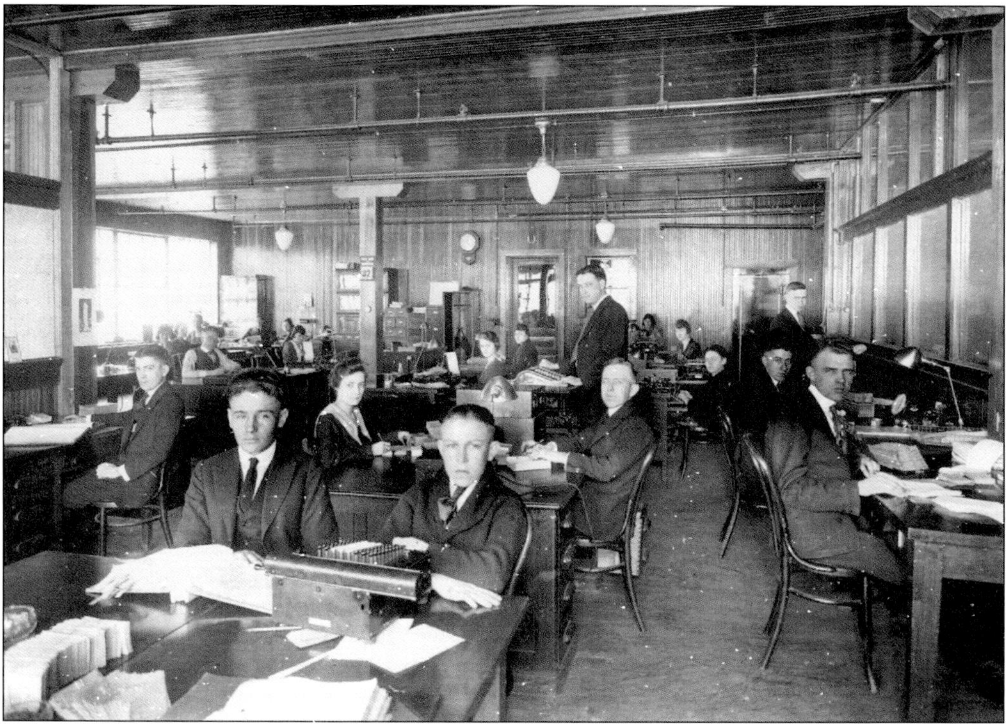

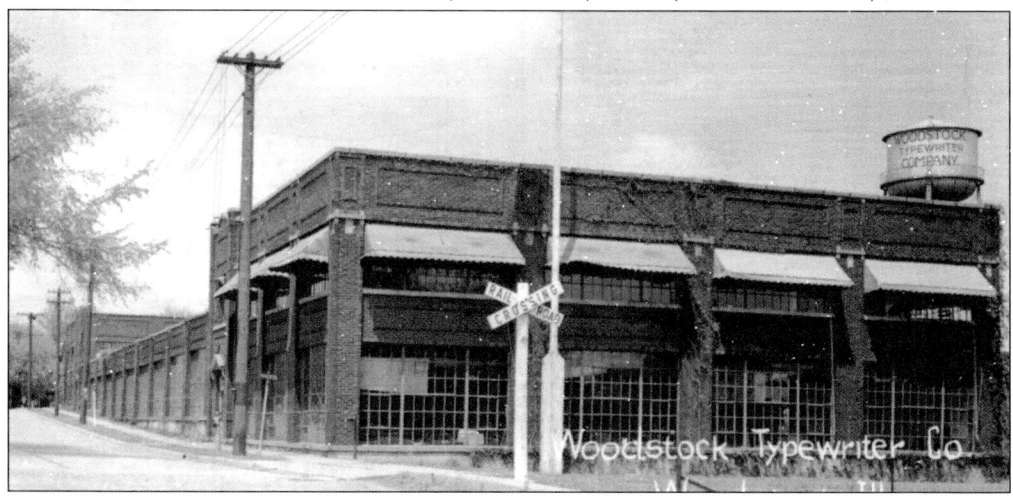

In 1919, some Woodstock Typewriter employees went on strike, and the plant shut down for six weeks. A compromise was reached, and management agreed not to discriminate against striking workers, to grant a nine-hour workweek, and to increase wages as soon as possible. Management held firm to maintaining a nonunion shop. Offices were located at the north and south ends of the building on the second floor. (Courtesy of McHenry County Historical Society.)

World War II gave tremendous exposure to the Woodstock Typewriter Company, as it was chosen by the government to supply machines for every army camp, navy ship, and outpost at home and abroad. As their use fanned out around the world, Woodstock typewriters were requested by other countries as well. In 1945, the *Woodstock Sentinel* described the company as a mecca for scores of representatives wanting to become agents for the machines. (Courtesy of McHenry County Historical Society.)

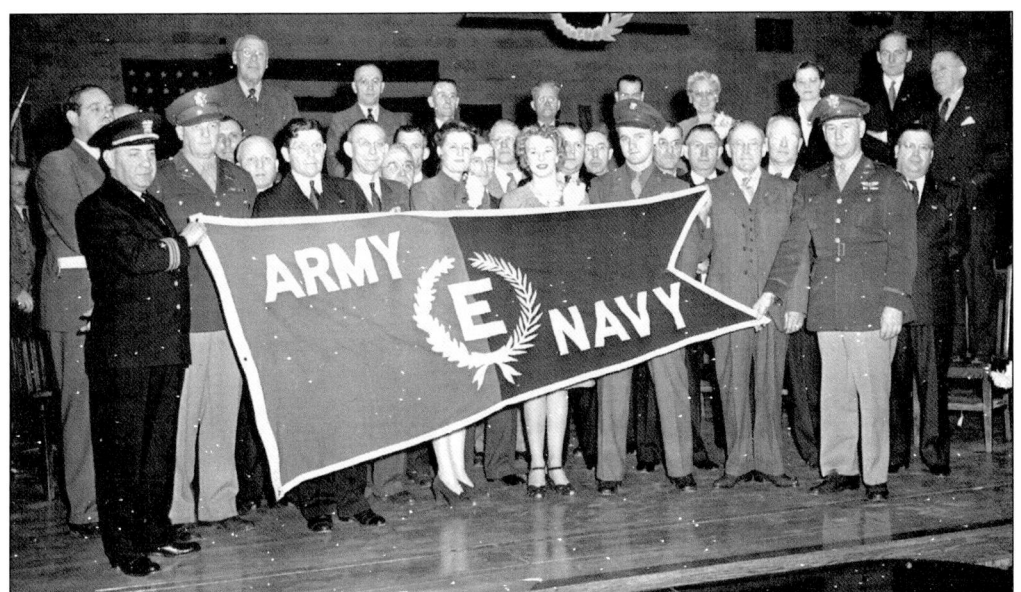

In recognition of the Woodstock typewriter's quality during use in World War II, the company was awarded the Army-Navy E Award. The ceremony was held at the Woodstock High School auditorium on November 24, 1944, emceed by John Harrington of radio station WBBM. An E Award flag was presented to company president Richard W. Sears, third from the left in this photograph, and token E pins were presented to five employees. All employees received a pin after the ceremony. (Courtesy of McHenry County Historical Society.)

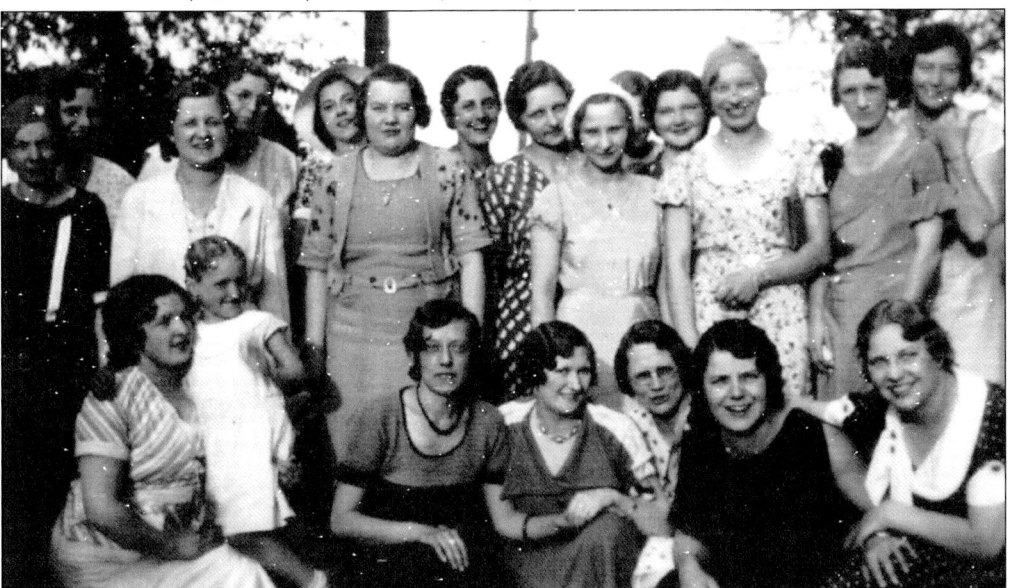

Domestic demand after World War II was very high, both because so many servicemen had been exposed to the typewriters during the conflict and because defeated Germany had been a major producer prior to the war. At this time, women continued as an important part of the workforce. In 1947, Century America purchased the Woodstock Typewriter Company. In 1949, Century America sold to R. C. Allen, which produced a typewriter under the Signature name. R. C. Allen closed the factory for good in November 1970.

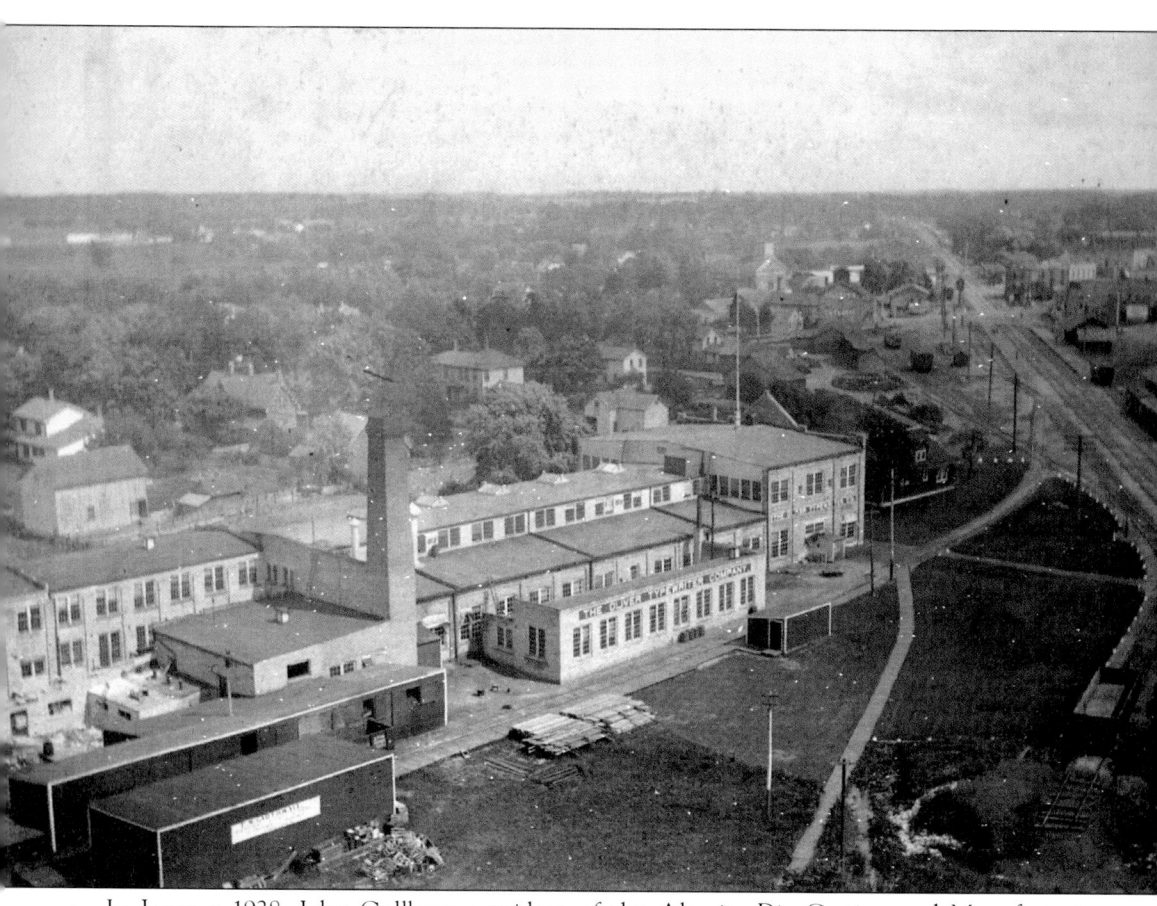

In January 1928, John Gullborg, president of the Alemite Die Casting and Manufacturing Company, inspected the recently vacated Oliver plant, accompanied by his friend Carl Swansson, a Woodstock barber. Gullborg was reportedly impressed by the transportation facilities and the size and condition of the buildings and was contemplating the relocation of his factory. He felt that labor conditions would be better in a small town. When Alemite moved to Woodstock, management tried to create ideal employee working conditions by providing a bright and airy atmosphere through many windows and maintaining a high degree of cleanliness (actually required to maintain quality castings). The executive offices were housed in the bungalow that had served the Oliver Typewriter Company. The grounds included shade trees and fruit trees, flowering shrubs, perennials, tennis courts, horseshoe pits, and a softball diamond. There were lawn swings, tables, and seats under the trees. Like many large companies, Alemite had an active recreation and social club that sponsored a baseball league, picnics, and parties. (Courtesy of McHenry County Historical Society.)

The die casting process began with the melting of ingots of aluminum or zinc in a smelting furnace at temperatures of 680 to 1,200 degrees. From there, the molten metal was conveyed to a die casting machine, where it was forced by compressed air into the die and the casting was formed. There was a loud percussive sound when this occurred. (Courtesy of McHenry County Historical Society.)

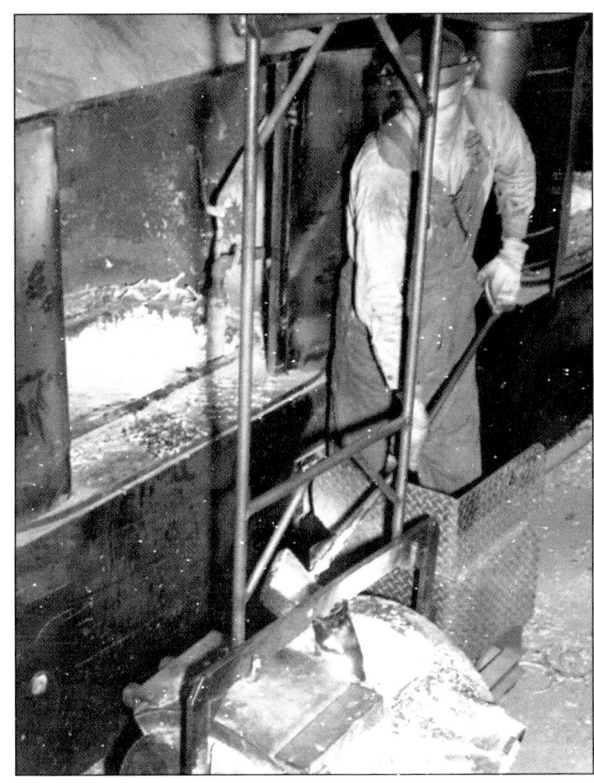

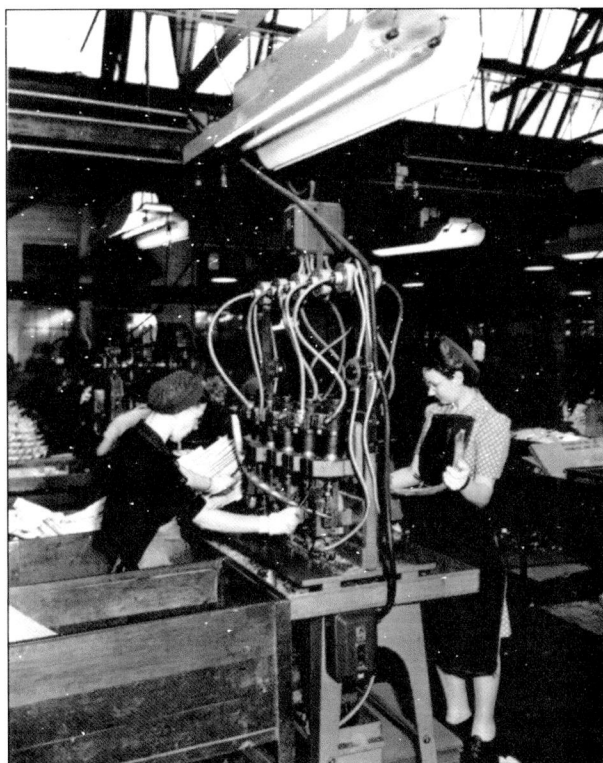

The casting was then transferred to the trimming department, where it was die or file trimmed and machined by punch or drill press. The workforce at Alemite always included women, but especially so during World War II. (Courtesy of McHenry County Historical Society.)

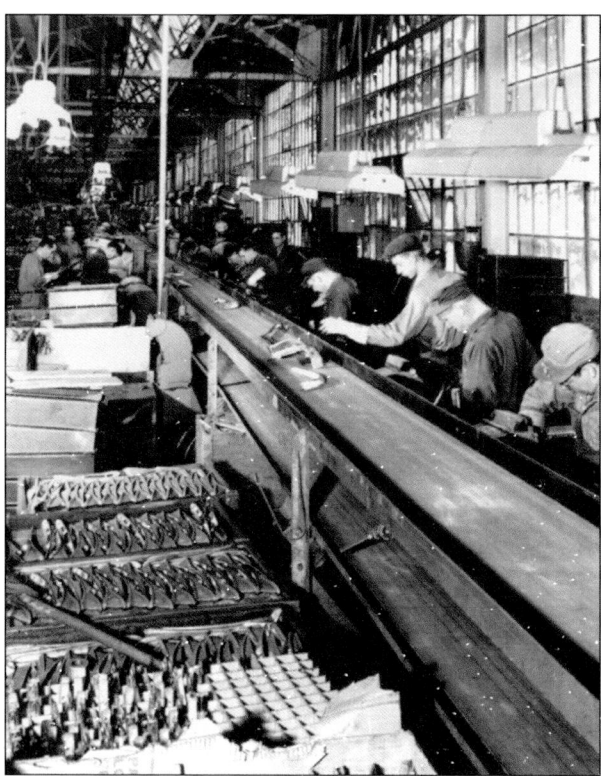

The castings had to be polished, buffed, and plated with copper, nickel, or chrome before the pieces were finally assembled, packed, and shipped. (Courtesy of McHenry County Historical Society.)

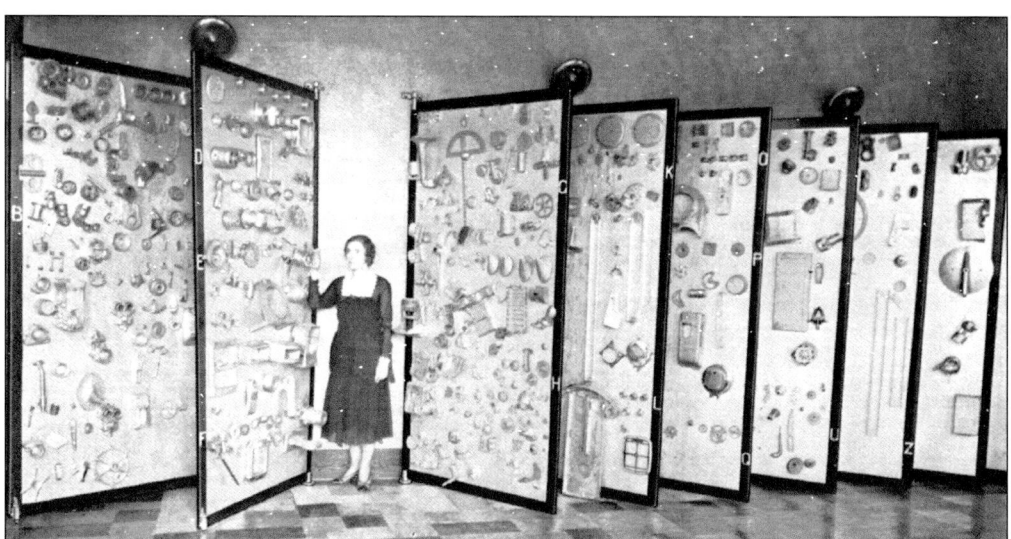

Die castings sped up production, reduced cost, and improved quality. These aspects were important to the manufacture of countless products, especially appliances and automobiles. Die castings required no machining to fit, and the outside finish was smooth so that no polishing was required. Alemite was one of the largest suppliers of die cast parts for the automobile industry. (Courtesy of McHenry County Historical Society.)

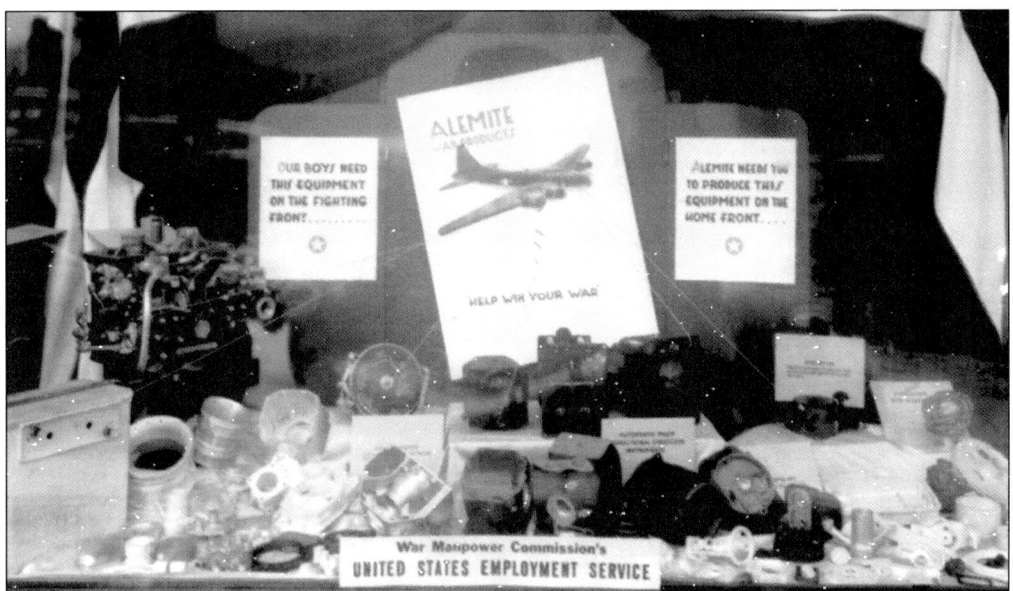

In 1935, the company became the Alemite Die Casting Division of Electric Autolite. Alemite's contribution to the war effort during World War II was considerable, as it produced mortar shells, timed fuses, bombshells, flares, voltage regulator and carburetor housings, and radar equipment. United States airmen used Alemite parts and cases for gyroscopes, oxygen regulators, and radio equipment. The Alemite name was dropped in the mid- to late 1940s, and local residents referred to the factory as the Autolite. (Courtesy of McHenry County Historical Society.)

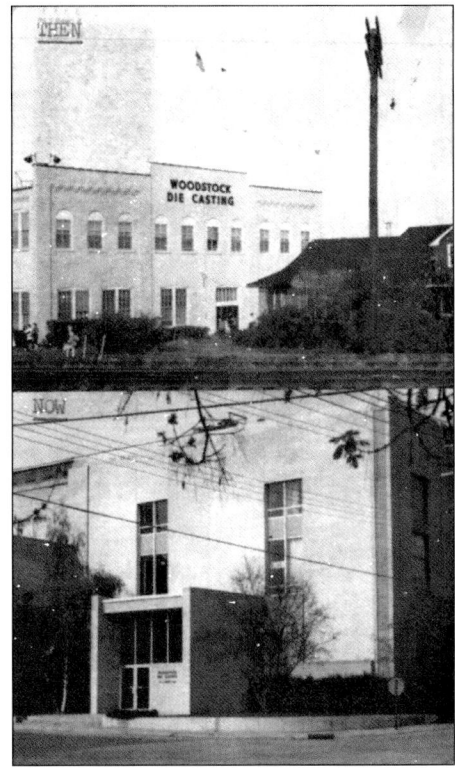

Autolite provided employment for members of many Woodstock families. An Autolite job meant steady work and good pay. In 1963, the plant became Woodstock Die Casting, and over the next 15 years, most of the defining architectural elements of the original Oliver Typewriter buildings disappeared due to remodeling and construction of new additions. In 1979, the plant was acquired by Allied Signal Corporation. (Courtesy of McHenry County Historical Society.)

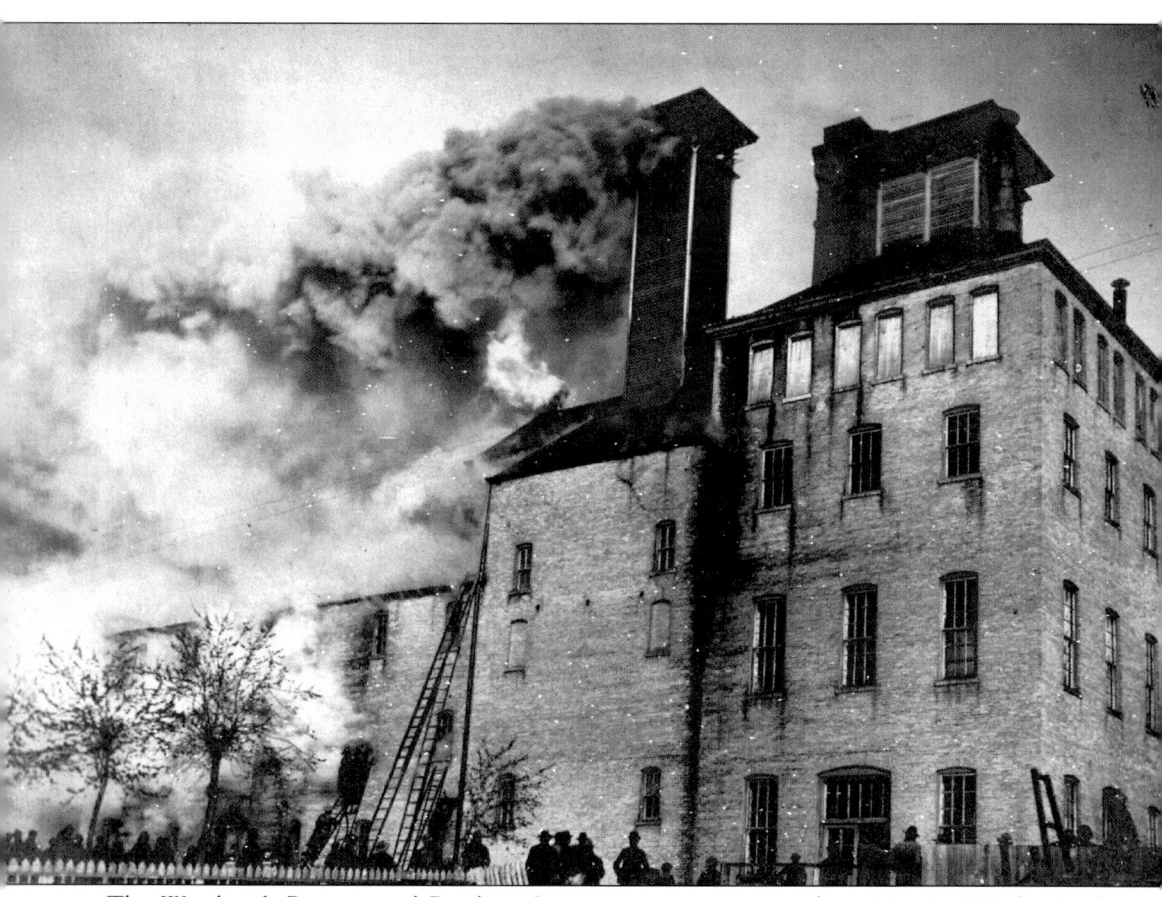

The Woodstock Brewery and Bottling Company was incorporated on May 1, 1887, by Jacob Zimmer, Henry Herman, and Emil Arnold, the proprietors of a brewery that had been destroyed by fire the previous year. John Bertchey first started a small brewery northwest of town almost as soon as Woodstock was selected as the county seat. According to reports of the 1886 fire, a large crowd stood watching helplessly as the buildings burned to the ground. It was noted that although the bottling house was destroyed, most of the goods were saved except for those consumed by the thirsty crowd. Simon Brink was hired to superintend construction of the new brewery facilities. The brewery used pure springwater and ice cut from the spring-fed artificial lake on the site. Woodstock beer was recommended for invalids by the best physicians, who were thoroughly aware of the brew's absolute purity. The 1887 brewery, shown here, employed 15 people and produced 60,000 barrels a year. (Courtesy of McHenry County Historical Society.)

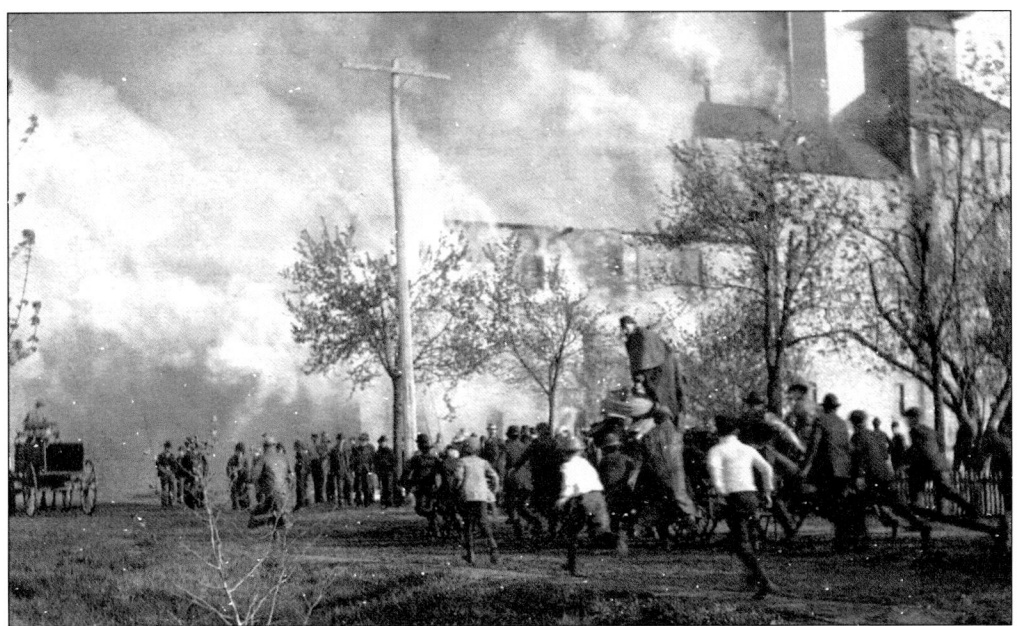

In May 1902, fire struck again and schoolboys raced to watch the brewery burn. The city, without enough hose to reach the nearest water main, was unable to throw a stream of water on the fire. When the Harvard Fire Department arrived on the scene an hour and a half later, firefighters connected the Harvard hose to Woodstock hose, and finally the public water supply could be utilized. By this time, however, the main building was already gone. (Courtesy of McHenry County Historical Society.)

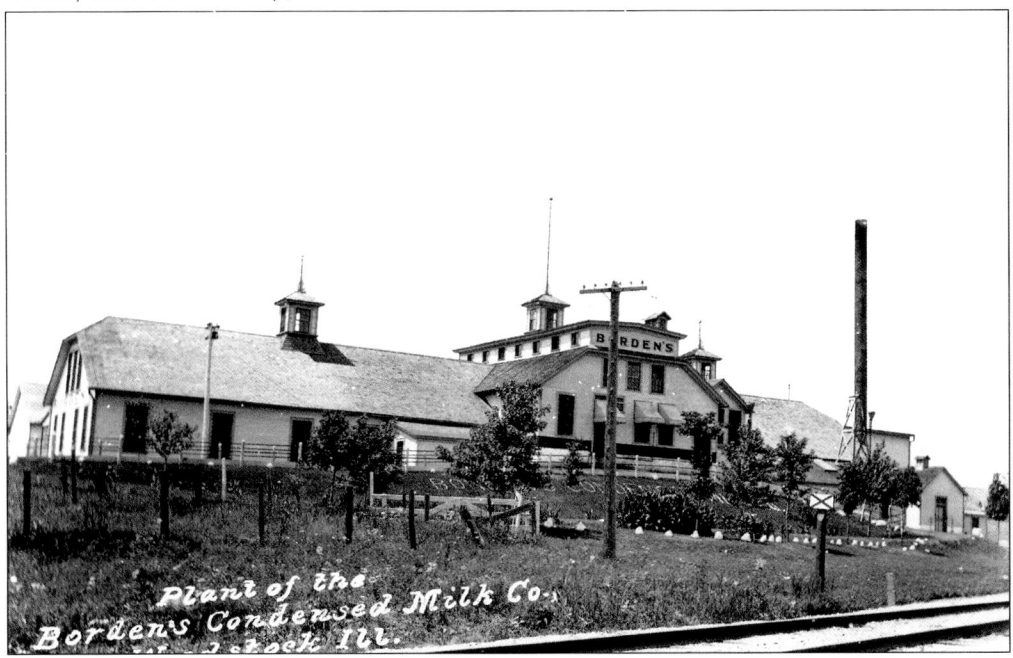

Borden's Condensed Milk Company built a plant northwest of town along the railroad in Woodstock in 1904. The facilities included a large icehouse, a bottle storage building, a coal storage building, and the main sterilizing and bottling plant.

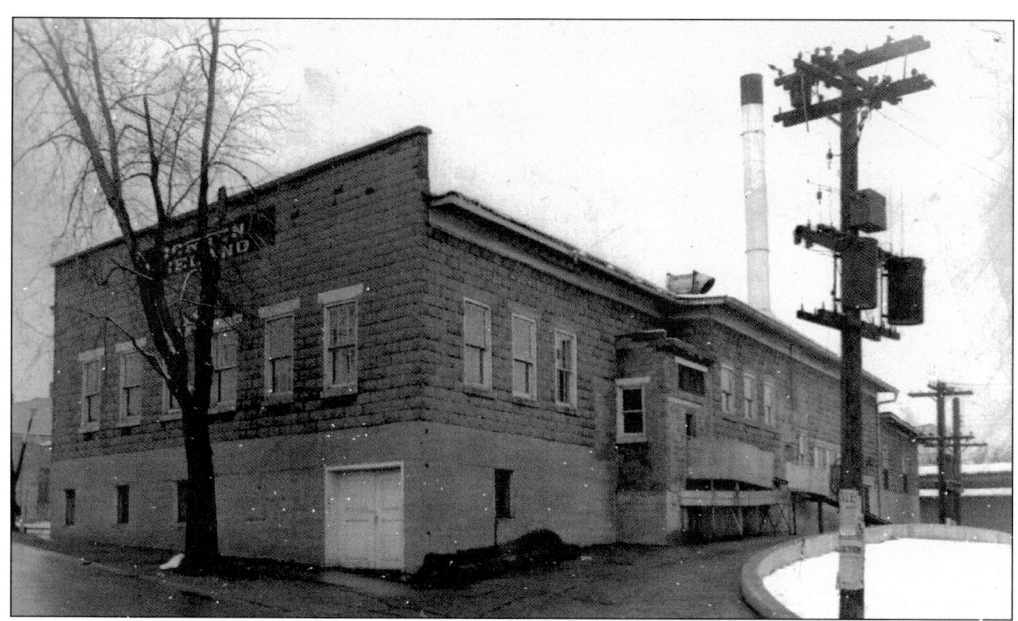

A second Borden plant was constructed along the railroad tracks at the corner of East Judd and Madison Streets. The plant was acquired by the Pure Milk Association in 1960, along with another in Hebron. (Courtesy of McHenry County Historical Society.)

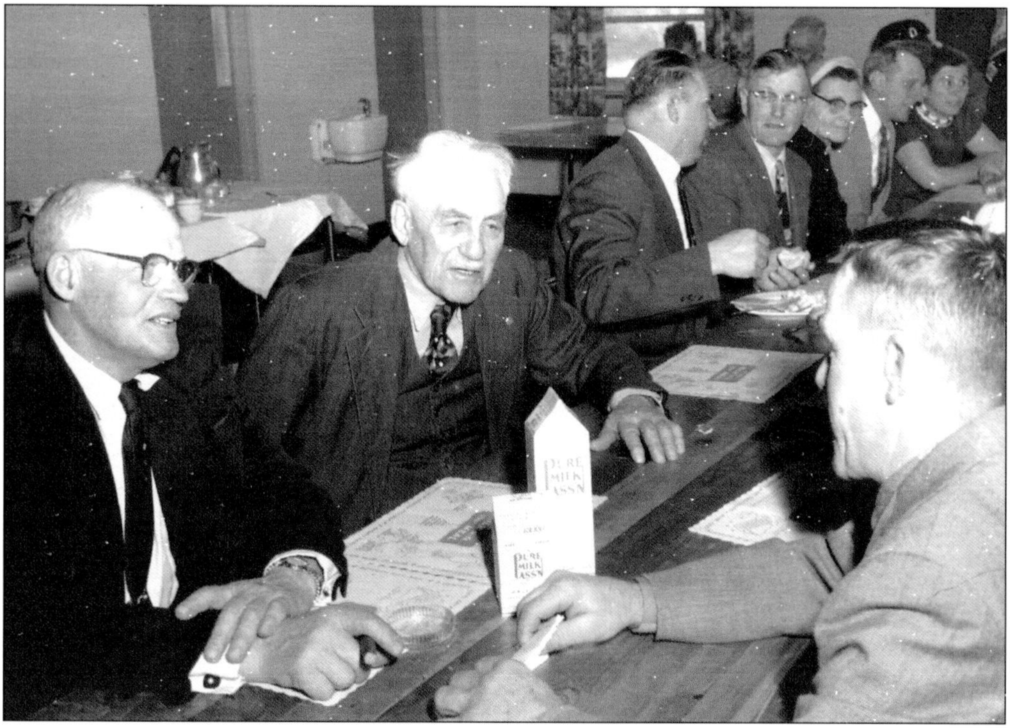

The Pure Milk Association formed out of a cooperative movement to create a market for milk from tuberculin-tested, tuberculin-free animals. Eventually the association concentrated on obtaining the highest milk prices for its members. (Courtesy of McHenry County Historical Society, Don Peasley Collection.)

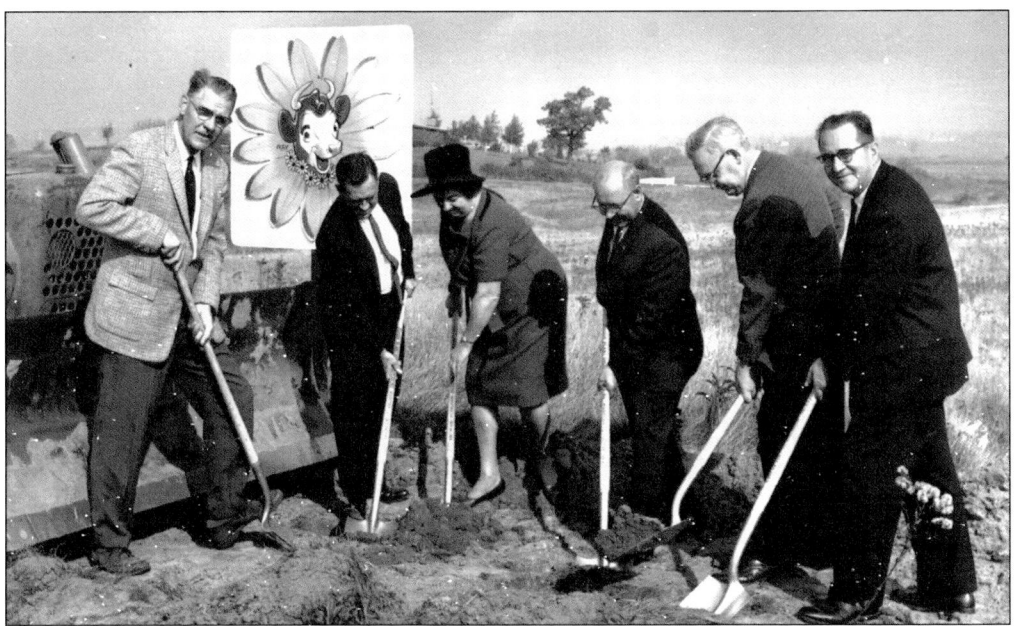

Borden selected Woodstock as the site of its new large modern plant. Mayor Francis Kuhn is among the dignitaries turning over shovels of dirt at this groundbreaking ceremony. The Borden plant was completed in 1964 at a cost of $5 million, and the Pure Milk Association's plant was closed. Today the Claussen Pickle Company occupies the Borden building. (Courtesy of McHenry County Historical Society, Don Peasley Collection.)

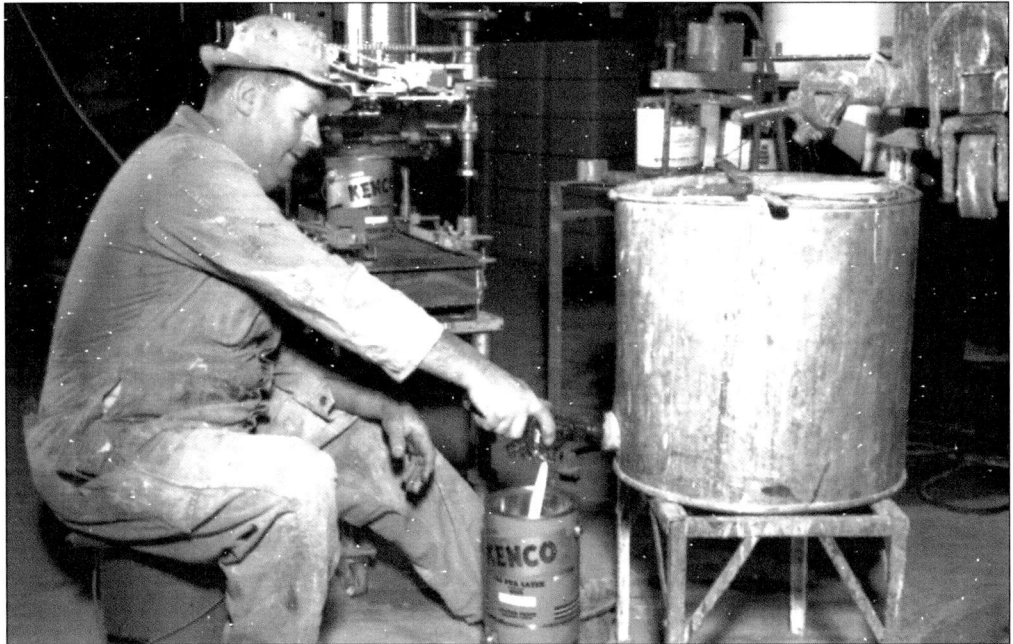

Louton Paint moved to Woodstock around 1950, locating at 214 North Seminary Avenue. This image and the two that follow are part of a collection of photographs taken by Commonwealth Edison in the early 1960s, when the company was contemplating the purchase of the Woodstock municipal power plant. (Courtesy of McHenry County Historical Society.)

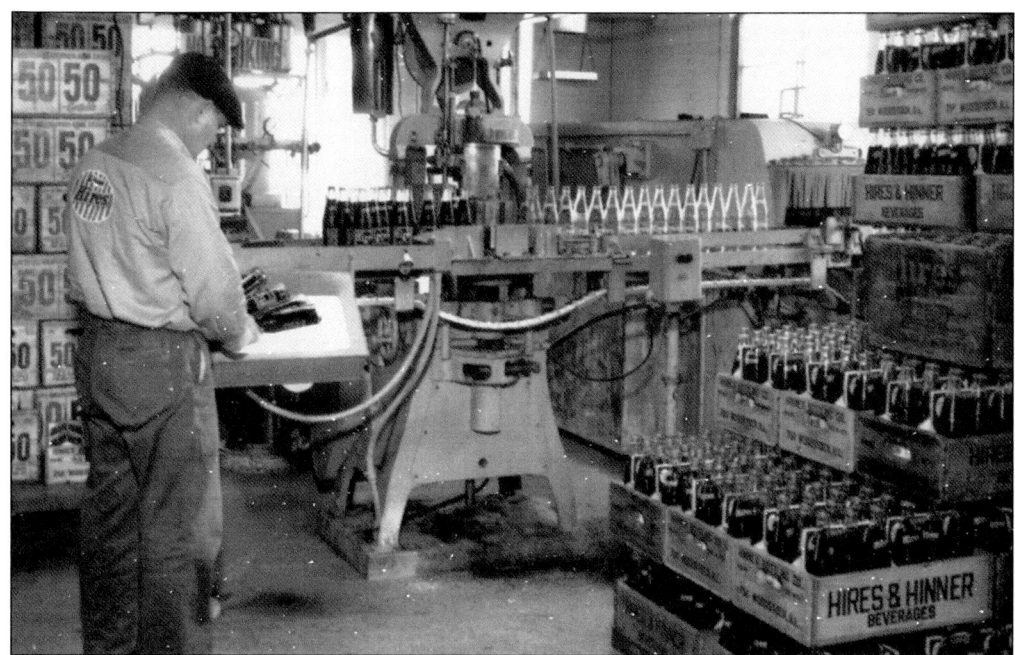

The Hinner Bottling Company was the only soft drink bottler in McHenry County when production began in 1947. The plant was located at the southwest corner of Greenwood Avenue and Route 47. Hires Root Beer was one of its major products. (Courtesy of McHenry County Historical Society.)

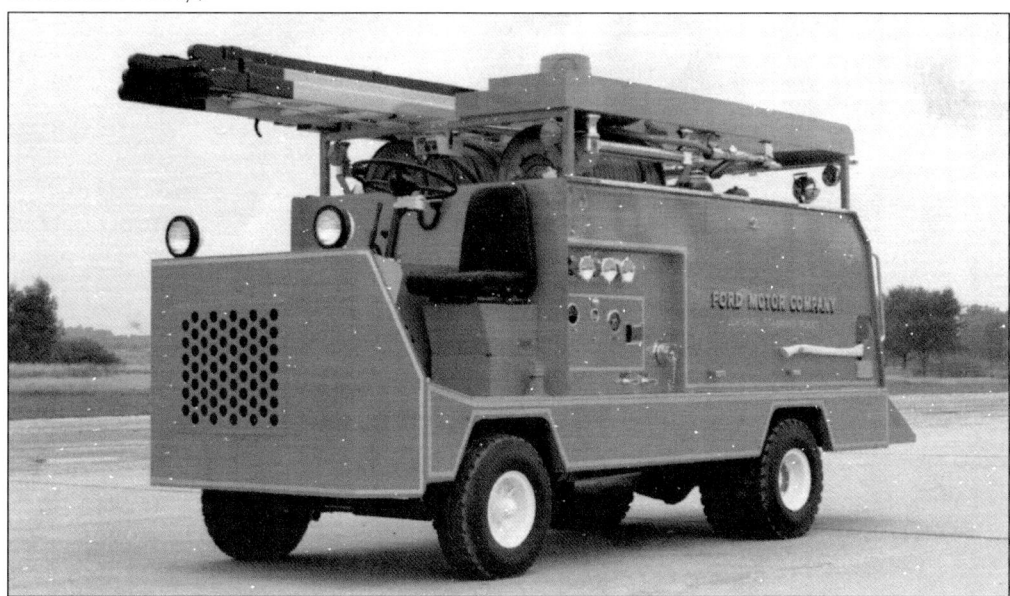

George Geiger started R and B Metal Products in 1952. Approximately 30 people were employed in the engineering and production of a variety of items, including seed treating equipment, dairy carton forming equipment, gas-fired toilets, various cabinets and controls, and a firefighting unit for in-plant protection. The finished Taskmaster was driven under police escort to the loading ramps at Peet Frate Lines, where it was readied for shipment. (Courtesy of McHenry County Historical Society.)

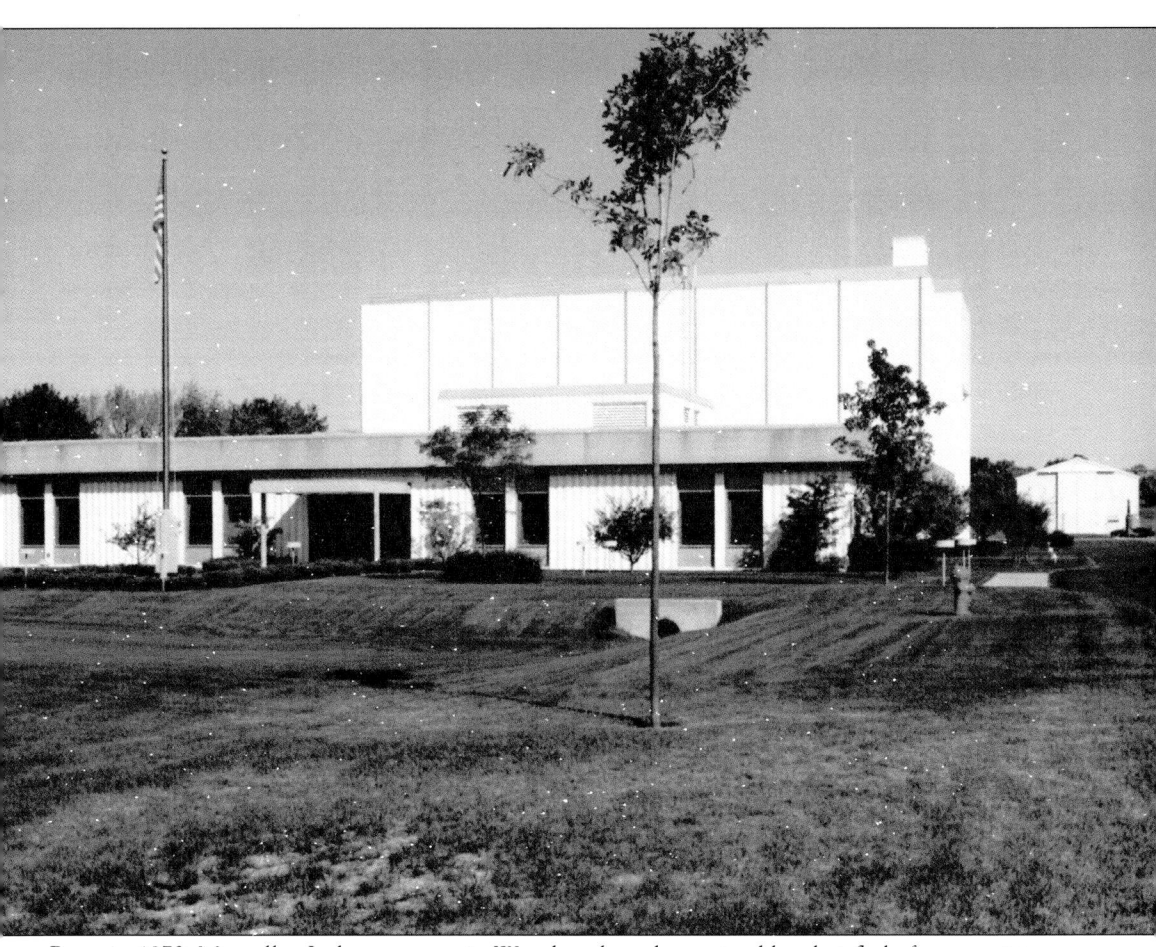

Born in 1873, Marcellus Joslyn grew up in Woodstock and practiced law briefly before acquiring an interest in a Crystal Lake company that produced Norway pine cross arms for electric poles. This led to the formation of the Citizens Electric Light and Manufacturing Company, with Marcellus serving as president. Norway pine supplies were soon exhausted, so the company moved to Chicago where transportation was better for shipping in southern yellow pine. In 1910, the business was renamed the Joslyn Manufacturing and Supply Company. When many new products were added, the company became a leader in the field of pole line hardware. Marcellus developed an innovative profit-sharing plan in the 1930s. In 1968, the company constructed the Joslyn Manufacturing Research Center in Woodstock. Marcellus retired to Southern California in 1958 and, in 1960, established the Joslyn Foundation, which gave over $6 million for the construction, remodeling, and purchase of bowling greens, clubhouses, and maintenance equipment for seniors' lawn-bowling facilities in Southern California. Funds were also given to hospitals, colleges, art museums, and other deserving groups. (Courtesy of McHenry County Historical Society.)

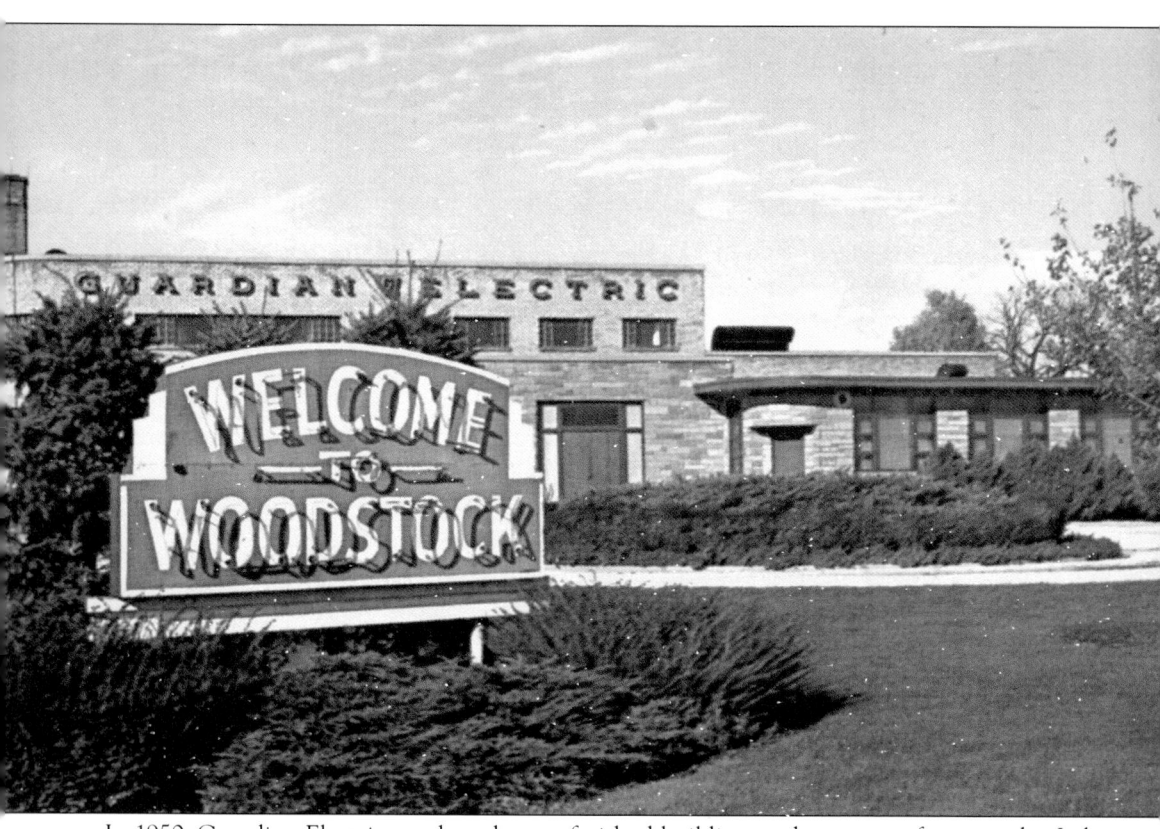

In 1950, Guardian Electric purchased an unfinished building at the corner of present-day Lake Avenue and Route 47, where contact switches, solenoids, and hermetically sealed relays would be assembled. Operations began in 1951. By 1967, 285 people were employed assembling commercial and aerospace relays. The Welcome to Woodstock sign was installed on the property in 1955. (Courtesy of McHenry County Historical Society, Don Peasley Collection.)

Four
AN EXTRAORDINARY SCHOOL

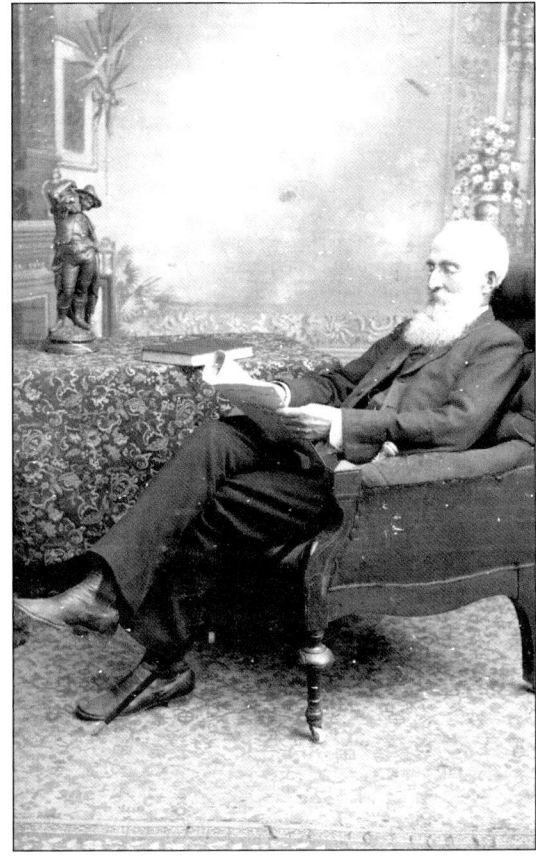

From its humble beginnings in 1848, the Todd School for Boys grew to offer facilities and programs that allowed students a chance to learn useful activities, express their creative talents, try a variety of physical activities, and study in an extraordinary environment. Rev. Richard Kimball Todd, along with his bride, came to Woodstock upon invitation to become pastor of the newly organized Presbyterian church. Recognizing the need for better schools, Reverend Todd taught a small group of students in his home in 1848. He also served as the county school commissioner from 1849 to 1855. In 1859, Reverend Todd opened the Woodstock Parsonage Institute, which burned to the ground in 1860 due to arson. Thankfully, the students were living in a separate building. For the next several years, classes were conducted a few blocks away in the Presbyterian church. The school, called the Woodstock University and the Woodstock Collegiate Institute during this period, drew most of its students from Woodstock and neighboring towns. (Courtesy of McHenry County Historical Society.)

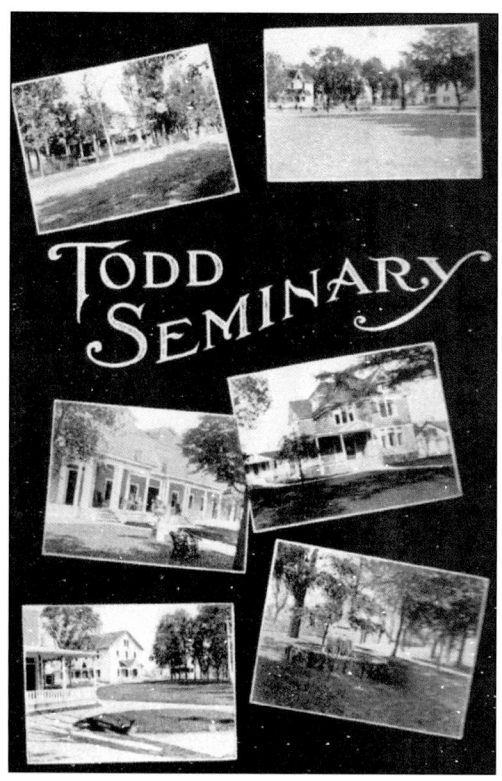

Noble Hill came to work for Rev. Richard Kimball Todd in 1890 and, in 1892, bought the school, which consisted of three buildings: Wallingford Hall, Clover Hall, and a barn. Hill later purchased additional land, bringing the campus to 14 acres plus the 40-acre Todd Woods. Hill's wife, Eliza Rogers, was well educated and very influential in the school's success. Todd Seminary for Boys celebrated its golden jubilee in 1898. (Courtesy of McHenry County Historical Society.)

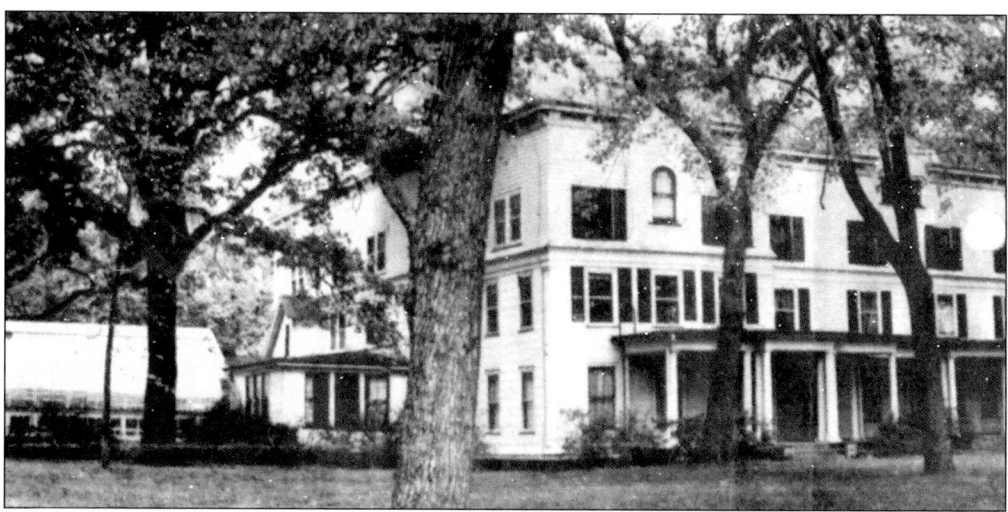

The oldest building on the campus was Wallingford Hall, named for Reverend Todd's father, Wallingford Todd. The structure originally consisted of two living rooms and two upstairs bedrooms. Eventually a third story was added. After Todd School closed, Wallingford Hall was used by the Woodstock Residence nursing home until its new facility was completed. It was demolished in 1964. (Courtesy of McHenry County Historical Society.)

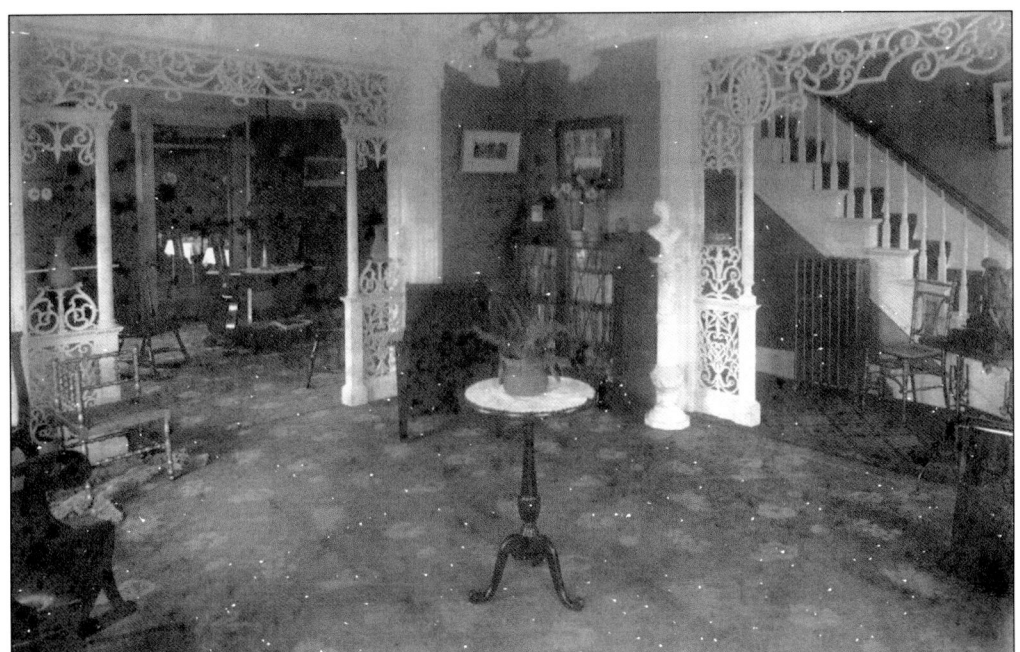

The Wallingford Hall living rooms remained relatively unchanged over the decades and as additions were constructed. Wallingford Hall later became the residence for the youngest students, aged 7 through 10. The very youngest had a six-bed dormitory supervised by its own nurse. (Courtesy of McHenry County Historical Society.)

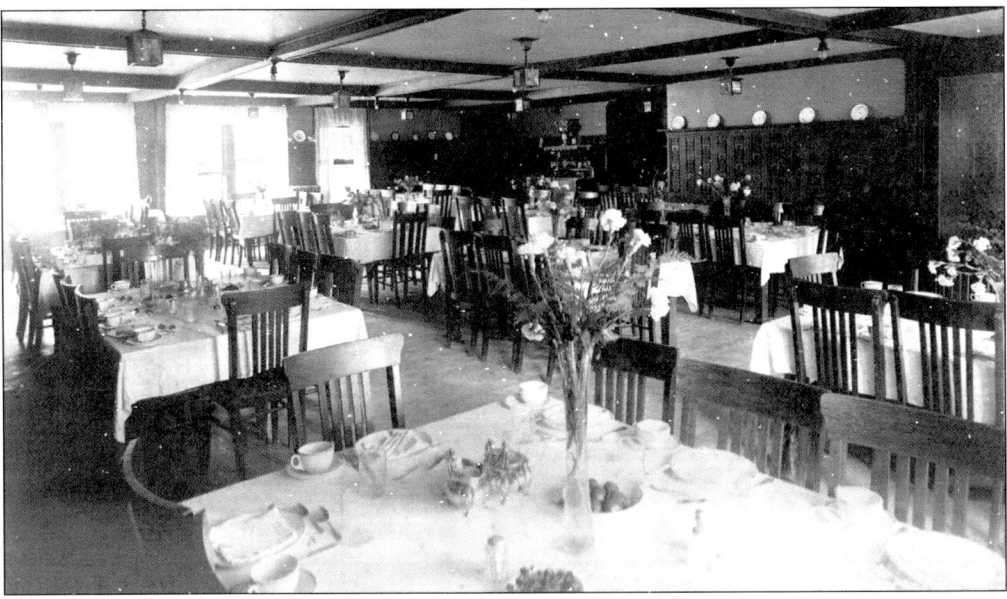

The school dining room was included in Wallingford Hall. A teacher sat at each table; students who did not eat well had to sit at a table with the nurse or the coach. Lena Paulson was the cook during Reverend Todd's tenure. One day while he was in Chicago, two boys wrote "Codfish Seminary" on the fence, as the students were tired of eating codfish every Friday. Furious, Reverend Todd told Paulson never to serve codfish again—and she did not. (Courtesy of McHenry County Historical Society.)

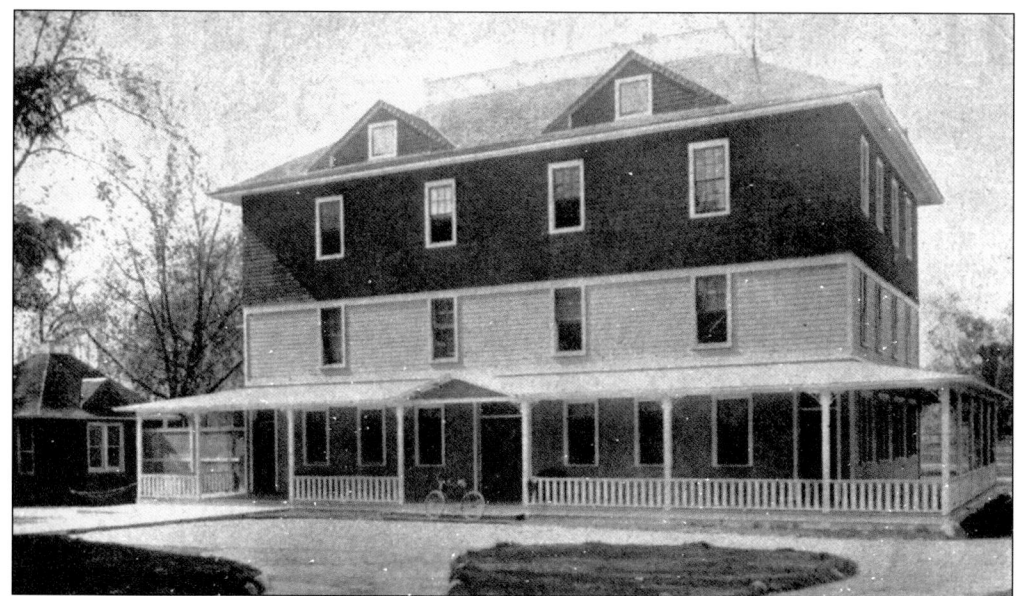

Clover Hall was named for Rev. Richard Kimball Todd's wife, Martha Clover. Upon completion of other facilities on campus, Clover Hall housed the 11- and 12-year-old boys. Like Wallingford Hall, it had brightly painted woodwork and furniture. (Courtesy of McHenry County Historical Society.)

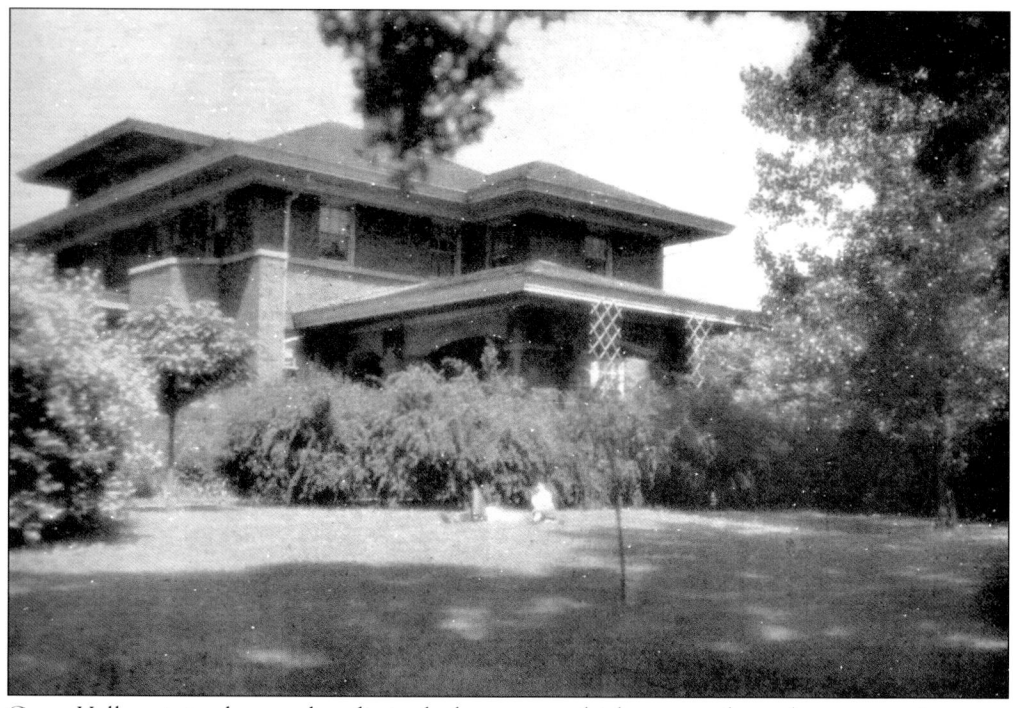

Grace Hall contained a sound studio in the basement, which gave students the opportunity to cut their own phonograph records, tape radio shows, and edit movie film. An electronic laboratory and darkroom were also available. Grace Hall housed 24 students, six faculty apartments, and a four-room suite of offices. (Courtesy of McHenry County Historical Society.)

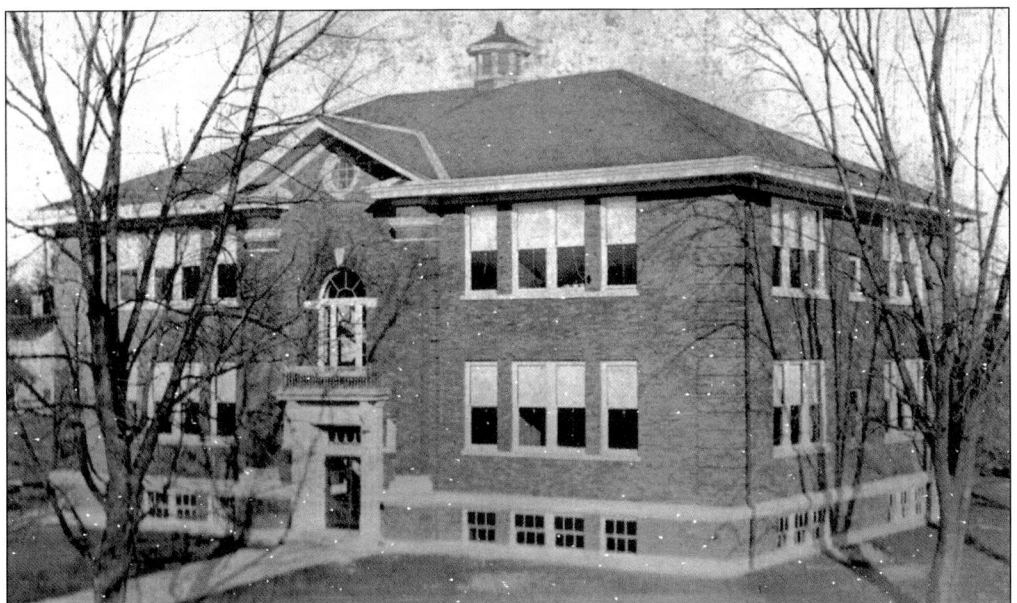

Rogers Hall was built in 1910 and named for Noble Hill's wife, Eliza Rogers. A wood shop, print shop, and machine shop were located in the basement, while classrooms, an office, and the library were found on the first floor. The typing room, chemistry and physics laboratories, and a 180-seat theater were located on the second floor. Scenery and costumes were stored in the attic, which also contained a projection booth. (Courtesy of McHenry County Historical Society.)

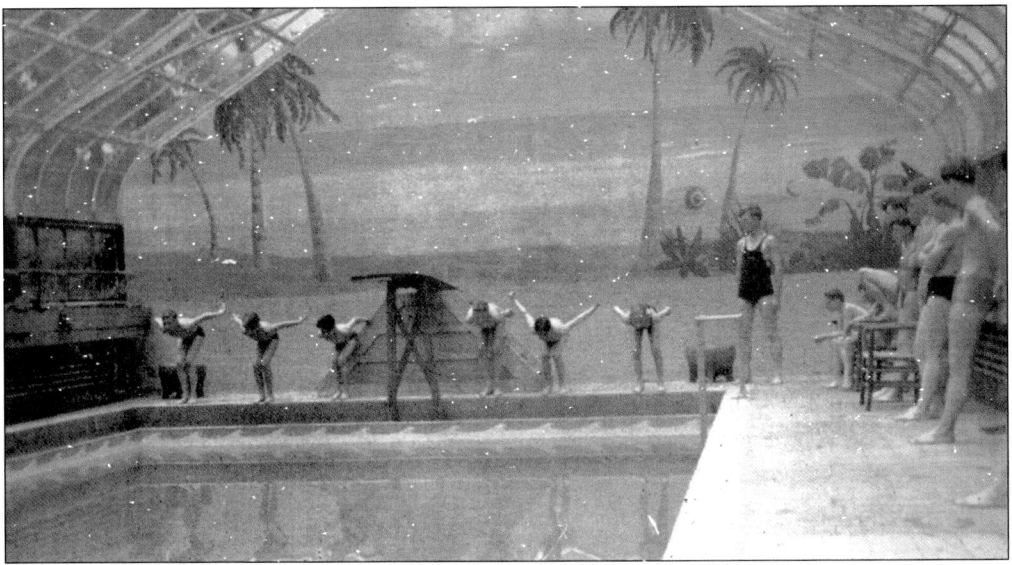

In 1930, Roger Hill purchased the school from his father and added to the facilities. An indoor swimming pool in a heated, glass-walled building was constructed in that same year. Students grew flowers, vines, and even tomatoes around the sides, and Mrs. Hill painted a mural at one end. The younger boys could travel directly from the pool to their second-floor dormitory without having to go outside. The shower rooms and mechanical equipment were located under the dining hall, and students could view the pool from dining hall windows. (Courtesy of McHenry County Historical Society.)

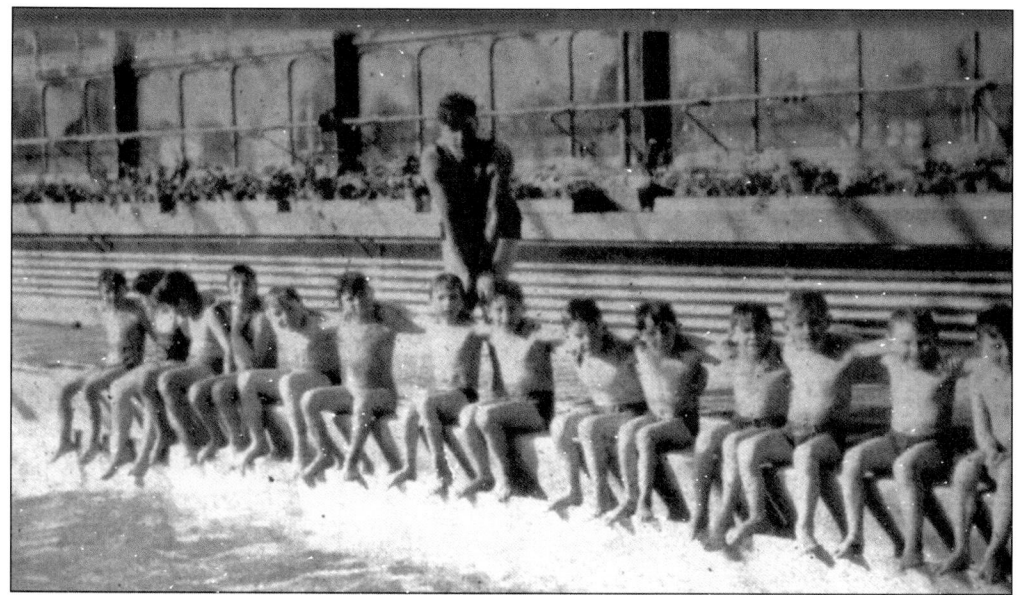

Physical education teacher Tony Roskie taught swimming and coached a very competitive swim team. At Todd, boys could play tennis, baseball, and football, run on the cinder track, or sled down the campus toboggan slide. Twelve horses were kept at the Todd stables. The boys learned to sail a schooner at Camp TOSEBO in Michigan, named through the first two letters in Todd Seminary for Boys. A fleet of sailboats was kept at Wonder Lake. (Courtesy of McHenry County Historical Society.)

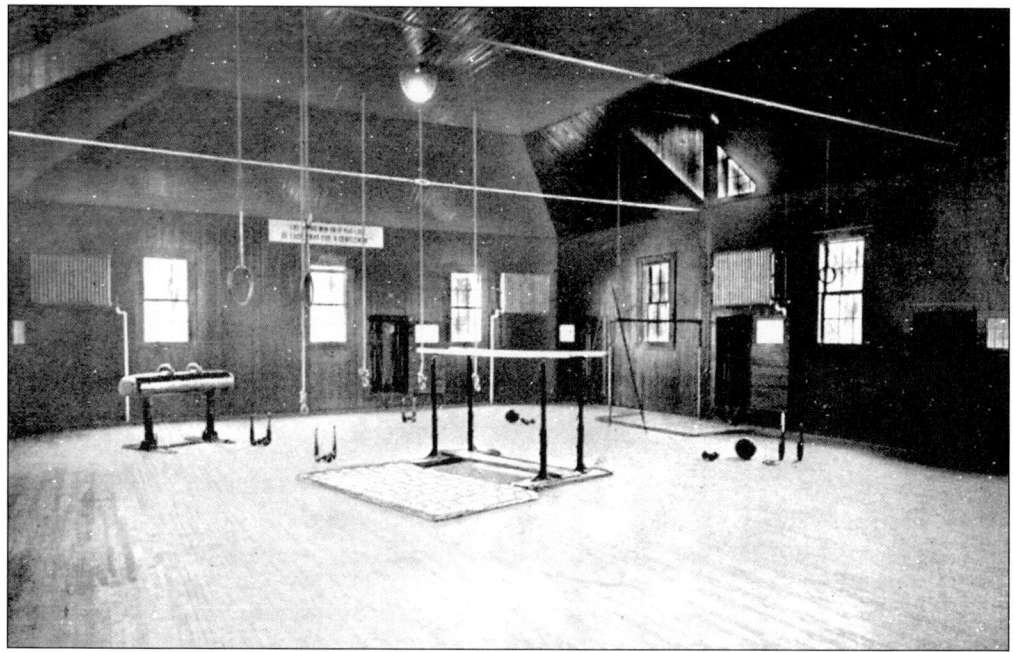

This gymnasium, eventually enlarged to allow spectator seating, contained a 70-foot-long basketball court, a bowling alley, and showers. Todd School competed against other schools quite successfully, while also conducting an active intramural program. (Courtesy of McHenry County Historical Society.)

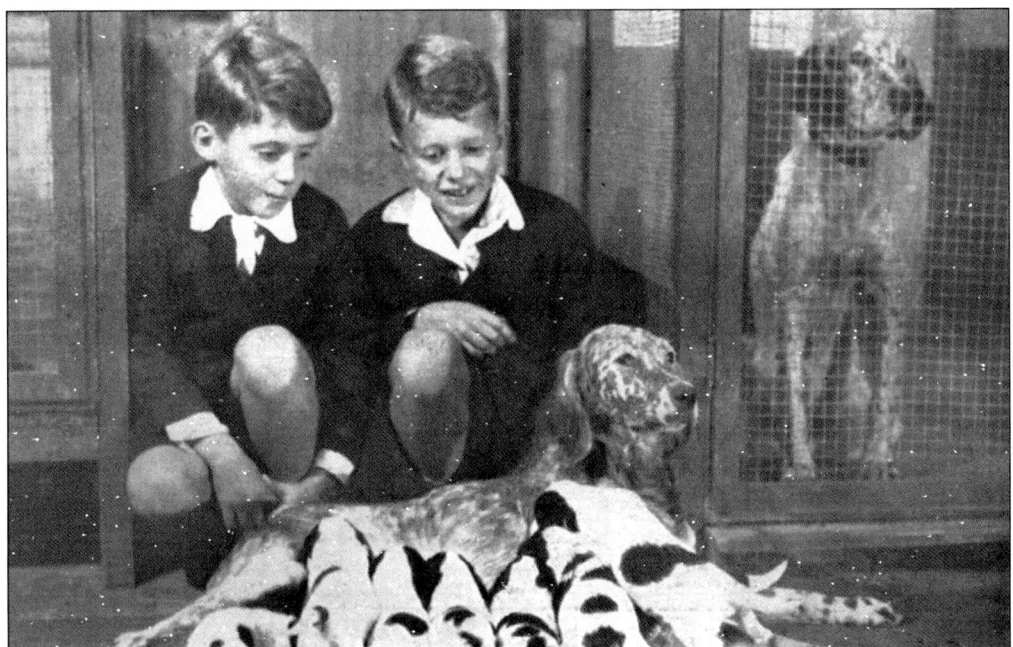

The Todd kennels were established in the belief that every boy should experience the love of a dog. The dogs were used in the animal husbandry curriculum, and students from fifth through eighth grade worked in the kennels. Older boys had a field trial club. Many Todd alumni, including award-winning reporter Sandy Smith, continued to train dogs throughout their lives.

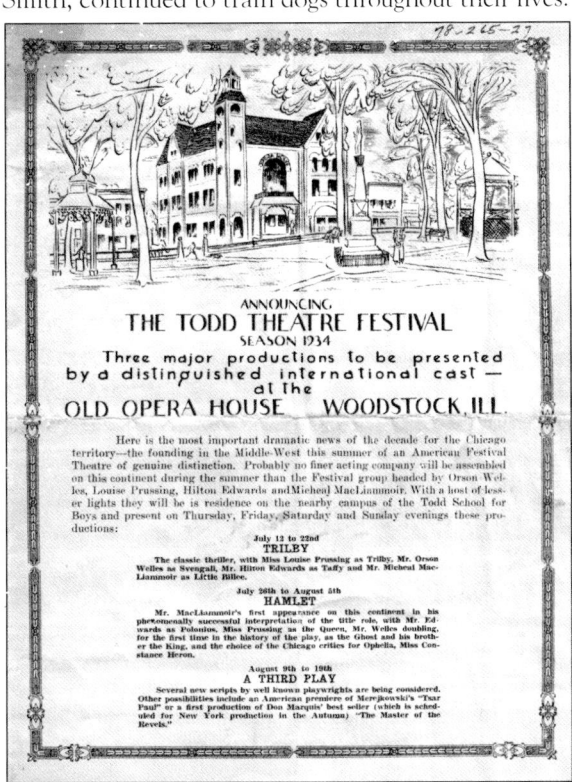

Orson Welles arrived at Todd School in 1926, following the death of his mother. Under Roger Hill's guidance, he developed a love of acting while writing, directing, and starring in school productions. Welles graduated from Todd in 1931, then traveled and performed abroad. In the summer of 1934, he returned to Woodstock to produce a festival of Shakespearean plays at the Woodstock Opera House. He and the cast stayed at Todd School during the summer. (Courtesy of McHenry County Historical Society.)

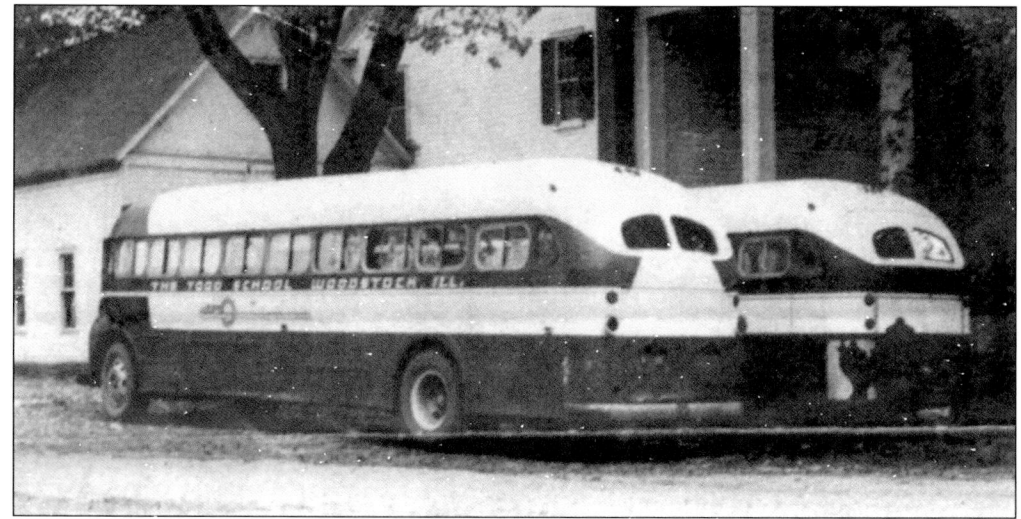

Students gave the name "Big Bertha" to the various Pullman buses transporting them to the places they were studying, such as Gettysburg or Harper's Ferry, and to Todd Island, a private island in the Florida Keys where students spent one month each winter. The Big Berthas contained complete accommodations in which 18 students could travel, study, eat, and sleep.

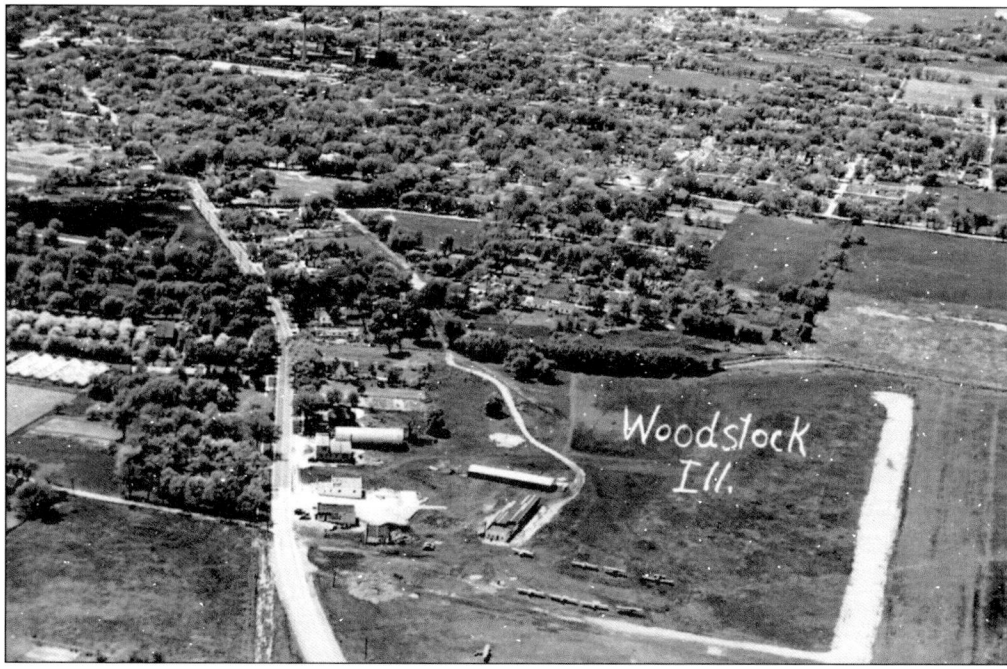

Actors, musicians, professionals, athletes, educators, and physicist Robert R. Wilson are all part of the Todd School story. Following his parent's divorce, Wilson came to live with his grandmother Nellie Fee Rathbone, a teacher and housemother who was a cousin of Grace Hill. He went on to work on the Manhattan Project, witness the first atomic bomb test in New Mexico in 1945, and help build the world's largest particle accelerator. By 1950, the Todd campus in Woodstock contained 250 acres with an airport and farm. When the school closed in 1954, the airport became the site of the new Marian Central High School. (Courtesy of McHenry County Historical Society.)

Five

CRIME AND CRIME-FIGHTERS

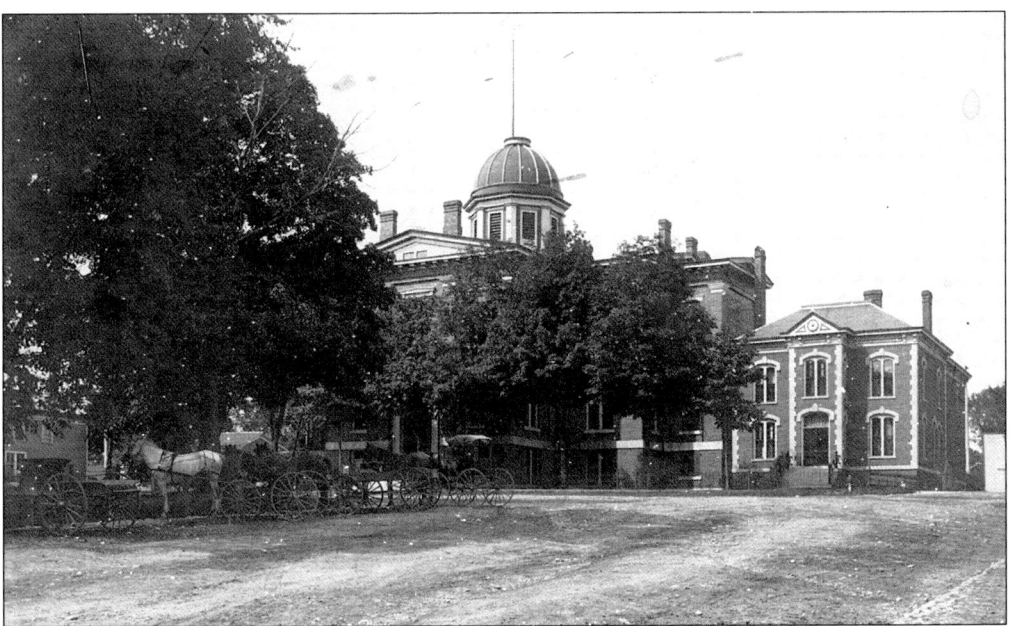

The first McHenry County Courthouse, located in the center of the square, was very small but contained jail cells and a sheriff's residence. The next courthouse, constructed in 1857, was designed with the jail in the basement. The sheriff resided in the courthouse itself. In 1886, Sheriff A. W. Udell reportedly came close to losing his prisoners. Children from a neighboring house had observed light shining through the brick wall of the jail. It was discovered that the prisoners had displaced bricks, creating a hole about two feet square, and were just about to escape. In 1887, a new jail and sheriff's residence was constructed next door. Sheriff Udell did lose prisoners from the new jail one evening when he and his deputy were away on business. Jim Russell, jailed for rape, and Mike Kelehan, jailed for burglary, managed to tear a section of pipe loose and use it to pry off sections of steel grate, which allowed them into a corridor with an unlocked door. The other prisoners chose to remain inside. (Courtesy Woodstock Public Library.)

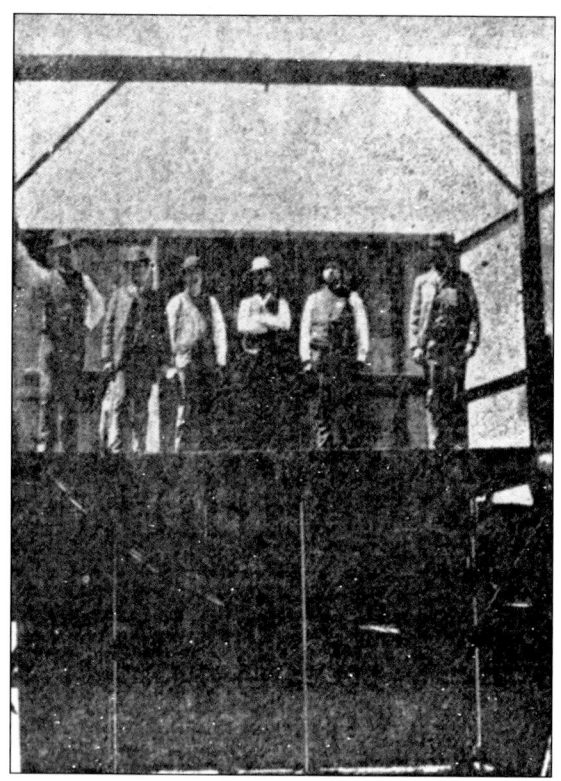

McHenry County's only legal hanging occurred on July 16, 1886. James Dacey of Chicago was convicted of shooting and killing Chicago alderman Gaynor in a saloon fight. He was moved to the McHenry County jail and held until his execution. A week before the hanging, Simon Brink, who would later oversee the construction of the Woodstock Opera House, constructed the scaffold for the hanging, assisted by his sons Fred and Charles. (Courtesy of McHenry County Historical Society.)

Willard Sherman would stop outside James Dacey's cell window and talk to him on his way home from school. A wall was built around the courthouse yard and people were given tickets to enter. Policemen were armed with wagon spokes because of a rumor that the Dacey gang would come to rescue him. Young Sherman walked through the gate without being stopped, crawled into a box, and found a knothole to look through. He saw Dacey emerge through the trapdoor with the rope around his neck and watched him die. Sherman grew up to serve Woodstock as a volunteer fireman for 58 years and a policeman for 20 years.

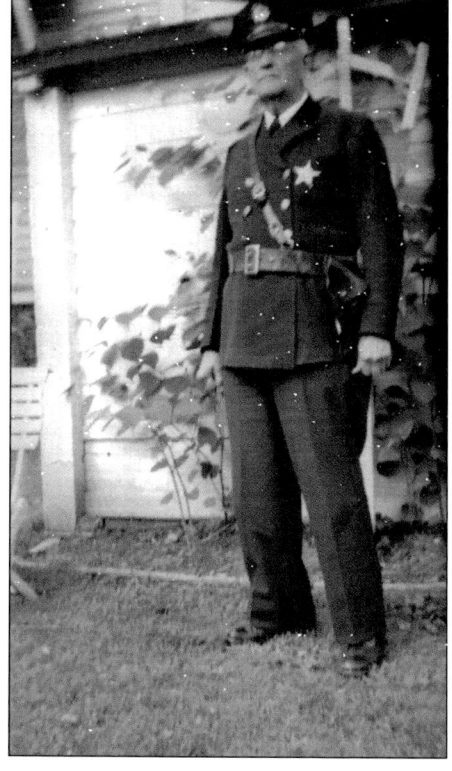

Among the infamous "guests" at the county jail was Eugene B. Debs. Debs and six other members of the American Railway Union were sentenced to prison in Woodstock in 1896 for contempt of court, related to their activities in the Pullman strike. They arrived by train under the charge of Deputy United States Marshal Donnelly and were met by Sheriff George Eckert and a large contingent of city residents who escorted them to the jail. Under Debs's direction, the men exercised rigorously each day before breakfast; they studied history and economics and debated each evening. Debs's introduction to socialism began during his imprisonment in Woodstock. (Courtesy of McHenry County Historical Society.)

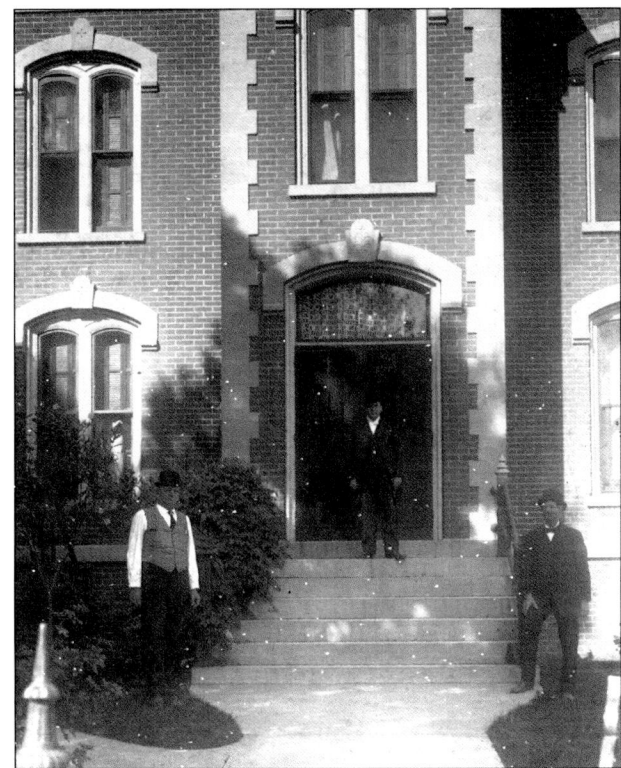

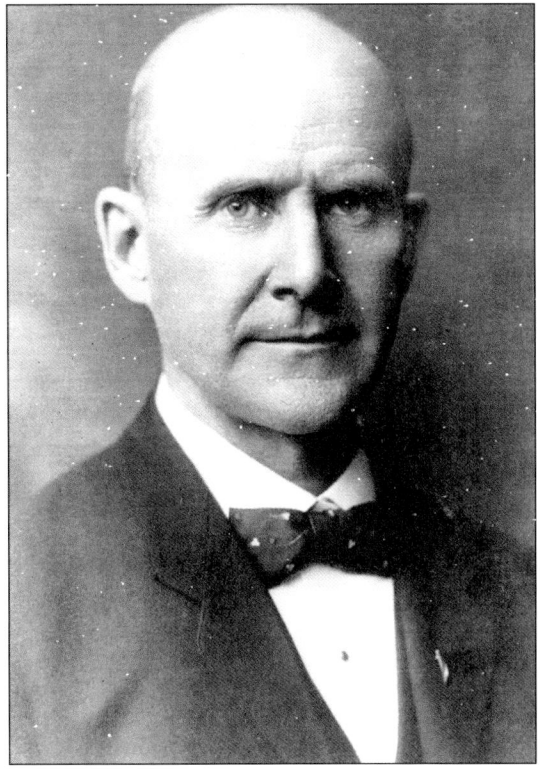

Sheriff Eckert extended extraordinary privileges to Debs and the others. They played football behind the courthouse, sunned themselves on the grounds, and dined with the sheriff's family. Debs was allowed to use the living room to receive visitors, including reporter Nellie Bly and *American Socialist* editor Victor Berger. He hired a secretary to assist with all his mail. A jail cell was set aside for the production of Debs's publication, the *Railway Times*. On the day he was released, Woodstock was jammed with crowds, and Debs was carried to the station on the shoulders of townspeople. (Courtesy of Bev Ganschow.)

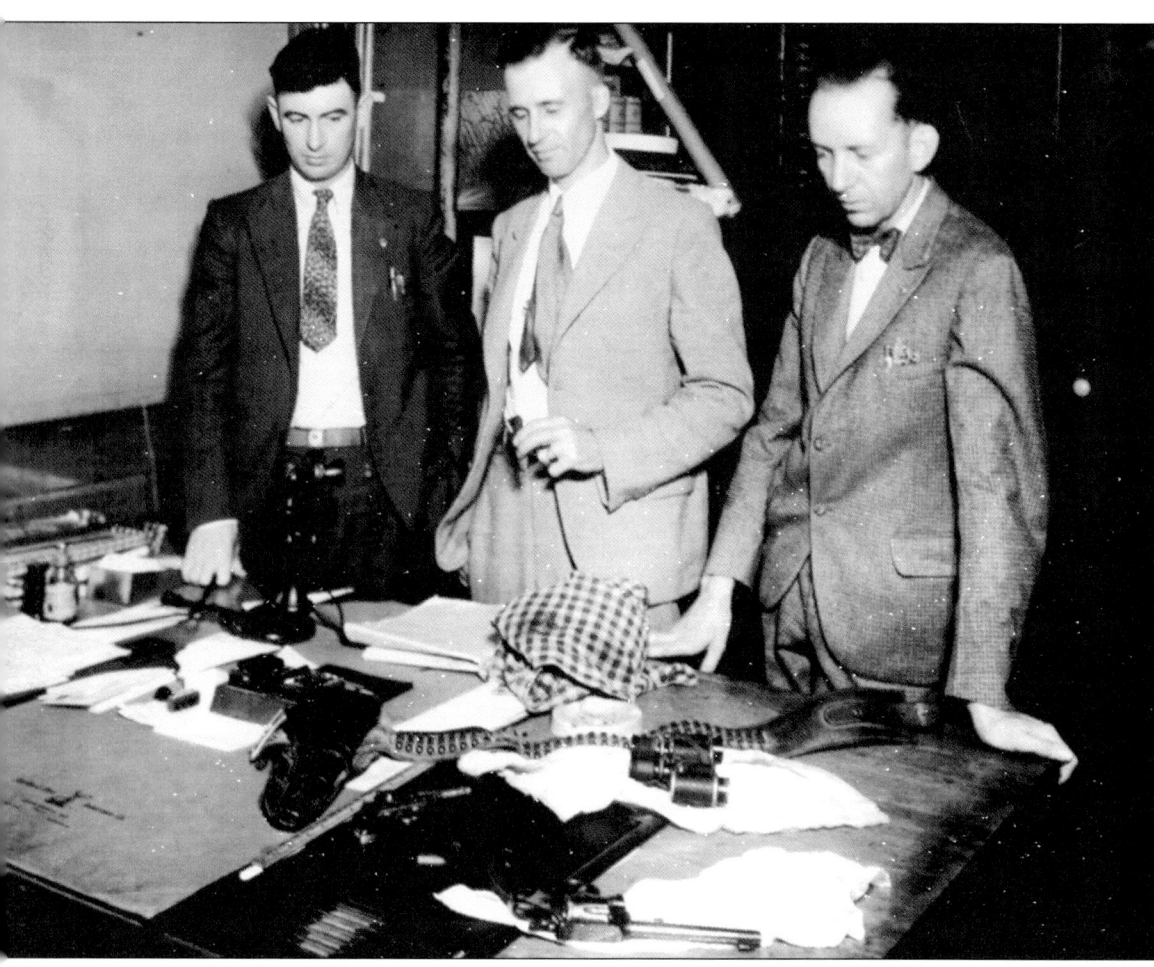

Deputy Sheriff Harold Reese, Sheriff Lester "Doc" Edinger, and newspaper reporter George Sullivan examine evidence from an unidentified crime. A local war hero, Edinger was elected sheriff at the age of 28 and served during much of Prohibition. With only two full-time officers and an estimated 25 to 30 speakeasies, Edinger had to deputize additional men before each raid. During Prohibition, beer runners made frequent trips from Chicago to Wisconsin by way of McHenry County. On several occasions, runners were caught, and at one time, 100 barrels of beer were stored as evidence in the jail basement. Because there were no federal prisons in Chicago, individuals held for federal crimes were placed wherever there was room, including the McHenry County jail. "Dapper" Dan McCarthy and Earl "Hymie" Wiess were among those prisoners. While they were held in Woodstock for a Chicago hijacking in 1925, Edinger put them to work laying bricks and carrying mortar for the red brick garage being constructed behind the county jail. (Courtesy of McHenry County Historical Society.)

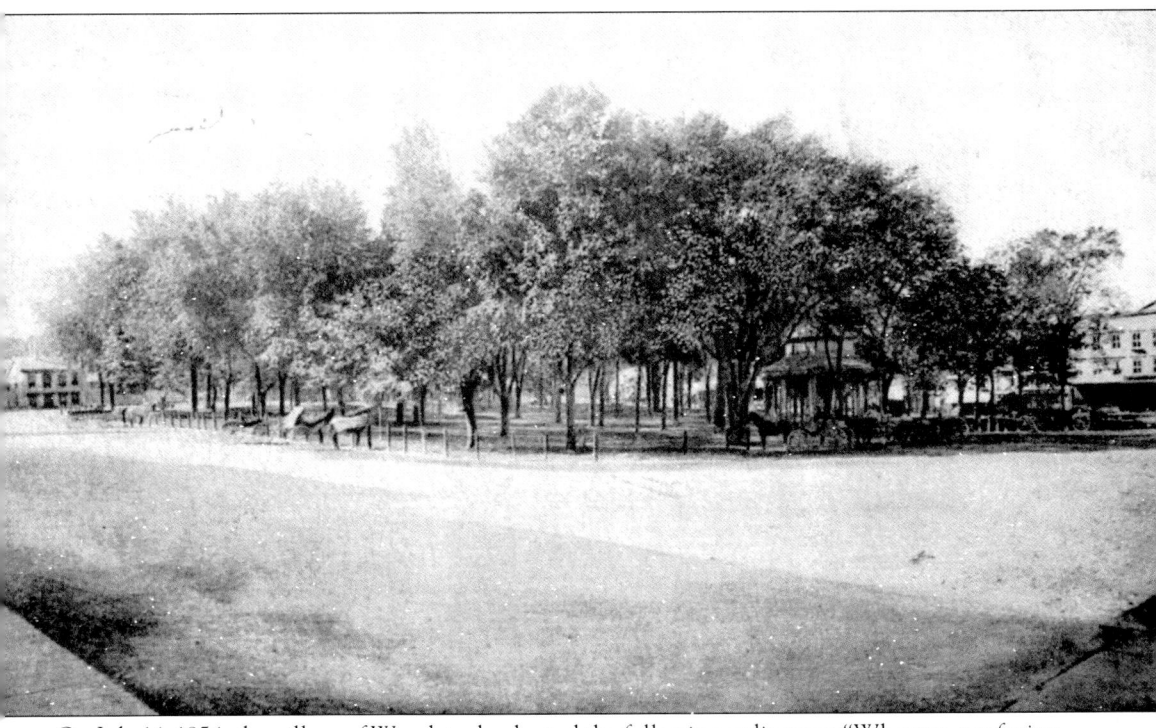

On July 14, 1854, the village of Woodstock adopted the following ordinance: "Whereas, confusion and turmoil seems to be the order of the day, and drinking and dissipation and street fights are practiced by many transient persons in this town and surrounding country, endangering the lives of peaceable citizens, and bringing disgrace upon our otherwise peaceable village, be it ordained . . . that a police force be and is hereby established . . . whose duty it shall be to suppress intoxication and rioting in the streets or other places, by arresting the parties making loud and unusual noises, if in their opinion said noise is made by means of intoxicating liquor, or when the parties may be in the act of quarreling or fighting, whether from said cause or otherwise, and commit such parties to the jail located in said corporation, and deliver him or her to them be peaceable or sober as the case may be, when they shall be conveyed before the police magistrate." Police officers investigated vagrants, transients, and hoodlums, the occasional domestic dispute or disturbance of the peace, and youthful pranks. Every so often, a burglary, horse theft, or arson would call for some real detective work. (Courtesy of McHenry County Historical Society.)

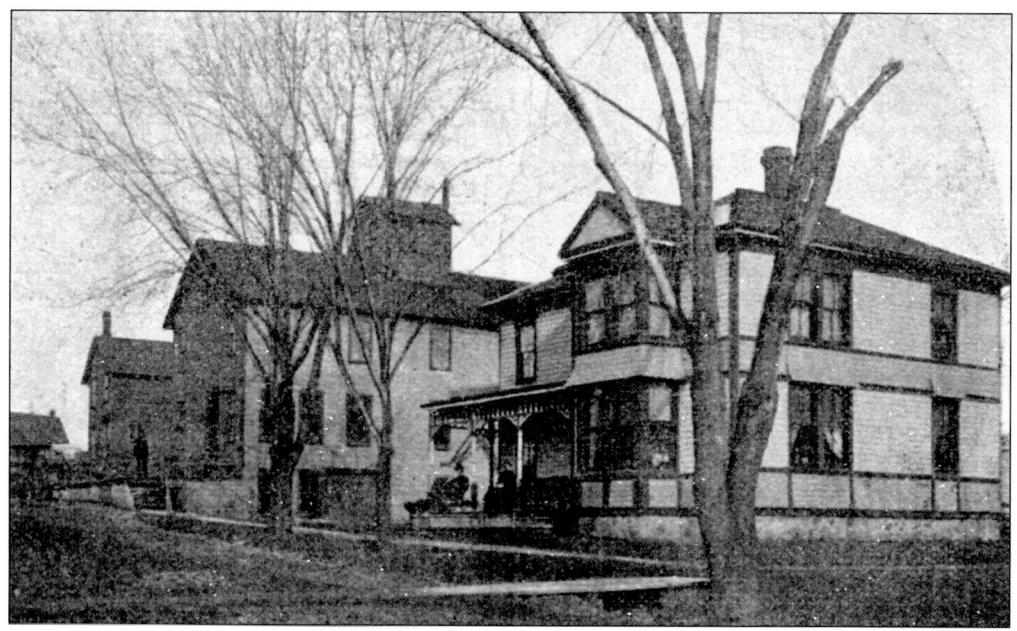

On February 28, 1902, Benjamin and Alice Ellsworth and 78-year-old boarder Amos Anderson were shot and killed in the Ellsworth house. Son Earl ran to the nearby lumberyard, revealing that Anderson had shot his parents and in turn his father had shot Anderson. The shootings had occurred in Anderson's attic bedroom. Since the Ellsworth family and Amos Anderson were well regarded in town, the bloody tragedy shocked Woodstock residents.

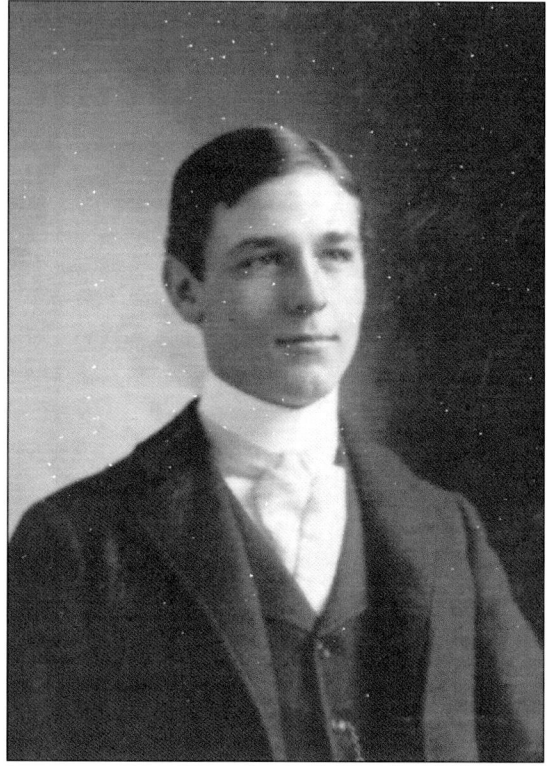

The state attorney did not accept Earl Ellsworth's explanation and so did surveillance on him and his girlfriend, Mary Lee. When it seemed that the relationship had ended, Mary was approached for information. Stating that Earl had admitted his guilt, she was prepared to testify but instead mysteriously disappeared, never to be heard from again. Ellsworth left town, and the Pinkerton Detective Agency was hired to follow him and elicit a confession. Earl Ellsworth was ultimately convicted and sentenced to life in prison. Some 18 years later, renowned trial attorney Clarence Darrow successfully obtained clemency, and Ellsworth moved to Wisconsin upon his release. (Courtesy of McHenry County Historical Society.)

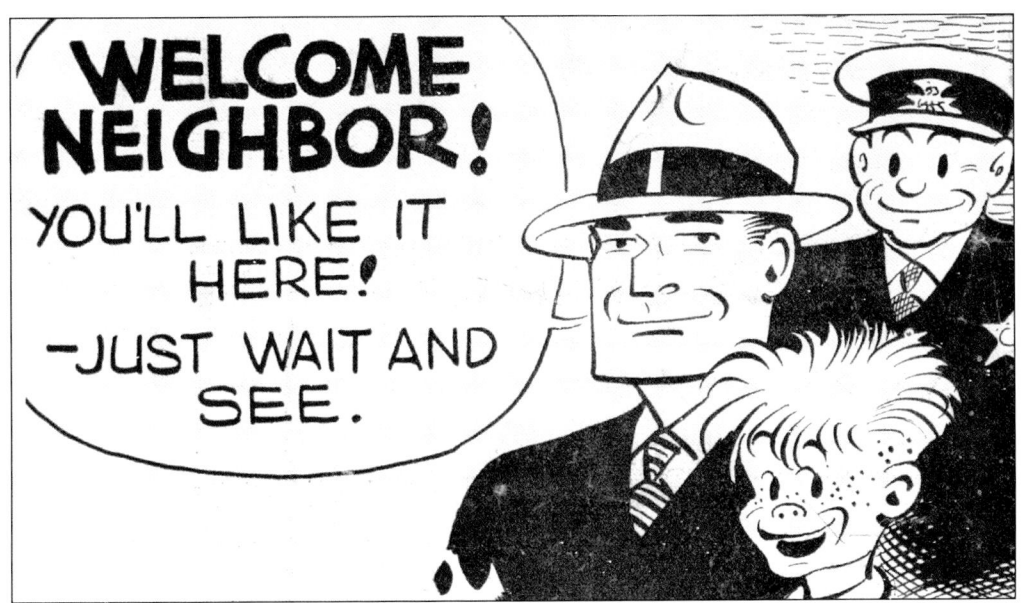

Woodstock's most legendary crime-fighter is Dick Tracy, the creation of Chester Gould. Gould and his wife, Edna, moved to a farm east of Woodstock in 1935. From his rural studio, Gould drew the comic strip character Dick Tracy for several decades. He also maintained a small office in town, overlooking the square, where his brother Ray lettered the comics. The "Welcome Neighbor" cartoon was created for a new resident booklet distributed by the chamber of commerce. (Dick Tracy ® 2006 Tribune Media Services Inc. Licensed by Classic Media, Inc. All rights reserved.)

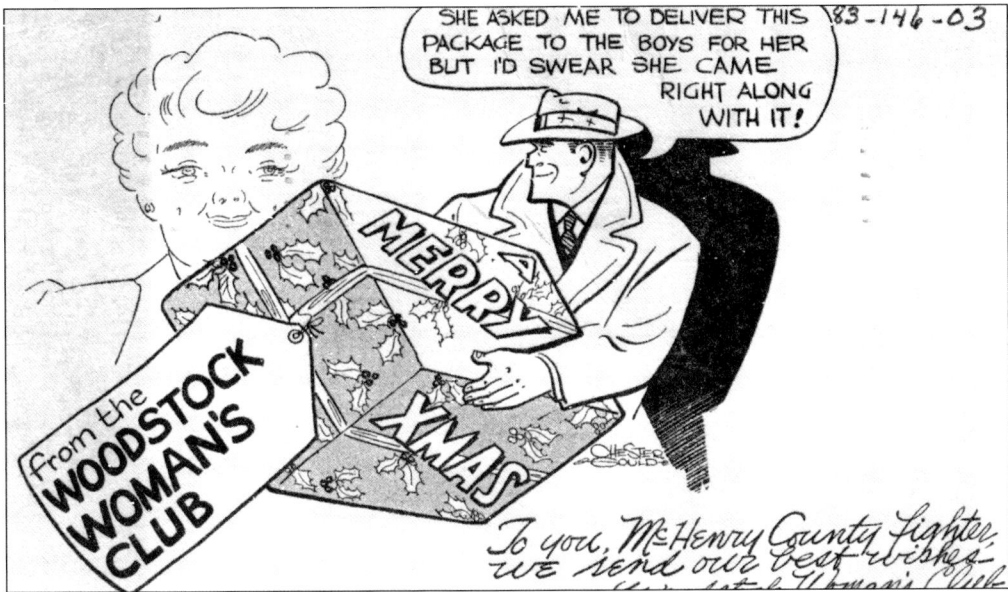

Chester Gould was very active in community affairs, giving original artwork to area residents and donating drawings for many causes. He chaired annual fund-raising drives for the McHenry County Easter Seals in the 1960s and provided Easter Seals with artwork for its national campaigns. In 1943, Gould drew the above cartoon for the Woodstock Women's Club to use as a Christmas card that was mailed to Woodstock servicemen. (Courtesy of McHenry County Historical Society; Dick Tracy ® 2006 Tribune Media Services Inc. Licensed by Classic Media, Inc. All rights reserved.)

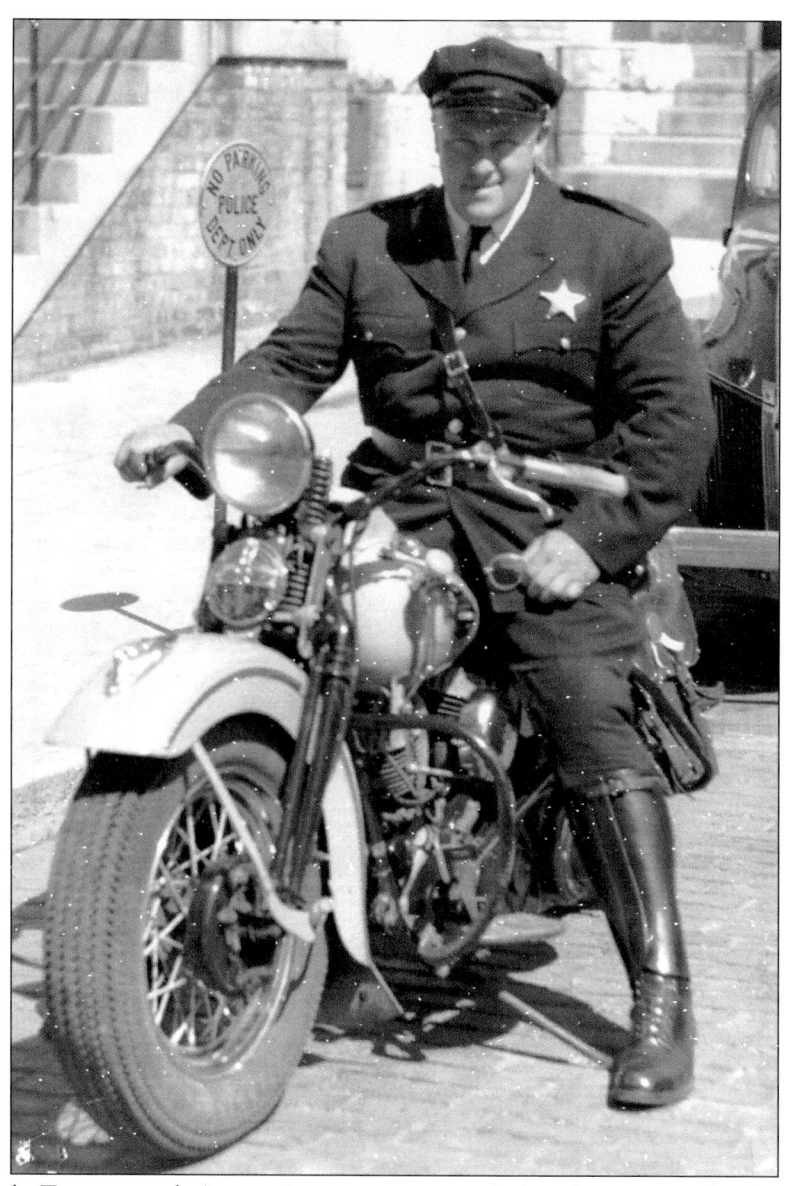

While Dick Tracy stirred America's imagination with his futuristic technology, he also introduced the junior crime-fighter idea. Chester Gould and Woodstock police chief Emery "Tiny" Hansman established the Woodstock Crimestoppers Club. Youngsters received Dick Tracy badges and decoder kits and listened to guest speakers from local, state, and federal law enforcement agencies. Bicycle safety, good citizenship, and companionship were stressed. On Friday or Saturday nights, Hansman would take a group of crime-stoppers to fish on Lake Michigan. Chester Gould underwrote expenses and would sometimes accompany them on these excursions. Upon their return, the crime-stoppers would distribute the fish to various service clubs for their fish fries. Woodstock native Hansman played football for the Chicago Cardinals in 1935 and served in World War II. Head of the Woodstock branch of the Salvation Army, he also conducted the first air raid siren test in McHenry County as Woodstock's civil defense director. At 370 pounds and six feet two inches tall, Hansmen was no small presence. (Courtesy of McHenry County Historical Society.)

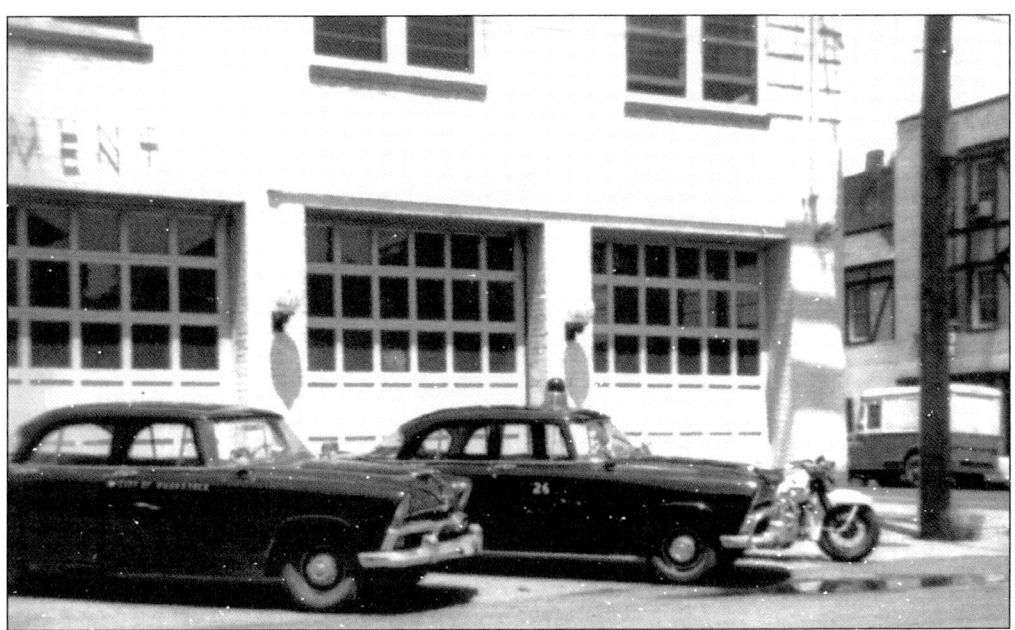

Tiny Hansman served as police chief for 14 years. His motto was to "keep people out of trouble and not get them into it." He believed that if you showed children that policemen were their friends, the young people would respect them. (Courtesy of McHenry County Historical Society.)

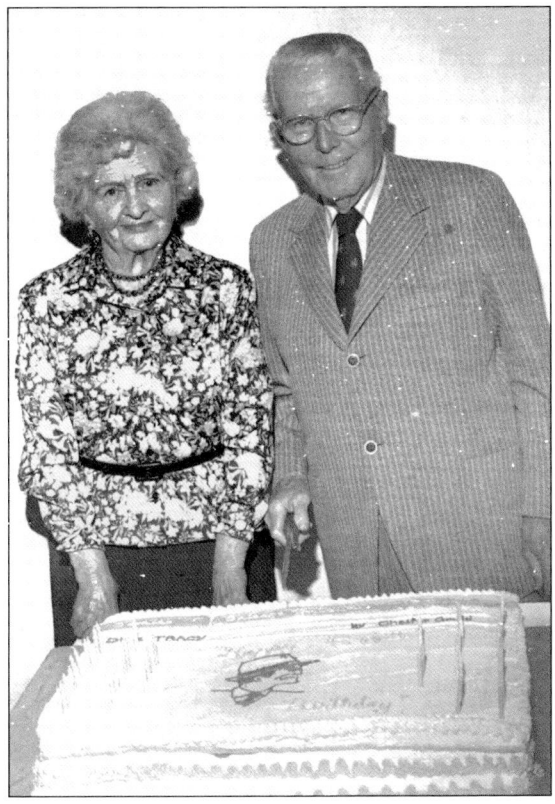

Chester Gould, and therefore Dick Tracy, also supported fund-raising for Memorial Hospital. Chester's wife, Edna, played a major role as chairman of the women's auxiliary. In 1981, the hospital staff surprised the Goulds with a party marking the 50th birthday of crime-fighter Tracy. Chester and Edna were at the hospital for a meeting of the capital fund drive committee, on which Chester served as the honorary chairman. After the meeting, a special cake, prepared and decorated by hospital staff, was unveiled. (Courtesy of McHenry County Historical Society.)

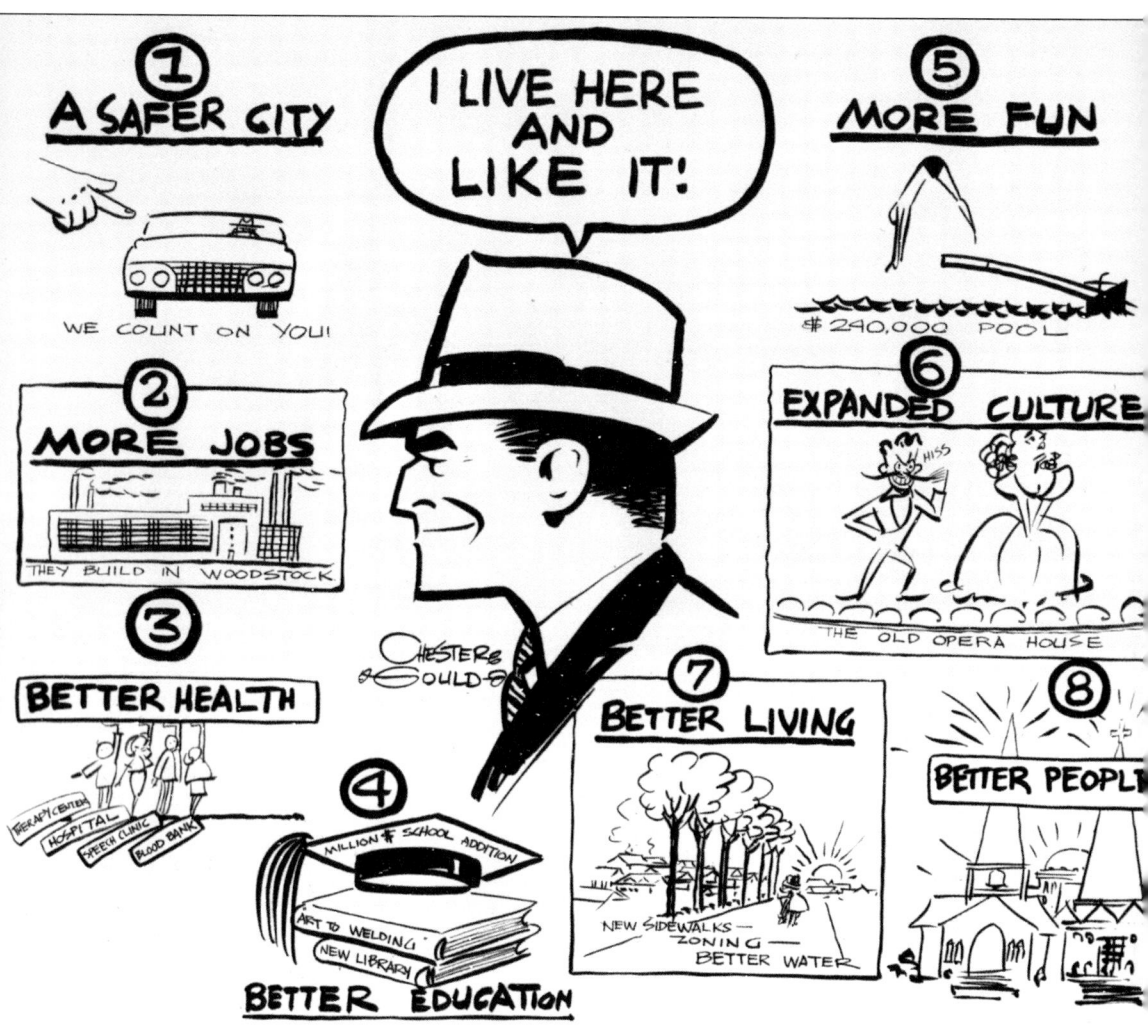

In 1963, Woodstock resident John Strohm, the editor of several national magazines and publisher of the *Woodstock Journal*, nominated Woodstock for All-American City honors, as sponsored by the National Municipal League and *Look* magazine. Chester Gould contributed to this effort by using Dick Tracy to tell the story. The drawing utilized the eight-point platform the nominating committee had developed. (Courtesy of Woodstock Public Library; Dick Tracy ® 2006 Tribune Media Services Inc. Licensed by Classic Media, Inc. All rights reserved.)

Six
WELCOME HOME

Woodstock citizens have a long and honorable tradition of serving the country in times of war. The Woodstock Light Guards was the second company in the state to organize when the Civil War began. The Woodstock Rifles soon followed. McHenry County furnished far more than its quota of men, and some gave their lives. The Women's Relief Corps, composed mostly of those who were left home while loved ones fought for the Union cause, was organized in 1893. This group looked after the welfare of indigent soldiers and their wives and children. At the beginning of the 20th century, the Women's Relief Corps began raising funds for the erection of a monument in the park that would pay tribute to "the boys in blue." The monument was created by Antonio Zoia and dedicated to the heroes of war, both living and dead. An unveiling ceremony was held on November 3, 1909.

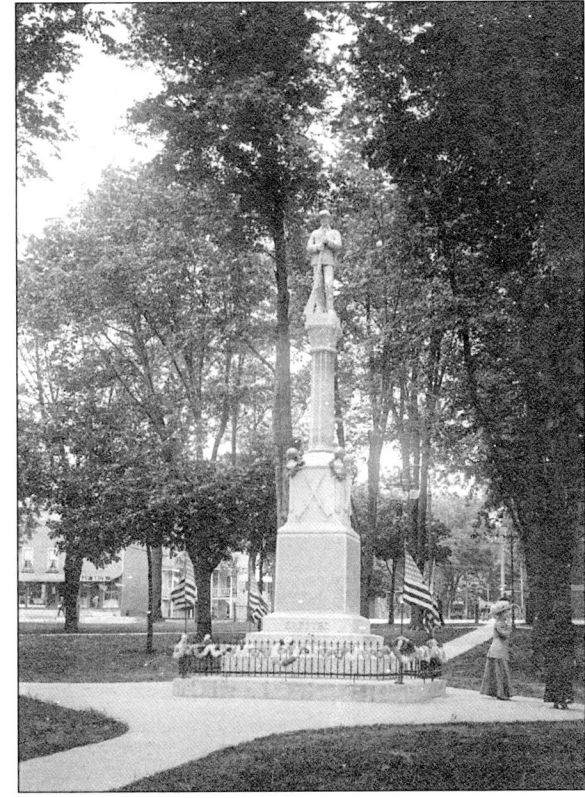

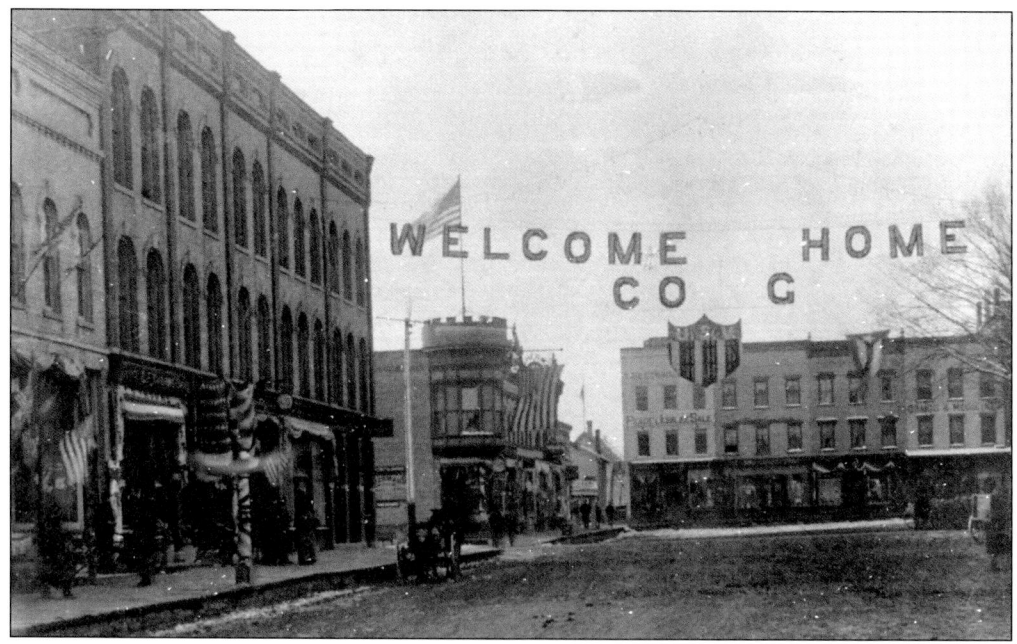

When the call came for the war with Spain in 1898, Woodstock's Company G answered with approximately 100 men. They sailed to Puerto Rico in July 1898 and were ordered home in November. Flags were flown around town, and the returning soldiers were greeted by a large banner spanning Benton Street.

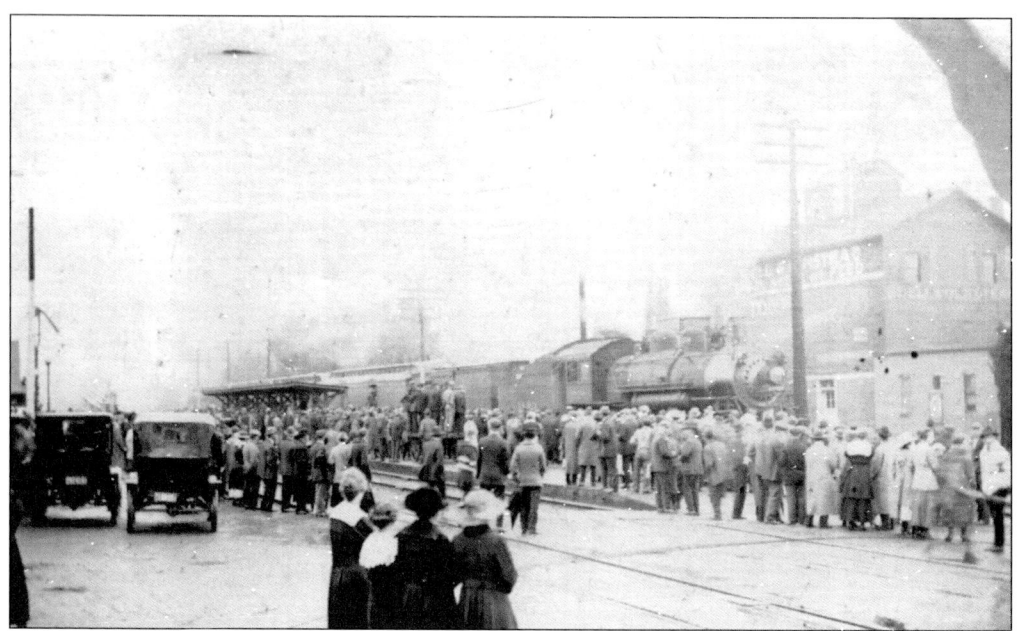

A throng of Woodstock residents saw their sons, husbands, brothers, and friends off to war at the Woodstock train station. In May 1918, Company G received orders for frontline service. The division took part in most of the major offenses during the summer and early fall of 1918 and was still in the frontline trenches when World War I officially ended with the armistice signing on November 11, 1918.

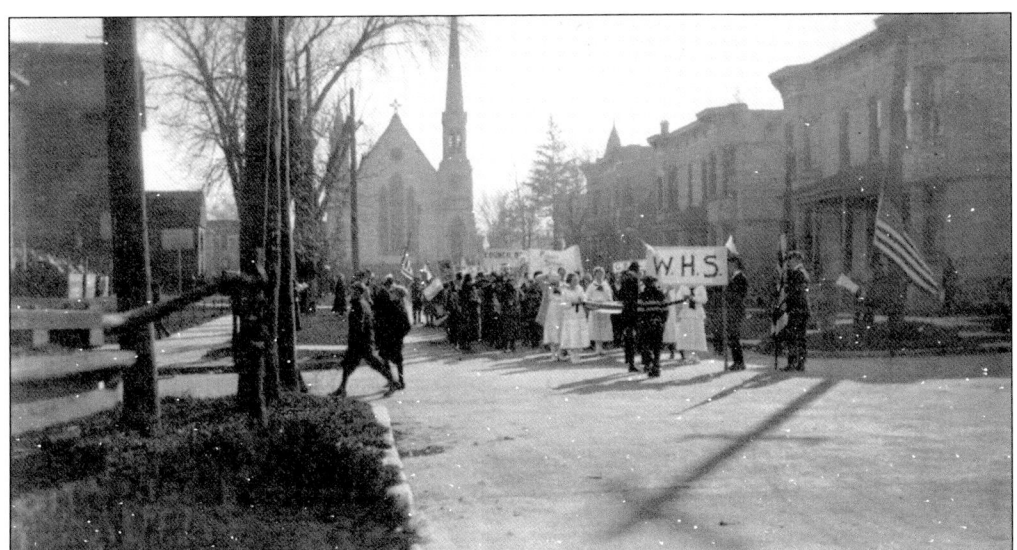

The news of peace was received at the Woodstock exchange of the Chicago Telephone Company, and word quickly spread around town. City government, newspaper men, and factory managers were told; factory whistles sounded around 3:30 a.m. Upon hearing the news, people quickly donned their clothes, grabbed anything they could use to make noise, and paraded through the streets. An official afternoon parade was hastily arranged.

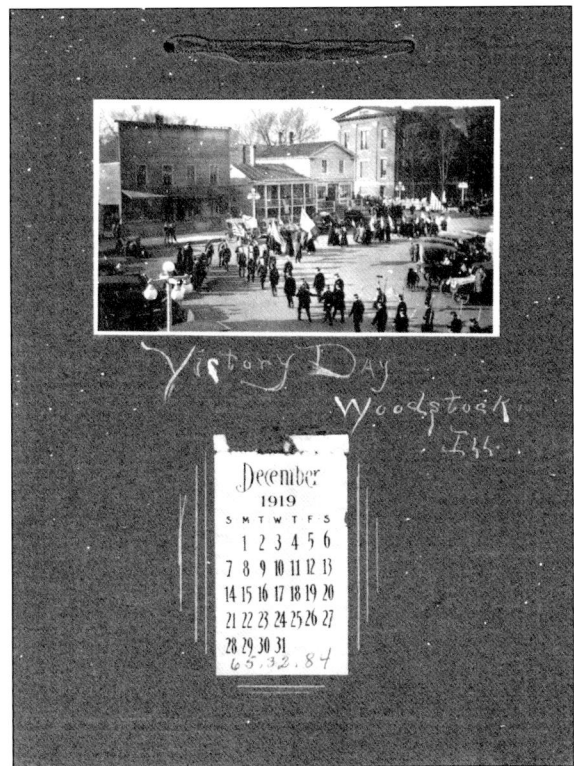

Civil War veteran George Eckert led the parade, followed by the city band, color guard, and members of the Women's Relief Corps. Schoolchildren, civic groups, politicians, and Oliver employees all participated. The city fire department's big red truck and about 100 decorated automobiles brought up the rear. This souvenir and many similar items were made following the 1918 Armistice Day celebration. (Courtesy of McHenry County Historical Society.)

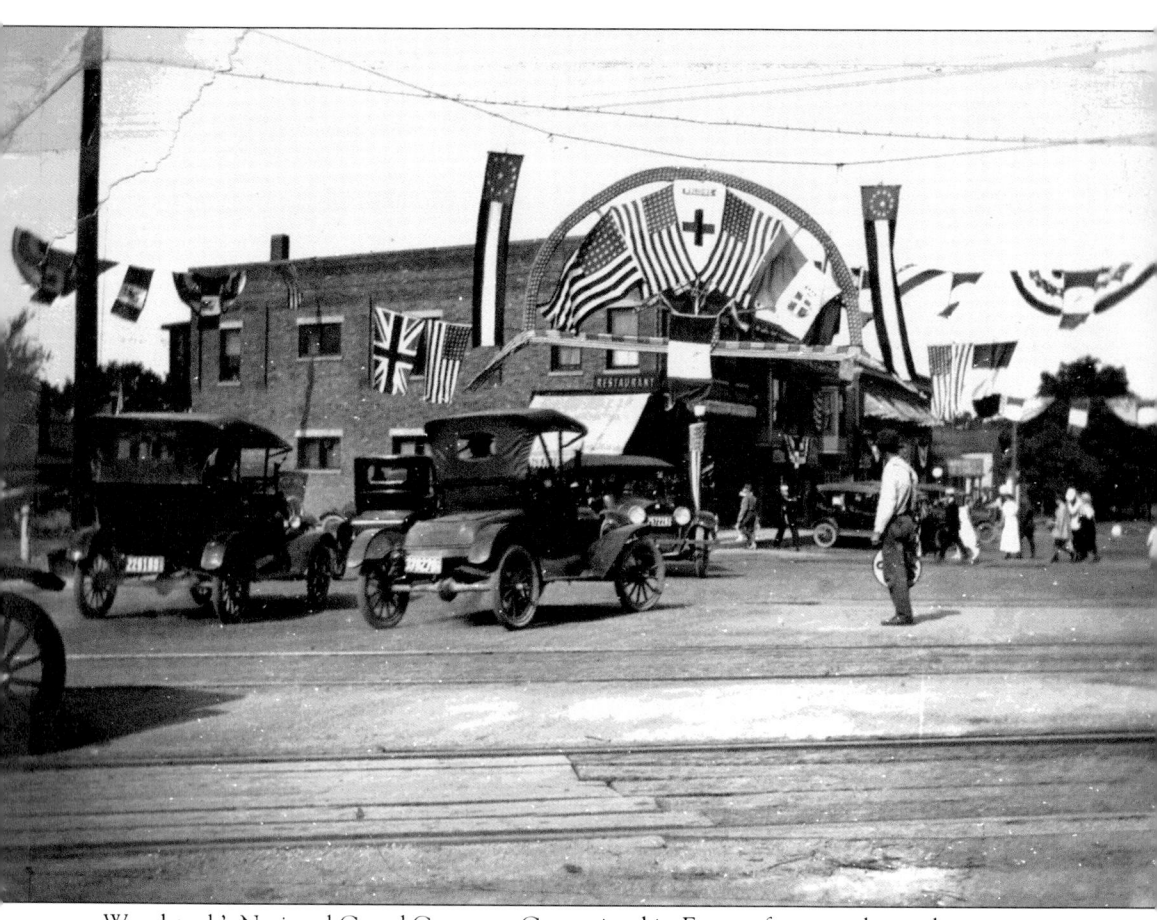

Woodstock's National Guard Company G remained in Europe for several months as occupation troops. By the time the men returned, the influenza epidemic of 1918 was waning, patriotism was high, and with the closing of the last saloons in the village of Union, McHenry County was officially "dry." Upon learning of the date of mustering out, officials hurried to make plans to welcome home area servicemen. On Tuesday, June 10, 1919, an estimated crowd of between 15,000 to 20,000 people from throughout McHenry County turned out to celebrate the homecoming of McHenry County servicemen who had fought in the Great War. Servicemen registered at the armory. As the parade stepped off at 11 a.m., the city and Oliver whistles began to blow. The procession was led by the city police force and the city band, followed by the officers and the platoons of men, each under the command of a sergeant. Crowds lined the streets and cheered as each platoon passed. In all, at least 750 men joined the parade. (Courtesy of McHenry County Historical Society.)

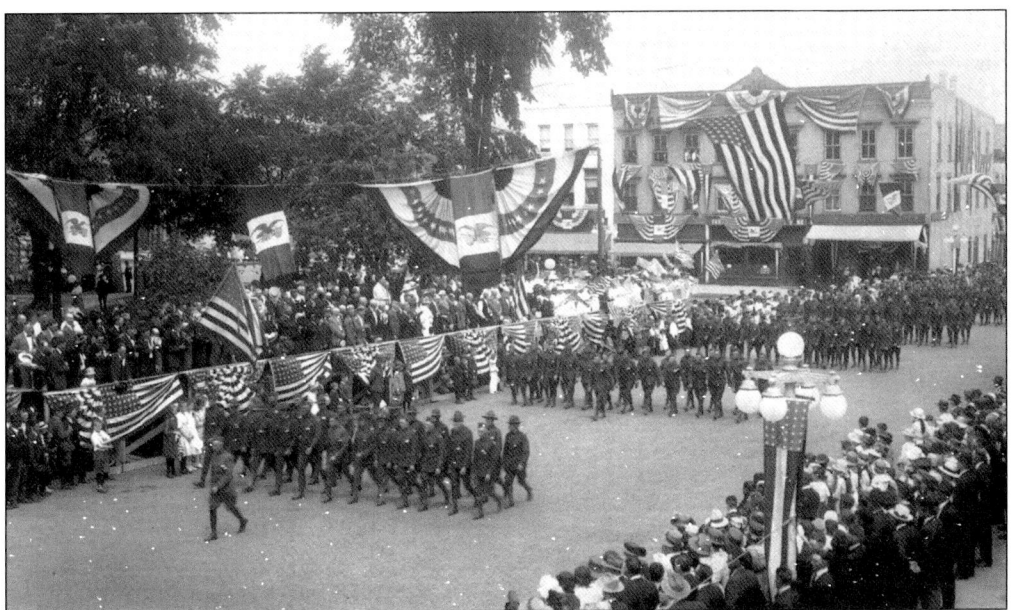

The town outdid itself with patriotic bunting and banners. A Chicago company had been hired to provide the decorations, and the business blocks looked superb. Oliver Typewriter Company had erected a huge black circle containing a yellow cross formed by electric lights—the symbol of the 33rd Division. The parade route led to the square, where the men passed the reviewing stand on Benton Street. On the stand were Grand Army of the Republic and Spanish-American War veterans, Women's Relief Corps members, and widows and gold star mothers.

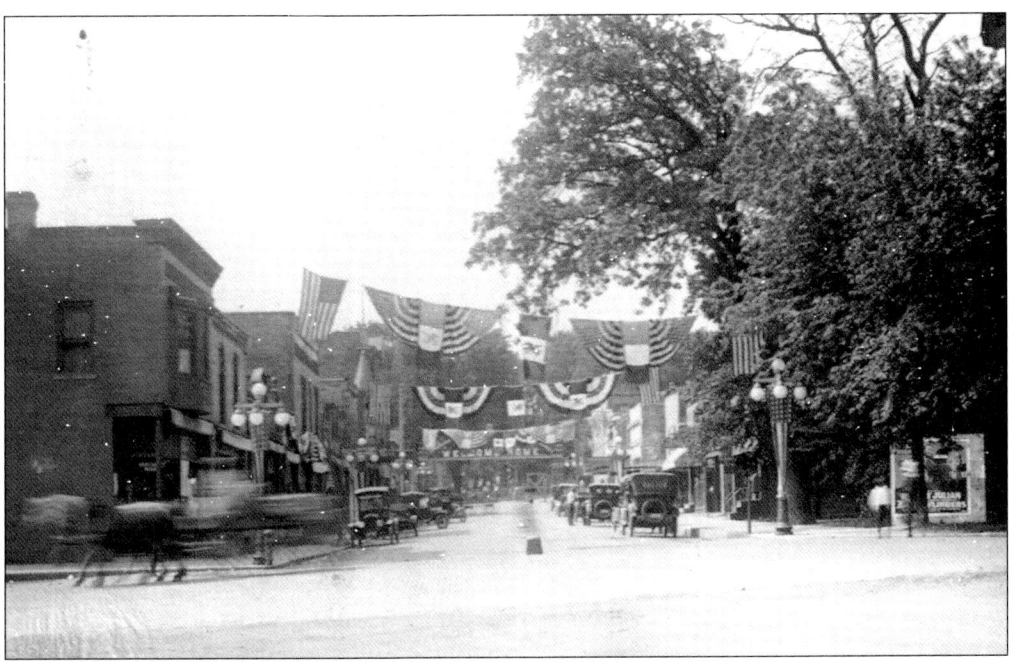

The parade headed south from the square and then circled back around and ended by passing under the victory arch constructed over Main Street at Cass Street. At every corner a civic, fraternal, or school group was in place with decorations, cheering or singing.

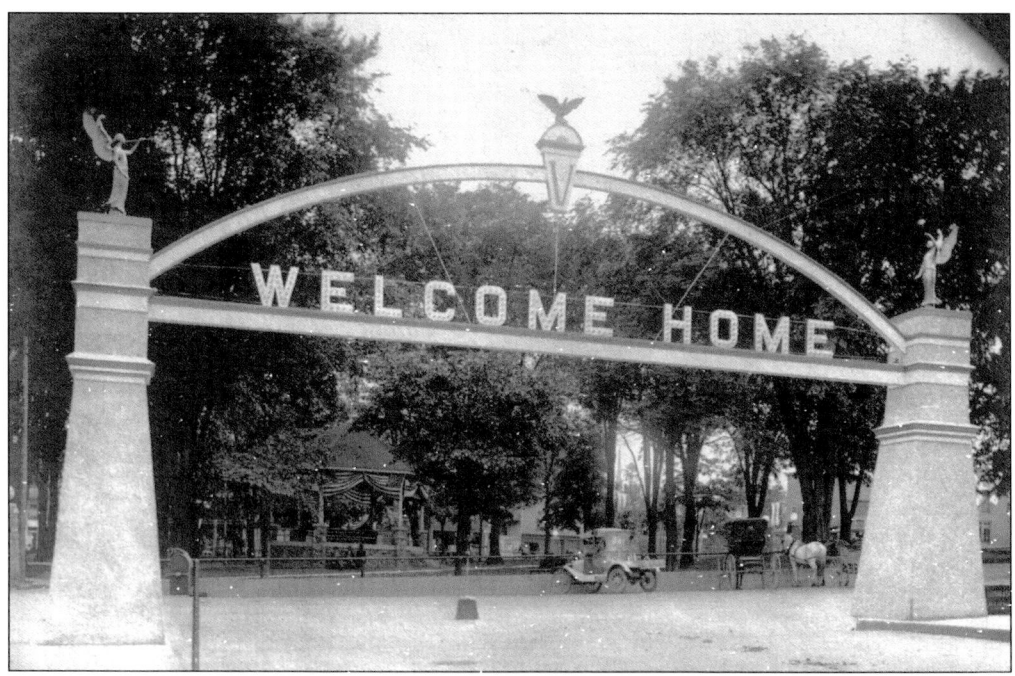

The victory arch was wired to light up at night. In the park in the square, tickets were distributed to all servicemen for a noon meal at the various churches. Each church served a complete meal of roast beef, potatoes, rolls, pickles, radishes, lettuce salad, coffee, brick ice cream, and cake.

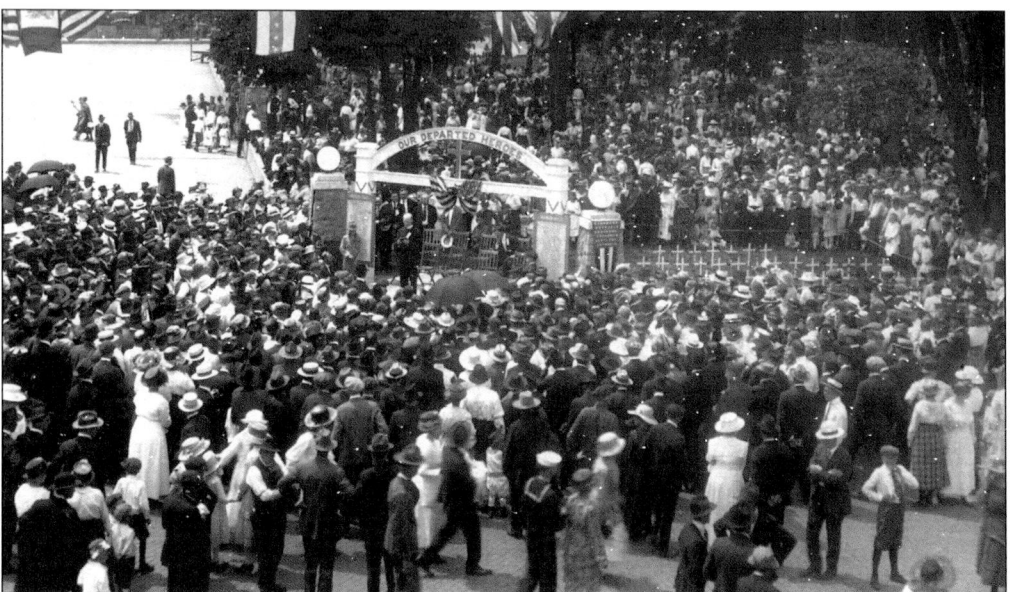

At 2:00 p.m., people gathered at the southeast corner of the park, where a miniature Flanders Field had been laid out. There were 57 white crosses and a six-pointed gold star, each representing a McHenry County serviceman who had died in the war. The field was covered with a mass of handmade red poppies. Rev. William Kilburne, the featured speaker, closed his address with the reading of "In Flanders Field," a poem by Canadian army officer John McCrea. Attorney Fred Bennett then called the roll of the honored dead.

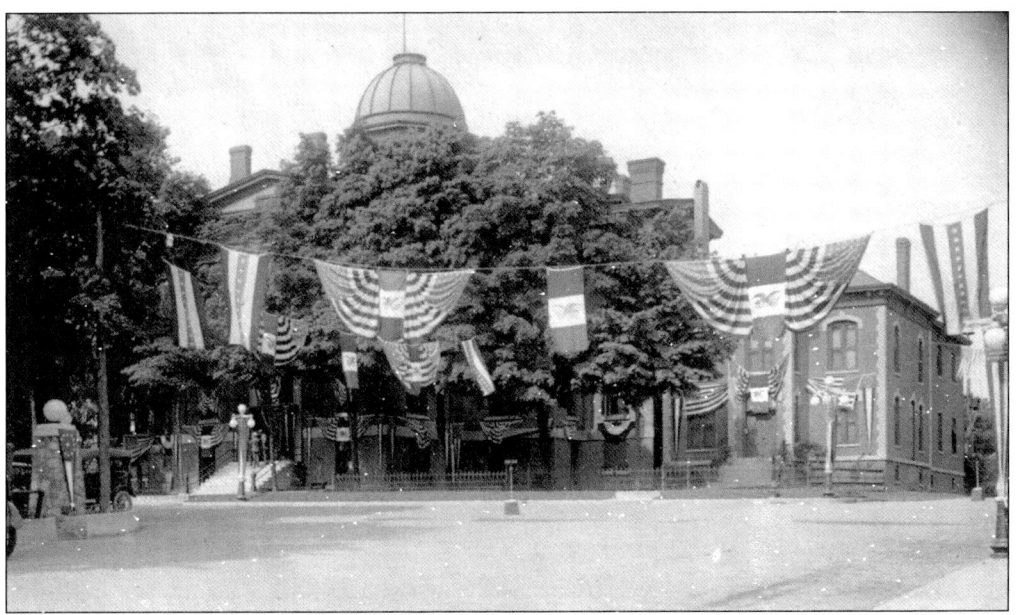

When festivities resumed, they included performances by musicians, dancing girls, and comedians. Beverages, gum, peanuts, and cigarettes were handed out to all uniformed guests. The brick pavement between the courthouse and city hall had been coated with paraffin to make a suitable dancing surface, and despite the very warm temperature, there were in fact many dancers. The entire event was captured on film and shown a couple of weeks later at the Princess Theater.

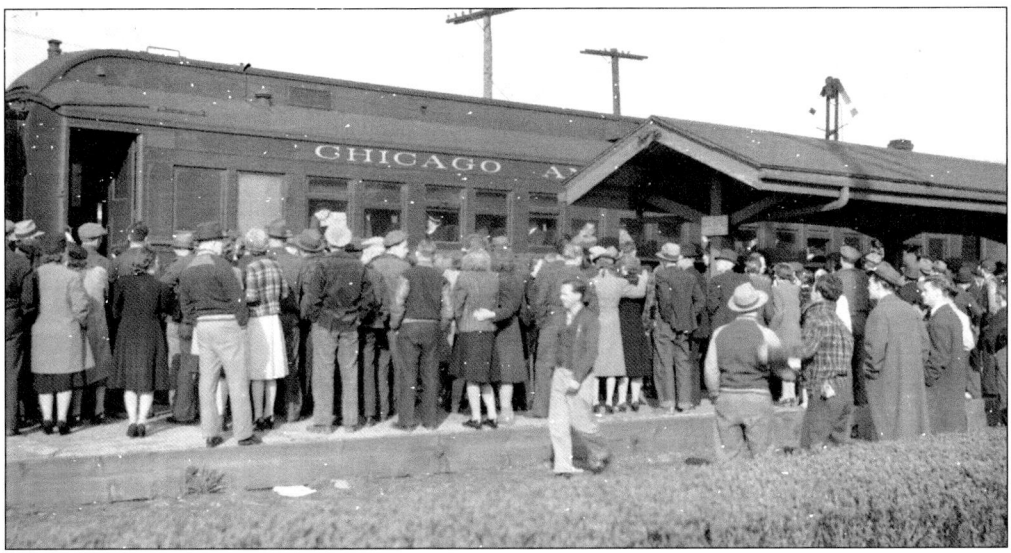

When Japan attacked Pearl Harbor in 1941, local youths rushed to join the service. Again Woodstock residents watched their love ones depart from the train station and greeted them there when they returned.

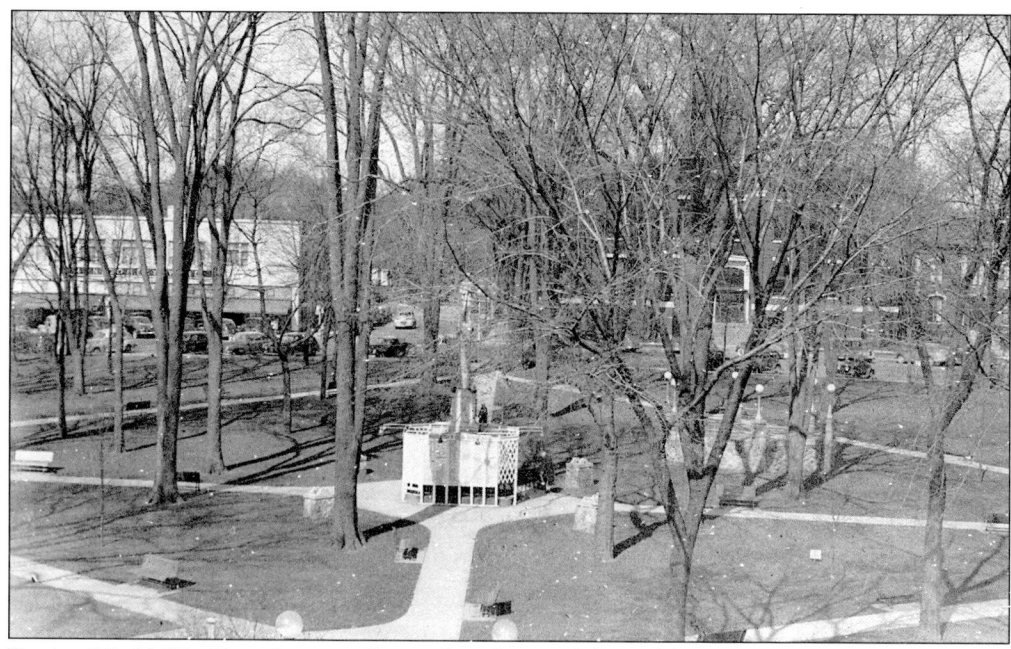

During World War II, an honor roll was placed around the Soldier's Monument at the direction of Mayor Raymond Johnson and the Woodstock City Council. The names were supplied by George Sullivan, editor of the *Woodstock Sentinel*'s serviceman's column. As of June 21, 1944, the honor roll included 1,200 names, of which 18 were designated a gold star.

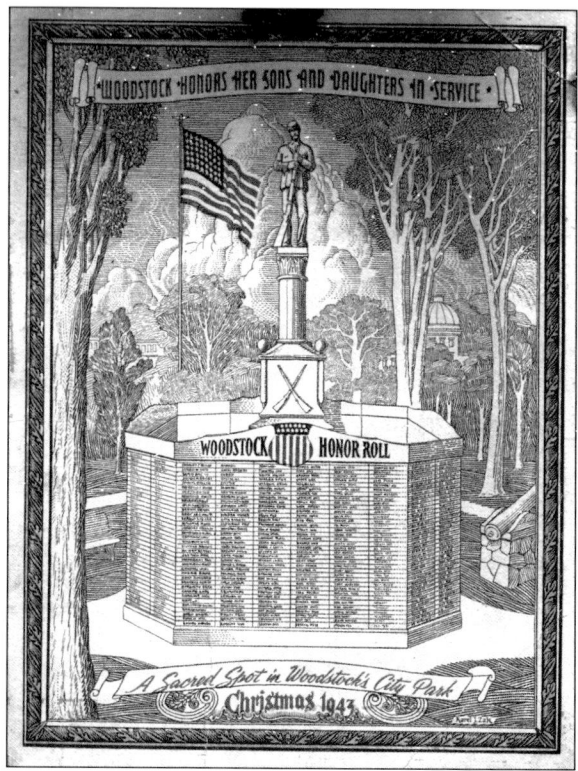

The drawing of the honor roll was given to *Woodstock Sentinel* customers as a Christmas card in 1943, and a copy was sent to every serviceman or woman from the Woodstock community. On May 8, 1945, victory in Europe was declared. Mayor Johnson asked the people of Woodstock to give thanks and prayers. They saved their celebrations for August 14, 1945, when Japan surrendered.

Seven
BE IT EVER SO HUMBLE

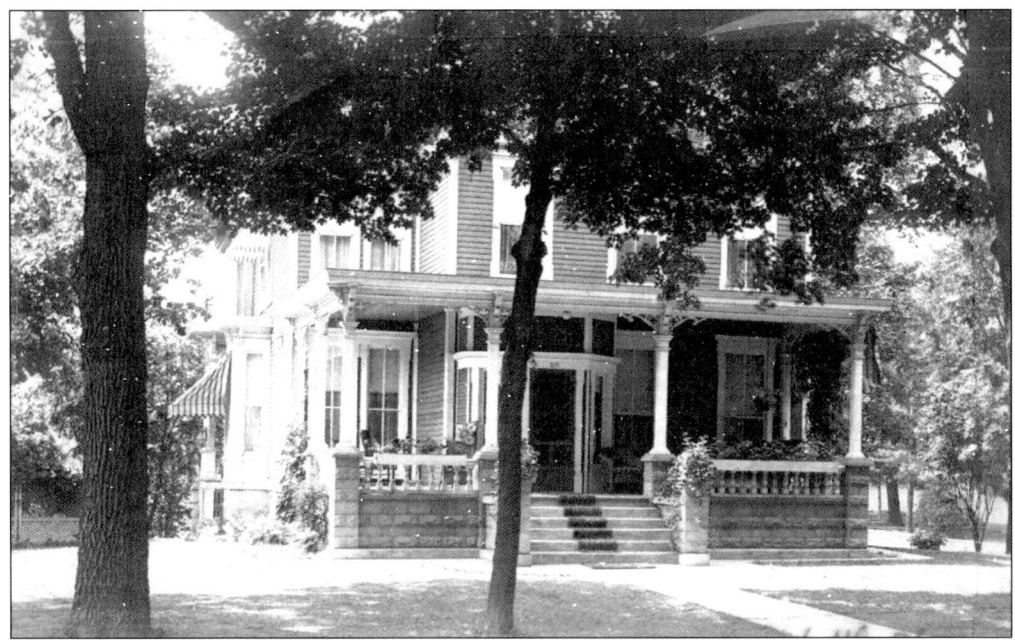

A. C. Belcher, a contractor who built many Woodstock homes, constructed the Amos K. Bunker residence in 1883. The first floor was divided into a parlor, library, sitting room, dining room, large sleeping room, bathroom, kitchen, pantry, and china closet. The second floor consisted of sleeping rooms and closets. Bunker, one of 13 children, partnered with his oldest brother, George, in the Bunker Brothers store on Van Buren Street. Amos was born in Woodstock in 1846.

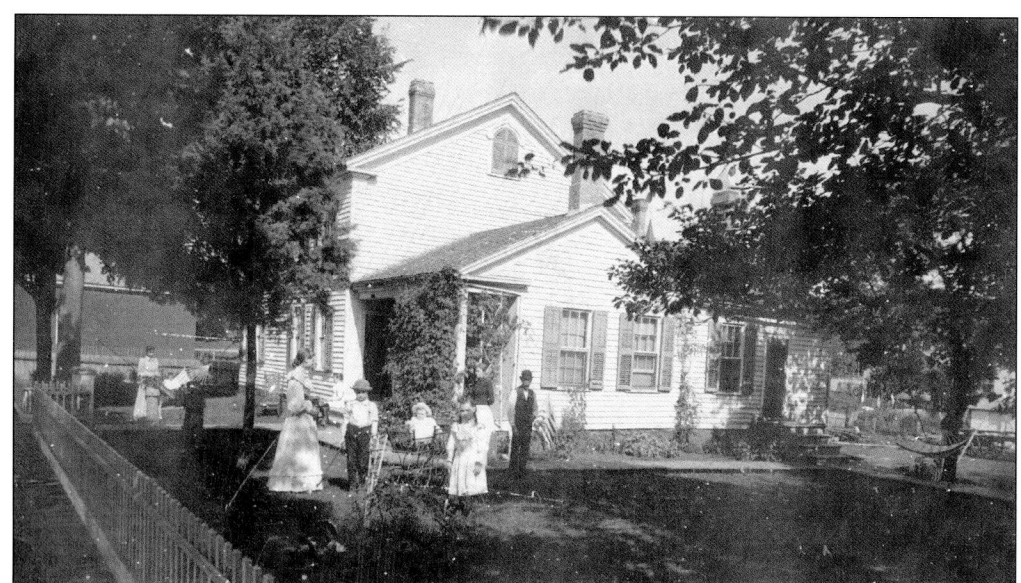

John A. Dufield, the owner of this home, was born in Woodstock in 1851 and started the *McHenry County Democrat* newspaper in 1877. He was described as an aggressive and popular newspaper man and a forceful writer. He served a term as postmaster, beginning in 1896. In 1903, he put a printing plant in the Kellogg building, where he offered specialty printing services such as souvenir advertising.

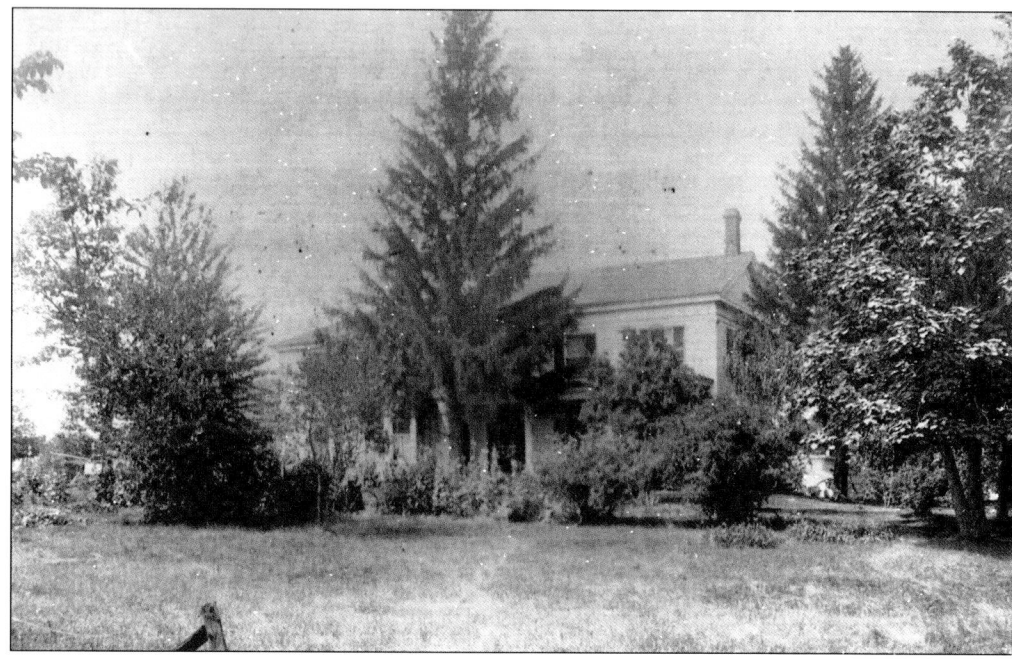

Merchant Frank M. Bunker lived in this Tryon Street residence, referred to as the 1890s House. Bunker had a two-year dispute with the city over the ownership of a seven-foot-wide strip of land running along his property line. Mayor John D. Donovan claimed the land belonged to the street and intended to have a sidewalk constructed on it. Bunker did not object to the sidewalk but still claimed he owned the land.

The Simon Brink house was built on North Street in 1868 and owned by family members for over 100 years. When the Woodstock Bicentennial Commission placed a plaque on the home in 1975, Simon Brink's granddaughter Amy still resided there. (Courtesy of McHenry County Historical Society.)

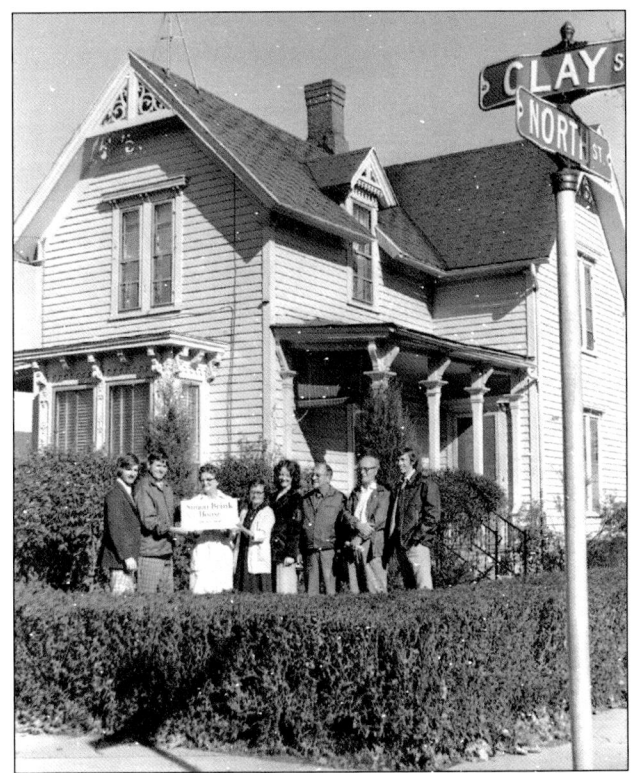

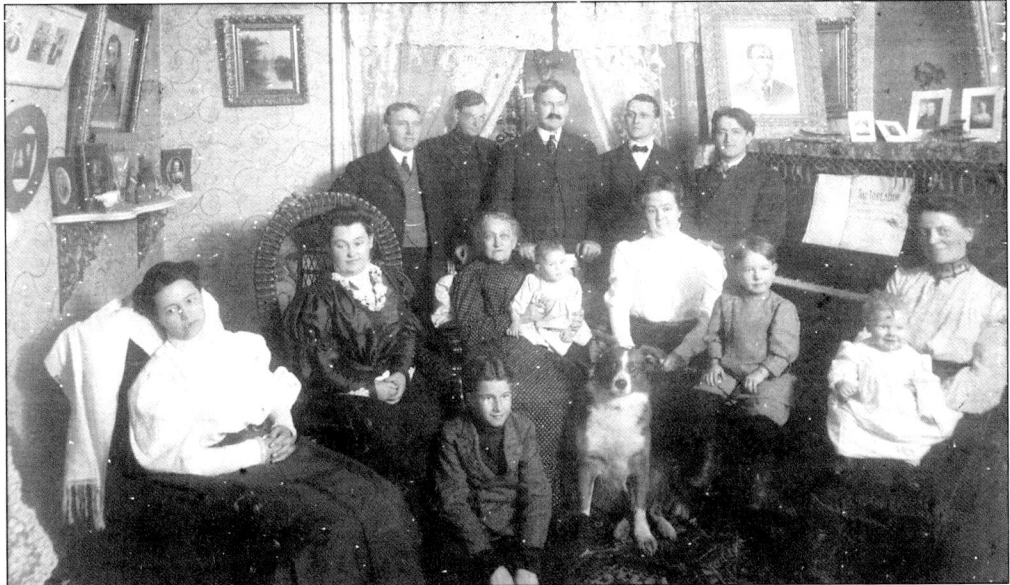

Simon Brink was the nephew of John Brink, a surveyor for the federal government in the 1830s and the first white man to see Lake Geneva. As a carpenter, Simon was in charge of many projects in Woodstock during the period from 1870 to 1900, including city hall, the Presbyterian church, and the Woodstock Brewery. A Civil War veteran, he also served as city clerk and postmaster. Simon's family is pictured here in the living room of the house. His portrait is on the piano. (Courtesy of Woodstock Public Library.)

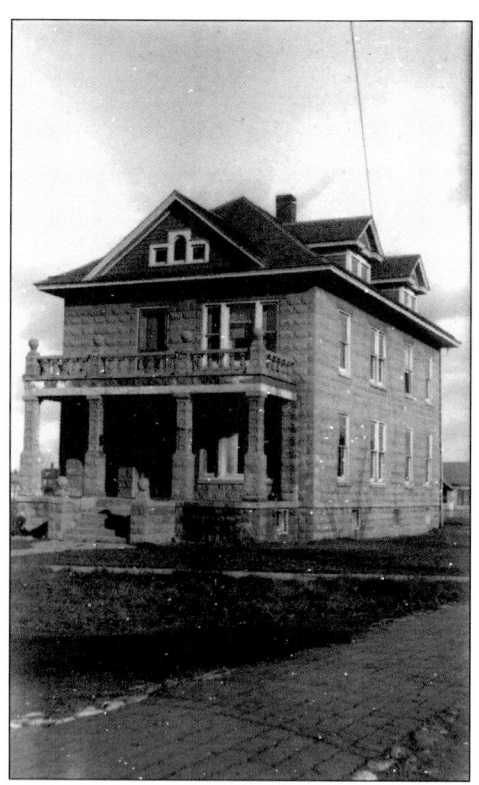

This Jewett Street concrete-block house with second-story porch was reportedly the residence of a man known as Oklahoma Johnson, a cement worker whose seal was found in many Woodstock sidewalks. (Courtesy of McHenry County Historical Society.)

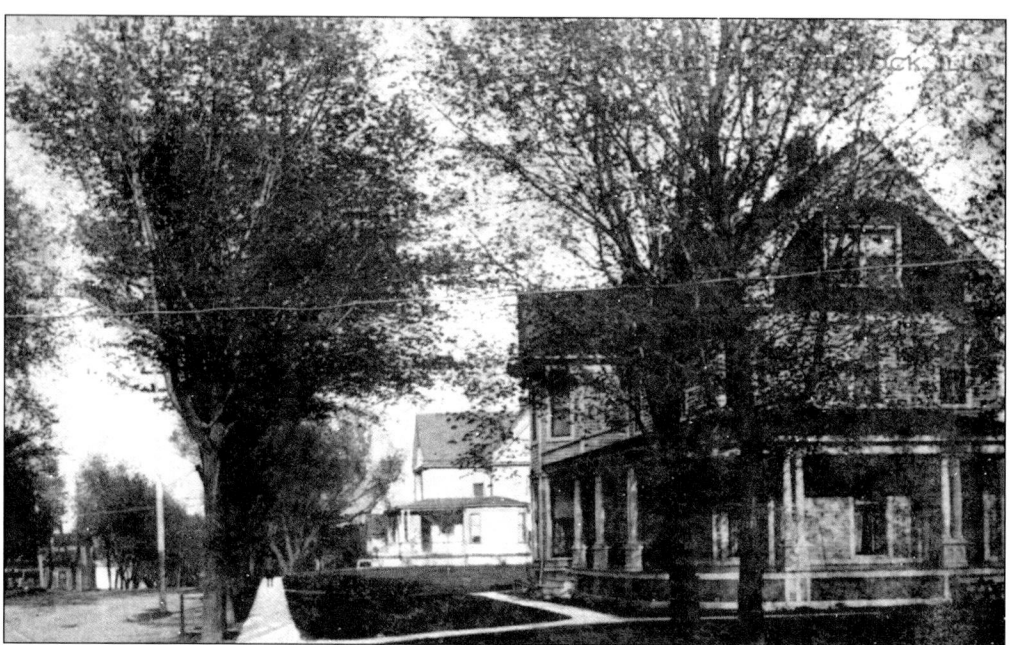

Most photographs of homes from the early 20th century show trees lining the streets. This view of the southeast corner of South and Dean Streets is no exception. Dutch elm disease later took a heavy toll on the mature, graceful trees in Woodstock's residential neighborhoods. (Courtesy of McHenry County Historical Society.)

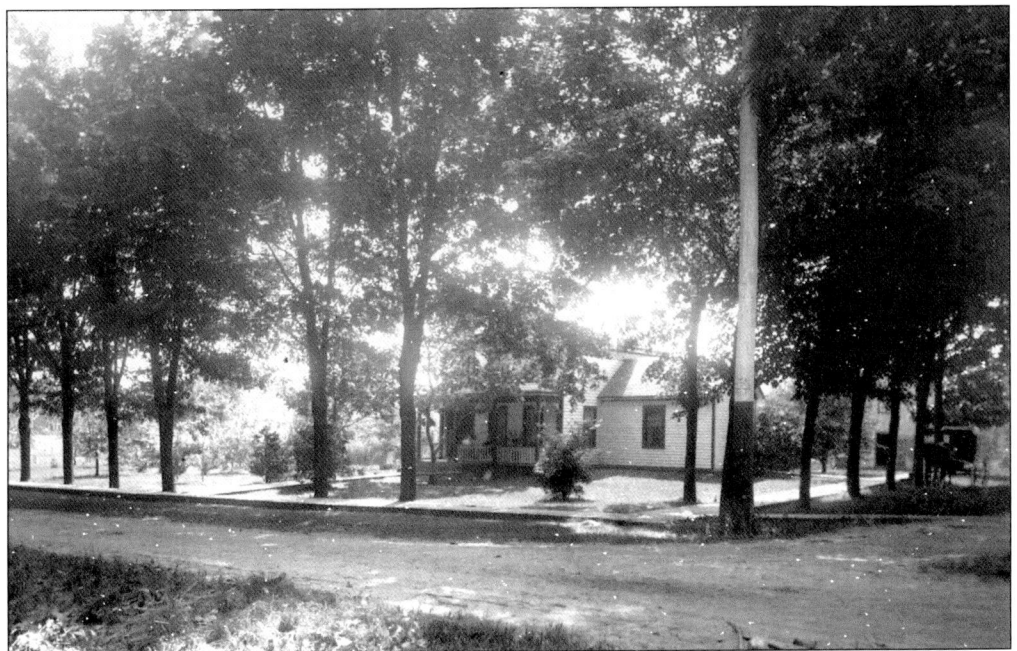

In 1905, Charles and Martha Stone purchased the house at the corner of Seminary Avenue and Grove Street from Elmer Bagley for $3,400. The horse and buggy in the tree bank belonged to Charles's brother Eric. The barn near the sidewalk was later moved back on the property. (Courtesy of McHenry County Historical Society.)

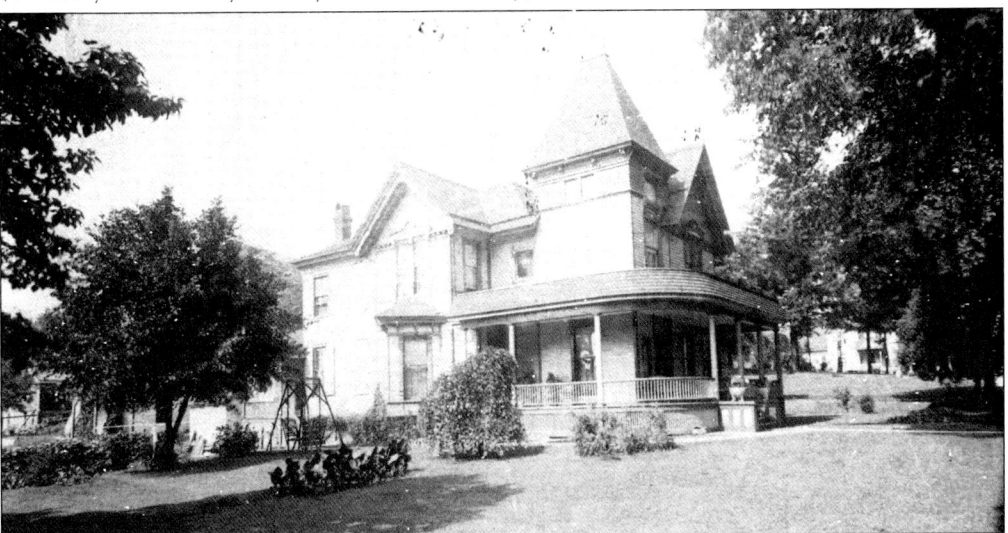

Erastus E. Richards, a prominent Woodstock resident, occupied this house. Born in England, he came to Woodstock with his parents in 1852. When the Civil War started in 1861, he enlisted in the 15th Regiment of the Illinois Infantry and served for 14 months. Upon his return, he was elected city clerk. Richards served several terms on the city council and also worked as a clerk of the circuit court. He was elected village president when Woodstock was a village and mayor after Woodstock incorporated as a city. Richards was the senior member of the abstract company Richards, Jewett, and Wright and president of the State Bank of Woodstock. (Courtesy of McHenry County Historical Society.)

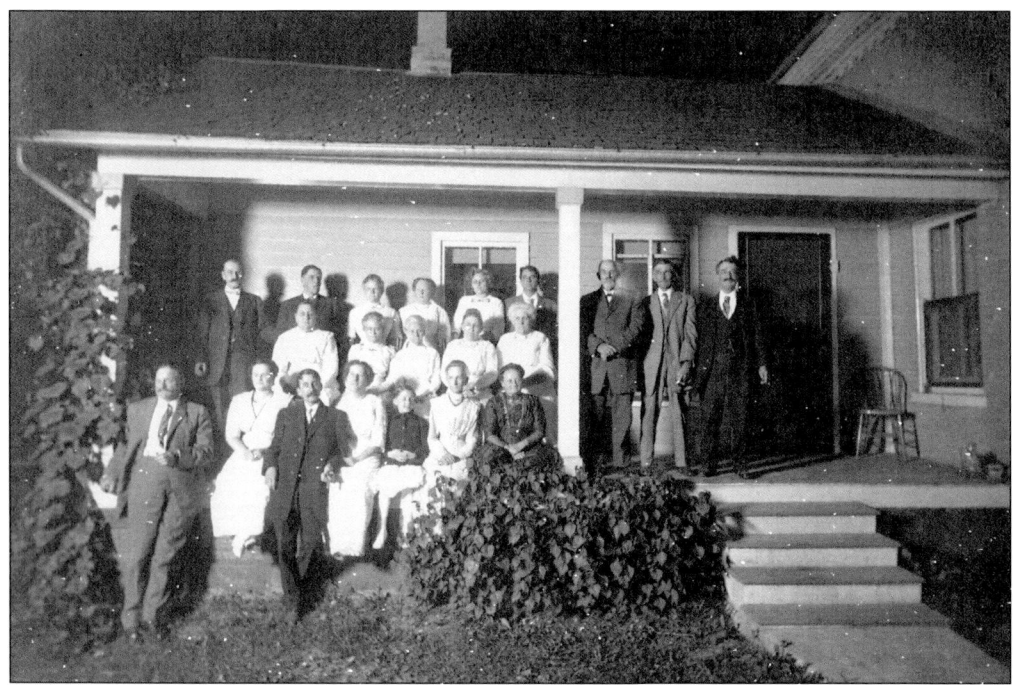

Friends and family gather to celebrate photographer Mel Tripp's birthday. Tripp's photographs of Woodstock events and buildings frequently appeared in newspapers and promotional publications at the start of the 20th century, and many were used in this book. Tripp is the third person from the left in the first row. (Courtesy of McHenry County Historical Society.)

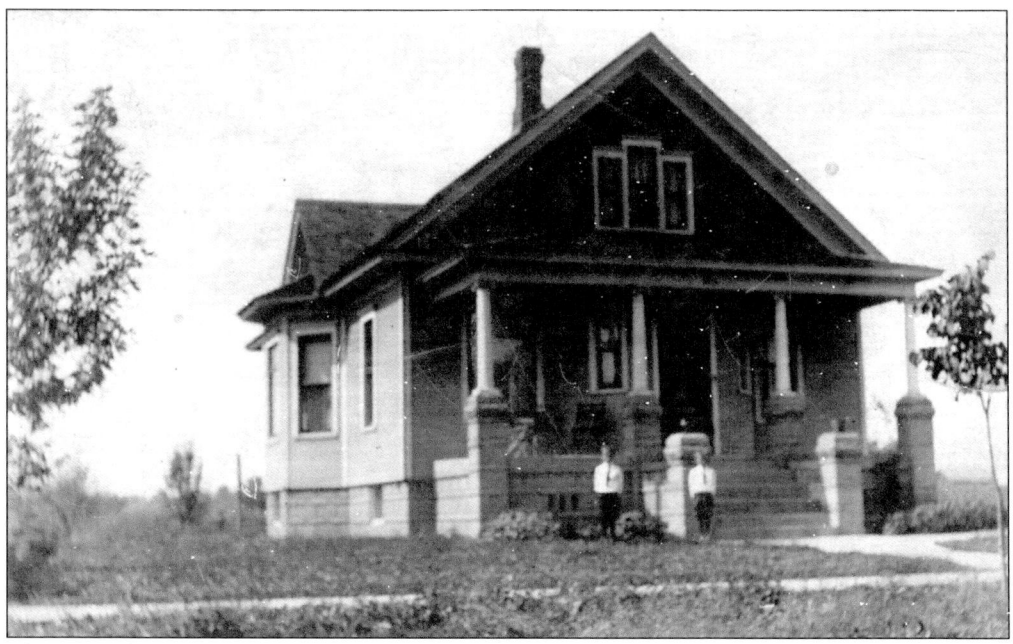

The Gustaf Persson house was located on Queen Anne Street. Posing in front of the house are the Persson boys—Stanley Gustaf and Arthur Eugene. (Courtesy of McHenry County Historical Society.)

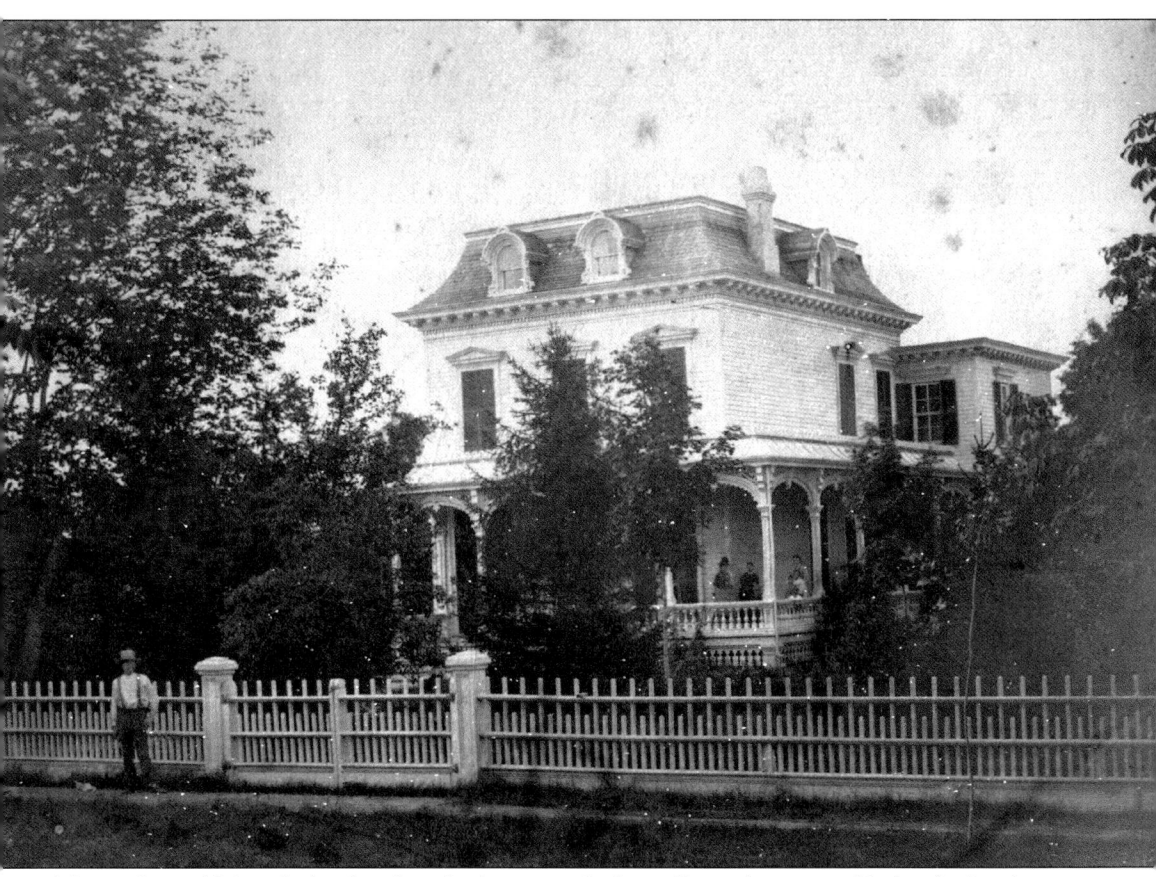

Merritt L. and Mary Joslyn lived in the house on Jackson Street known as Under the Lindens, about three blocks west of the square. Merritt was the son of Lindsey Joslyn, one of McHenry County's pioneer residents. He practiced law in Woodstock from 1851 until shortly before his death in 1904. He served as an organizer and captain of the Woodstock Rifles, the first unit from town to enter the Civil War. The Woodstock Rifles became Company H of the 36th Regiment, Illinois Volunteer Infantry. Merritt served twice as village president and was also elected state representative and state senator. A biographer of his time in the state senate wrote the following: "He was aggressive, irrepressible—the facetious, ironical, vigilant watchdog of the Senate, on the Republican side. Nothing of the dangerous or doubtful character in the way of legislation escaped his unfailing vigilance or his brilliant humor and withering sarcasm by way of condemnation." Merritt was later elected mayor but resigned to accept the appointment as second assistant secretary of the interior under Pres. Chester Arthur. (Courtesy of McHenry County Historical Society.)

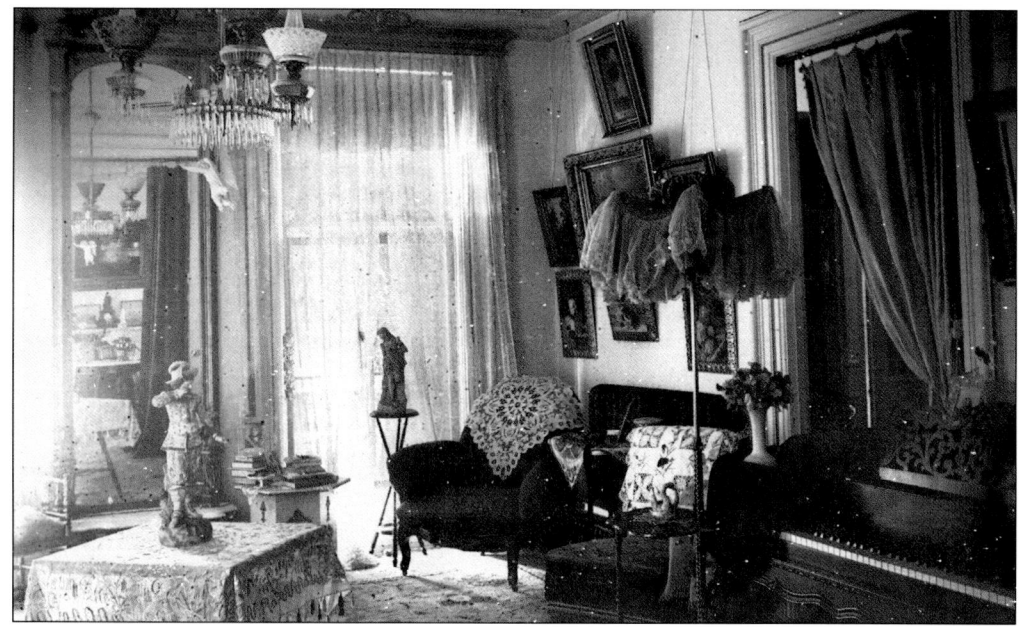

Mary Joslyn (née Robinson) was described as well educated, beautiful, and a queen among women. Active in civic and cultural affairs, she organized Woodstock's Chautauqua circle and participated in the Congregational Sunday school and Women's Christian Temperance Union. The Joslyns entertained many guests, including visiting dignitaries and politicians, in their Jackson Street home. (Courtesy of McHenry County Historical Society.)

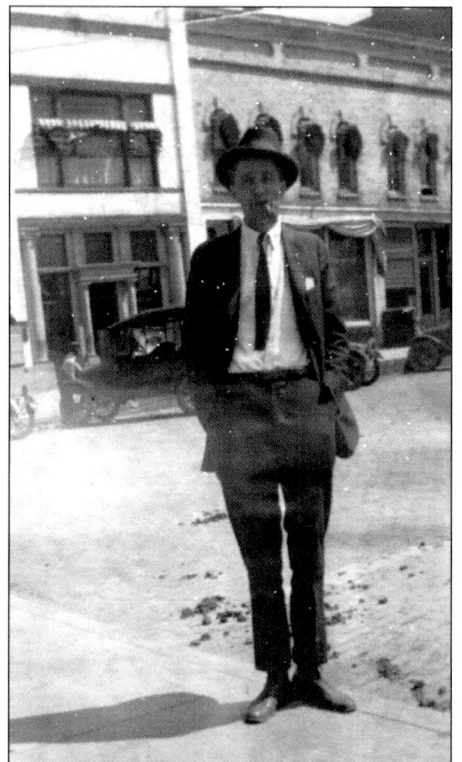

Merritt and Mary Joslyn had four daughters and two sons. David R., born in 1866, left his parents home of wealth and refinement at age 14 to try farming. He later graduated from the Chicago College of Law and returned to Woodstock. An extraordinary orator, he used his skills both in the courtroom and in patriotic and civic affairs. He went on to raise his family at Under the Lindens. His son, David R. Joslyn Jr., born in 1893, was admitted to practice law in 1914. After serving overseas in World War I, he returned to Woodstock to work with his father. His family resided in the home of his great-grandfather David W. Robinson. (Courtesy of McHenry County Historical Society.)

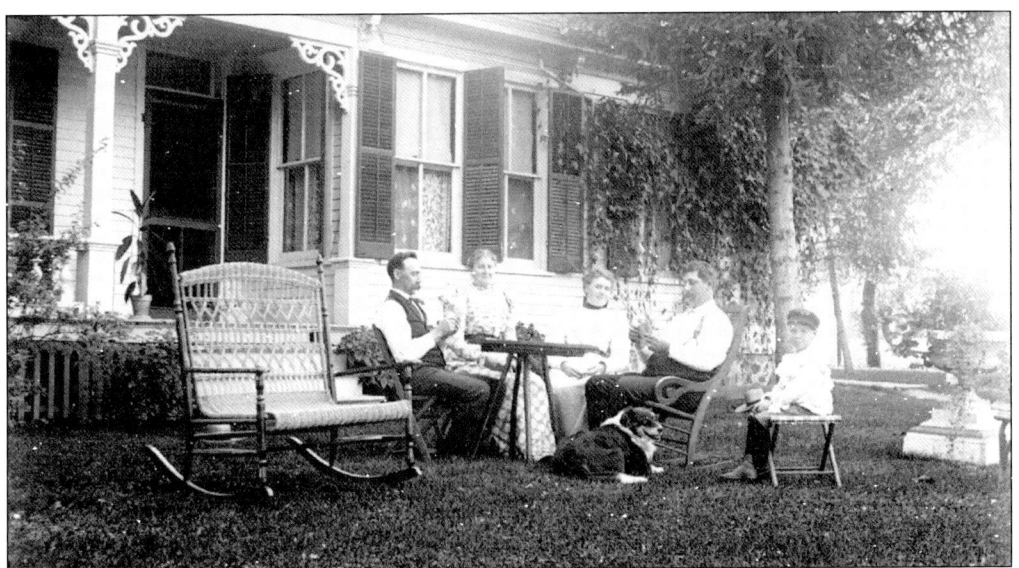

A. J. Olson was orphaned at age 10. At age 15, he made his way to Chicago and found employment driving a milk wagon, later becoming the proprietor of the business. After serving on the Chicago City Council and in the state legislature, he moved to Woodstock and held various public offices, including alderman, mayor, and state senator. Olson built a house called the Larch on McHenry Avenue. Pictured here, from left to right, are Charles A. Stone, Jane Olson (A. J.'s wife), Martha Stone (Charles's wife), A. J. Olson, and an unidentified child. (Courtesy of McHenry County Historical Society.)

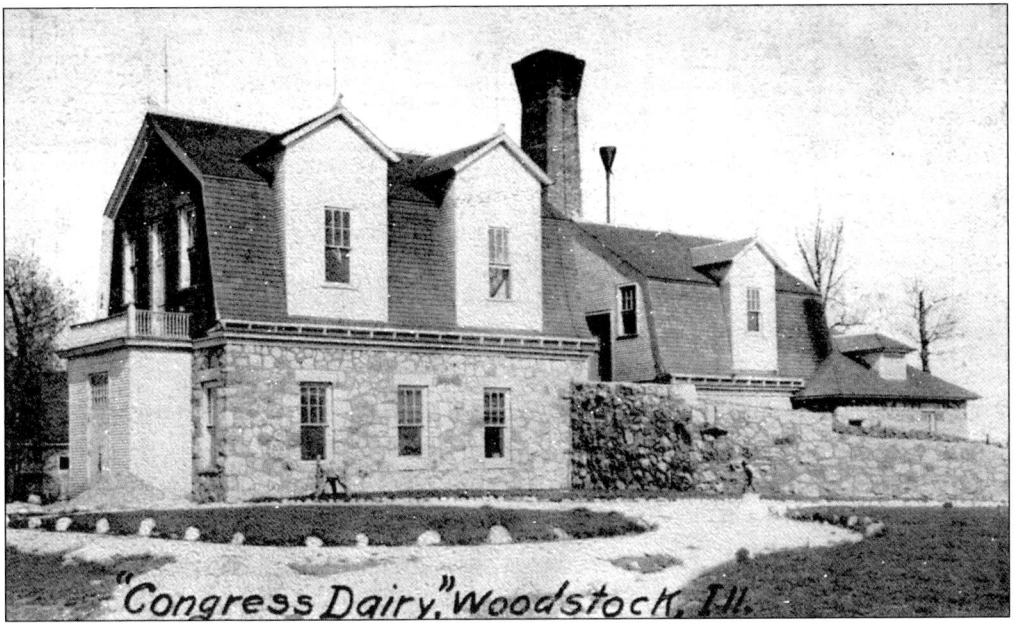

A. J. started the A. J. Olson Creamery (later the Congress Dairy) during a time of milk strikes and controversy over dairy herd testing. He aligned himself with those opposing mandatory herd testing and worked in the state senate to pass legislation that would allow the state to compensate farmers for the destruction of their cattle. (Courtesy of McHenry County Historical Society.)

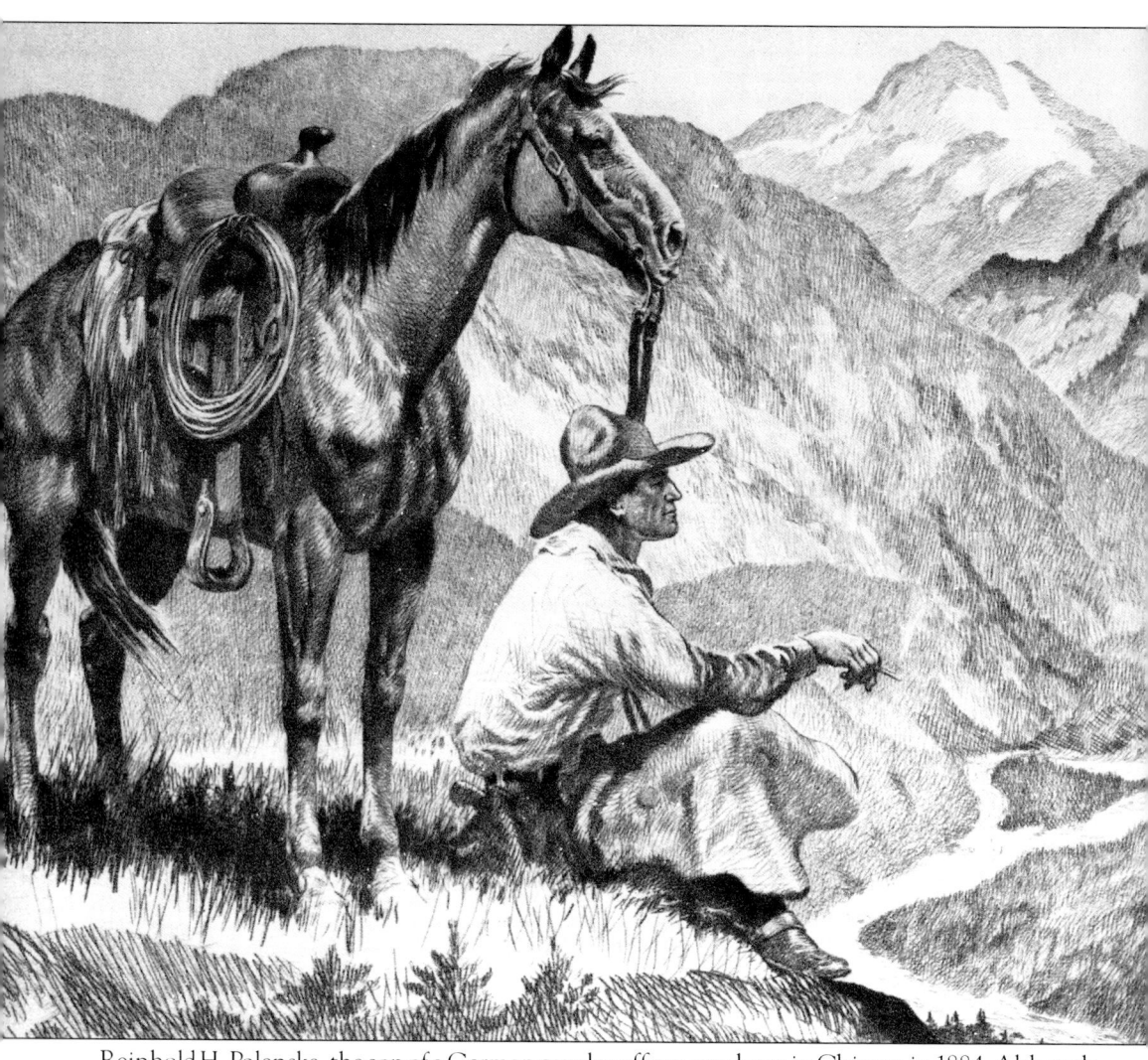

Reinhold H. Palenske, the son of a German cavalry officer, was born in Chicago in 1884. Although interested in art, he was encouraged by his father to enter the real estate business. Palenske was first employed drawing newspaper sketches for $15 to $18 a week for the *Chicago Journal* and then the *Chicago Daily News*. He was married in 1907. Later he worked for Hearst Publications in Chicago. After 10 years of creating newspaper illustrations, he started his own business, employing over 30 artists. During this time, he enrolled in the Chicago Art Institute. After three lessons, Palenske's instructor discovered who he was and asked him for a job. He never returned. Palenske then went to work as an advertising account executive handling the Canadian Pacific Railroad account. For 30 years, he and his wife spent time in the Rockies. He taught himself the complicated art form of etchings, in which each tiny line is hand cut into copper. Palenske's favorite subjects were animals, the outdoors, and the Native Americans of the Canadian Rockies. The etching *Our Country* is shown above. (Courtesy of Bev Ganschow, Old Courthouse Arts Center.)

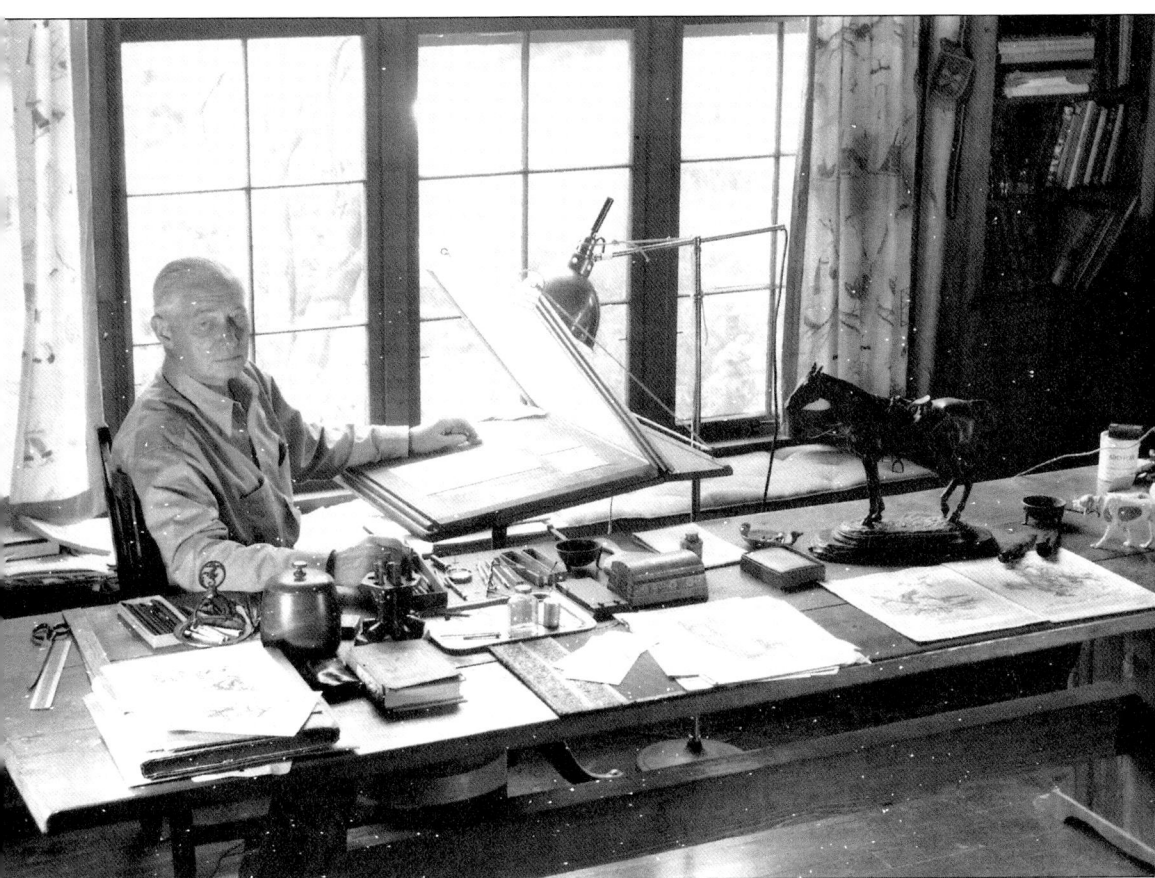

On Palenske's worktable is a copper plate on which he etched his drawings with a diamond-point instrument. In the mid-1940s, he signed a contract with Brown and Bigelow, the world's largest producer of calendars. He and his wife moved to their rural Woodstock country estate where he did most of his work. Neighborhood children called him "Mr. Peter Rabbit" because he hid goodies in the woods and told them that Peter Rabbit had left them. Upon his death, Paul Harvey eulogized the "gentle and generous heart which stopped last night . . . in Woodstock, Illinois." Harvey ended his radio show by saying that what made Palenske really great was not just the artist but the man. (Courtesy of Bev Ganschow.)

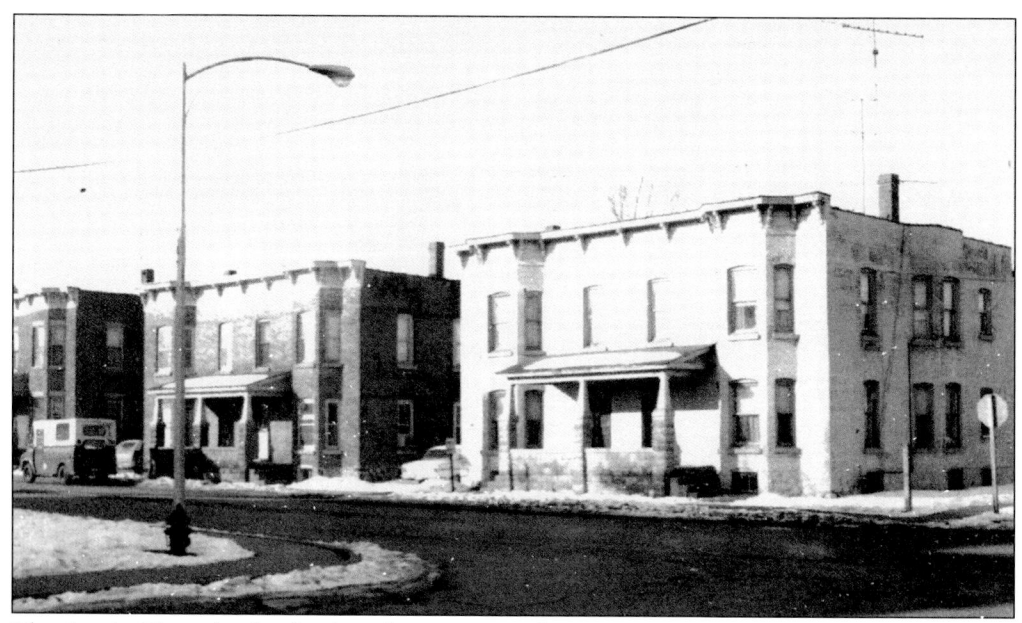

The Austin Flats, the first brick multi-apartment flats, were constructed on Washington Street in 1899. The Class Flats, consisting of the three buildings on Throop Street shown above, were started in 1905. Originally, the front porches stepped down to a sidewalk. When Throop Street was widened, the porches were removed and replaced with stairs leading to the side. In 1907, the Sherman Flats and Cunningham Flats were built on Jefferson Street.

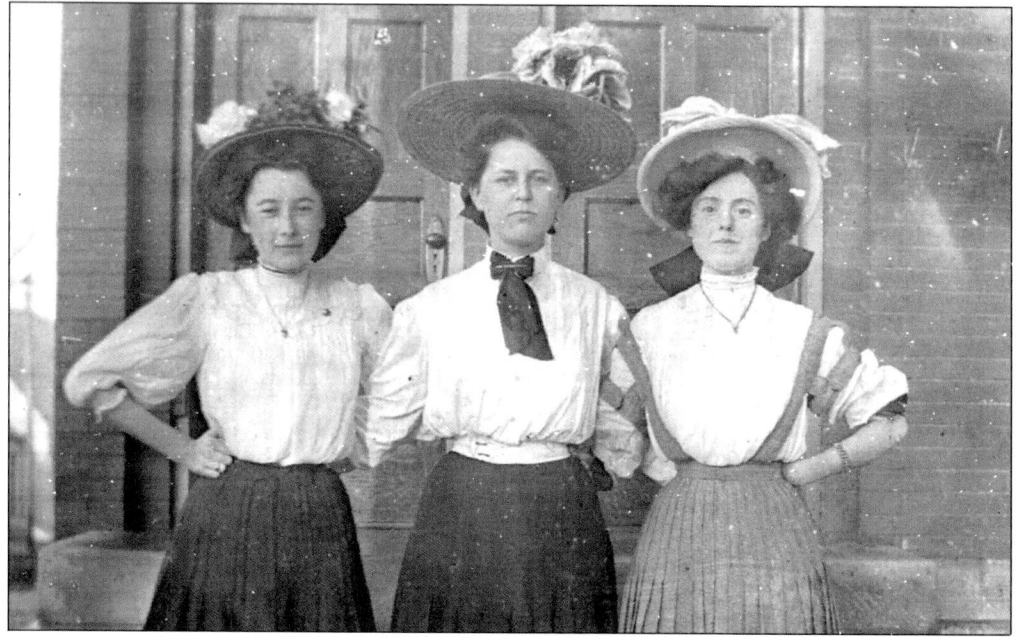

Also in 1907, the Charles and Allen Flats were constructed on Dean Street. The building consisted of four units centered around a light well. Each unit had its own outside entrance like the entrances behind the girls in this 1910 photograph. The front rooms were finished in oak, and the rear rooms were trimmed with Georgia pine. Hardwood floors were used throughout. (Courtesy of McHenry County Historical Society.)

Eight
Old-fashioned Fun

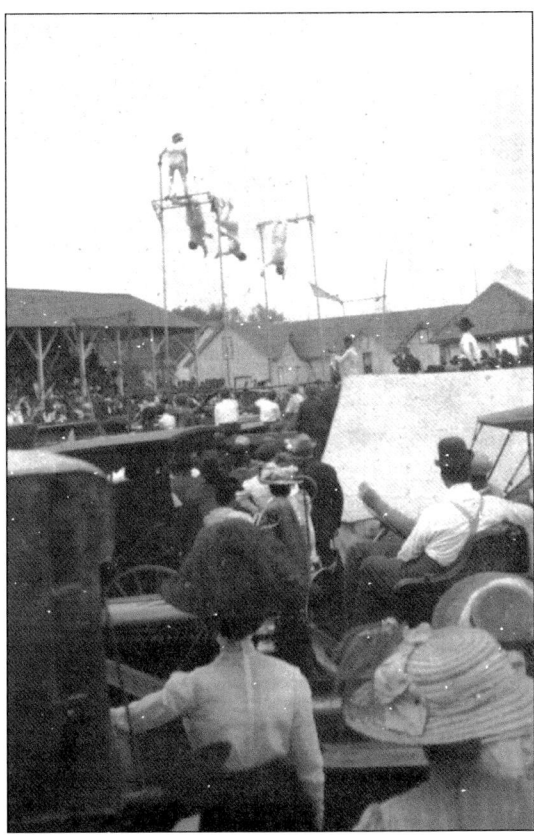

In the fall of 1936, just months before he passed away, Charles F. Dacy wrote a letter to his friends in Woodstock in which he reminisced about his youth. He stated that today's youth could never imagine the dullness of children's lives in a small town in the early days. There were hardly any amusements, except what they improvised themselves—no picture shows, radios, telephones, automobiles, or bicycles. The most thrilling enjoyment of the gang was usually the surreptitious reading of nickel and dime novels. He recalled the day when a group of boys and a couple of girls left for Cary, where there was a boat that the boys had built. The group intended to spend the night there before embarking for New Orleans. Before morning, however, they boys' irate fathers had arrived, smashed the boat, and put an end to the adventure. With little in the way of organized entertainment, the arrival of the Fourth of July, the circus, and the county fair were things to look forward to attending. An acrobatics demonstration was held at the 1910 county fair. (Courtesy of McHenry County Historical Society.)

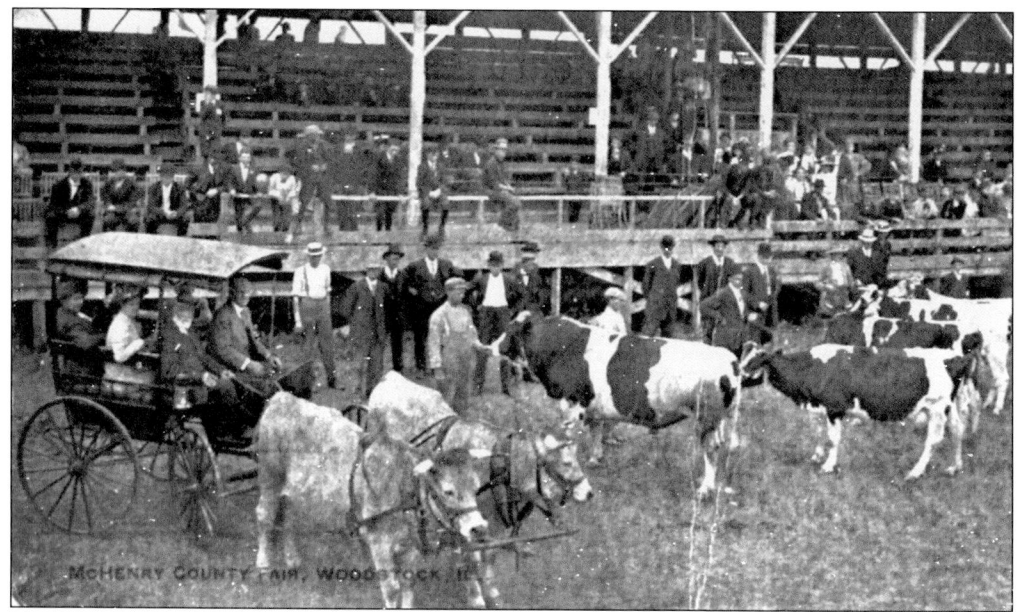

The first county fair was organized in 1852. Early fairs were held on the streets of various towns, where rail pens were built to hold livestock and rooms rented for exhibiting fine arts. By 1859, the McHenry County Agricultural Society had purchased 10 acres just east of town, and livestock sheds had been erected there. In the 1860s, 12 acres were added. Through the influence of fair secretary A. S. Wright, many noted guests, such as generals, governors, diplomats, congressmen, and senators, attended the fairs.

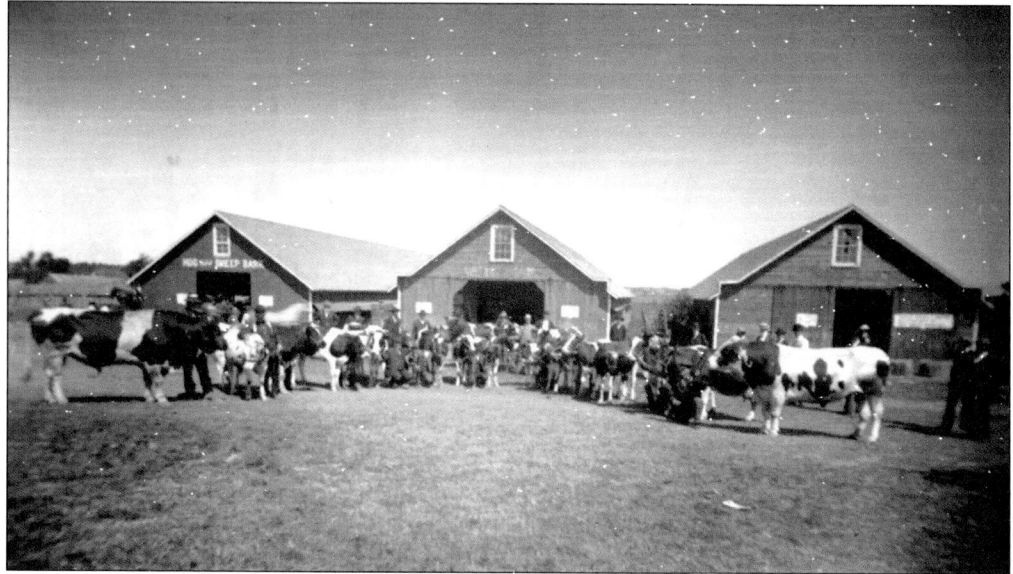

Fairs of the 1880s included performances by various local bands, horse races, bicycle races, and sporting teams, along with exhibits in the two-story agriculture hall and the floral hall. On the designated Old Soldiers Day, many national and local orators arrived at the train depot. In the 1890s, large cow stables were constructed at the north end of the grounds, and boxed stalls for racing horses were built at the south end. The grandstand was enlarged with seats placed at a greater incline, resulting in a better view. (Courtesy of McHenry County Historical Society.)

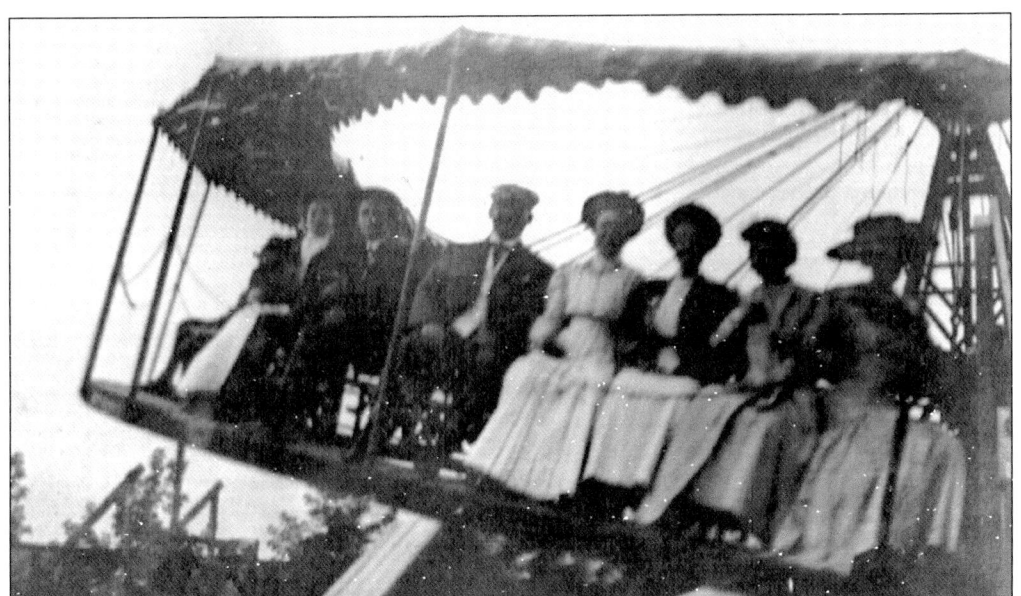

George Hunt left a written account of fair improvements during his tenure as fair secretary, beginning in 1903. He tells of the construction of a manufacturers' building where visitors encountered a large refrigerator with dairy product exhibits, including a giant carved butter cow and dairy maid. A women's building and a large dining hall were also added. The carnival rides were a great thrill to people attending the fair in 1910. (Courtesy of McHenry County Historical Society.)

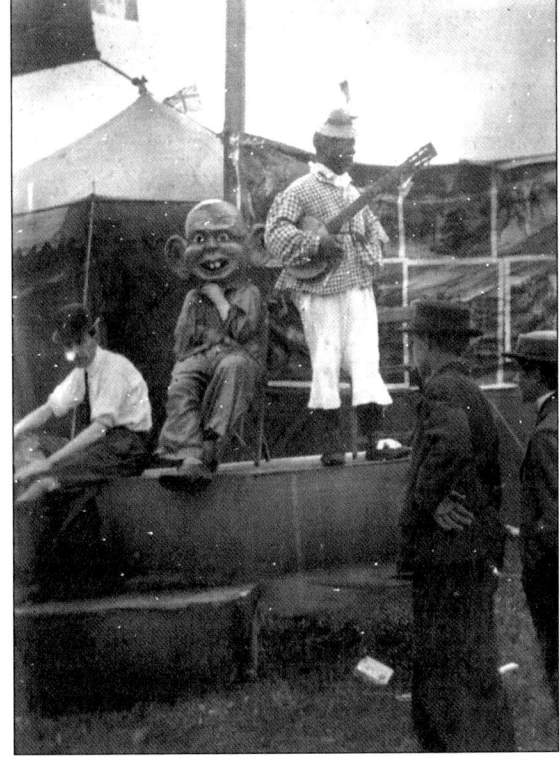

The 1910 fair also brought other carnival performers. In 1914, the year the Panama Canal opened, a miniature replica of the canal was exhibited. Visitors listened to a lecture and watched as white boats passed through the locks. The Clifton-Kelly Carnival, also a part of the fair, was described as a clean, moral enterprise free of dancing girls and freak shows. (Courtesy of McHenry County Historical Society.)

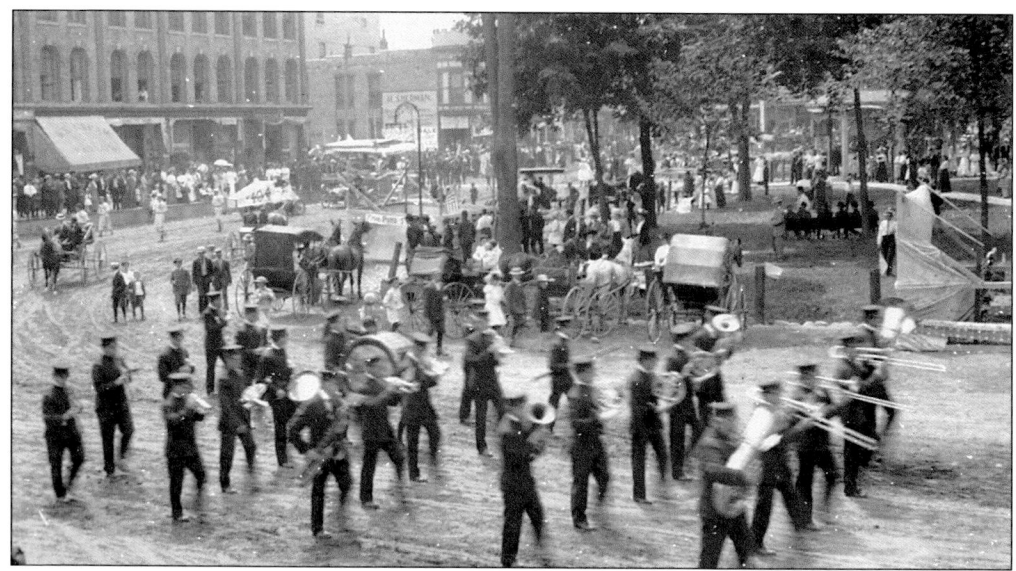

The National Day, or Fourth of July, in 1879 was celebrated in Woodstock by an estimated crowd of 4,000 people, including large delegations from neighboring communities. The festivities included speeches, a reading of the Declaration of Independence, and musical performances. The town marshal was complimented for sending home those who had become intoxicated, rather than arresting them. In 1910, the Oliver Typewriter Band was among the parade attractions. (Courtesy of McHenry County Historical Society.)

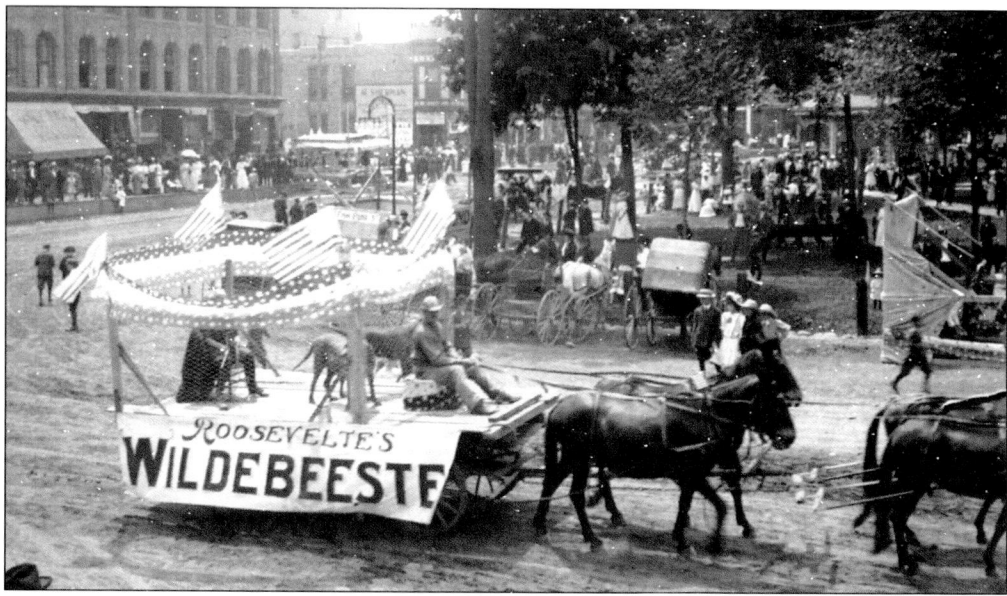

July 4, 1910, was celebrated from early morning until late in the night. The morning parade consisted of Mayor John D. Donovan's decorated automobile carrying a bevy of happy girls, followed by the Oliver Typewriter Band, the North Crystal Lake and Woodstock Reds baseball teams, the fire department, two "Roosevelte Wildebeestes," Mr. Bates and his "mules and ragamuffins," the members of Company G, and the Mills Brothers Military Band. (Courtesy of McHenry County Historical Society.)

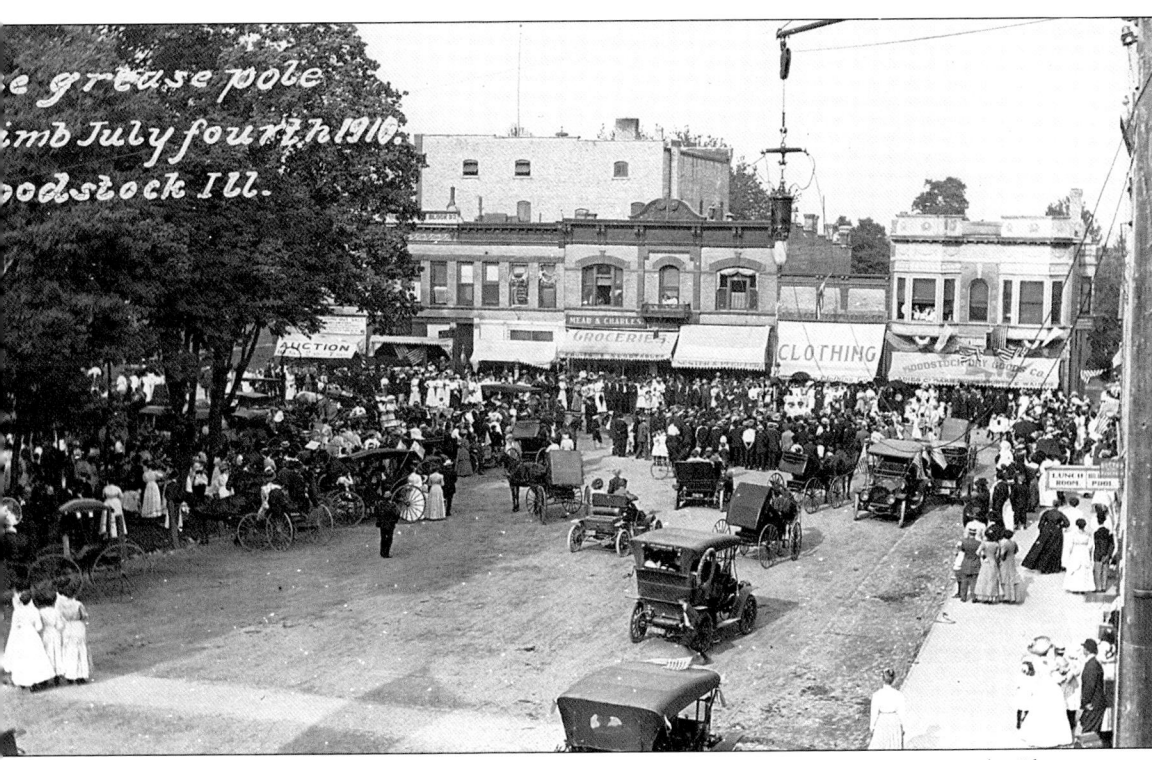

The parades were typically followed by events such as a blueberry pie–eating contest and a "fat man's race" for those weighing 200 pounds or more. A greased pole climbing contest was part of the fun in 1910. A baseball game and horse races at the fairgrounds were attended by a large crowd. The Oliver Typewriter Band performed a concert in the afternoon and again during the evening fireworks. At night, the park was brightly illuminated with a grand display of Chinese lanterns. (Courtesy of Woodstock Public Library.)

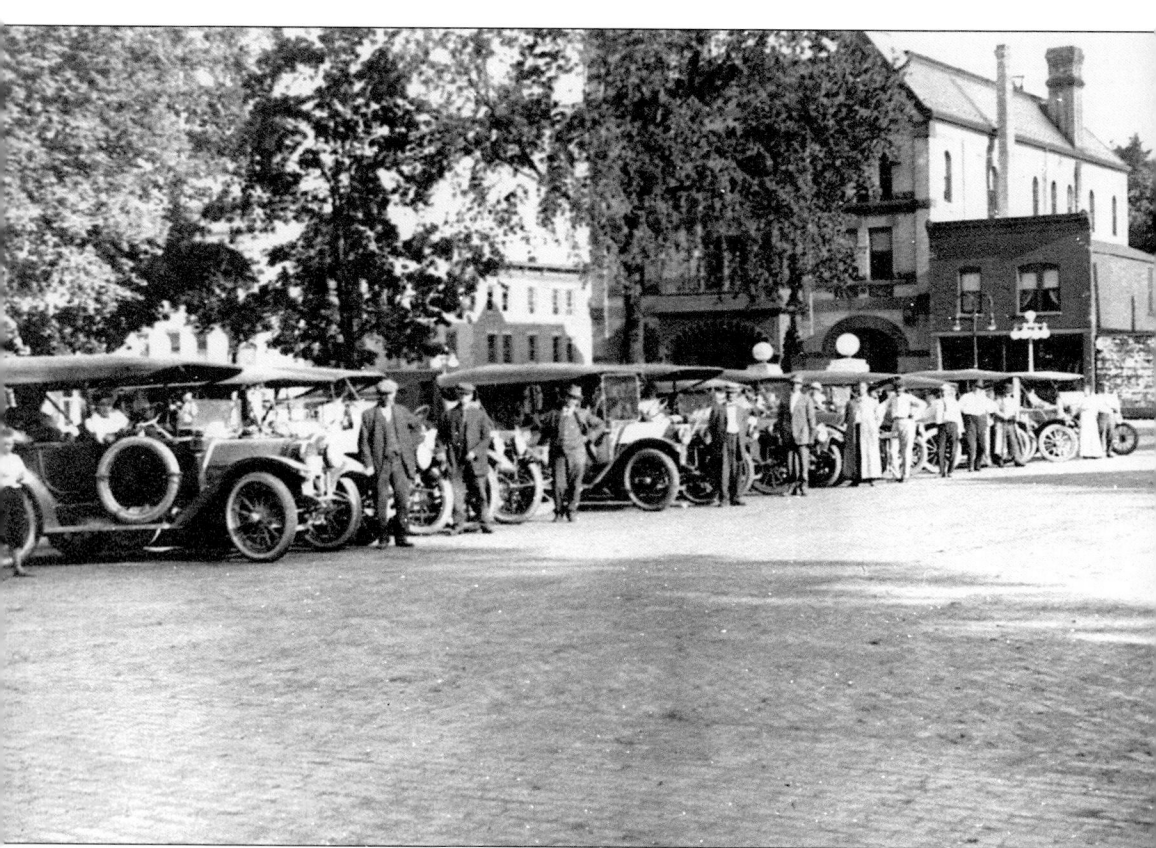

Automobile rides were enjoyed by adults and children alike. The first automobile, appearing on Woodstock streets in 1901, reportedly frightened residents as the driver tried to gain enough momentum to make it up a hill. Sunday afternoon tours started almost as soon as there were enough residents with cars to form a group. Drivers and passengers generally dressed up for these occasions. (Courtesy of Woodstock Public Library.)

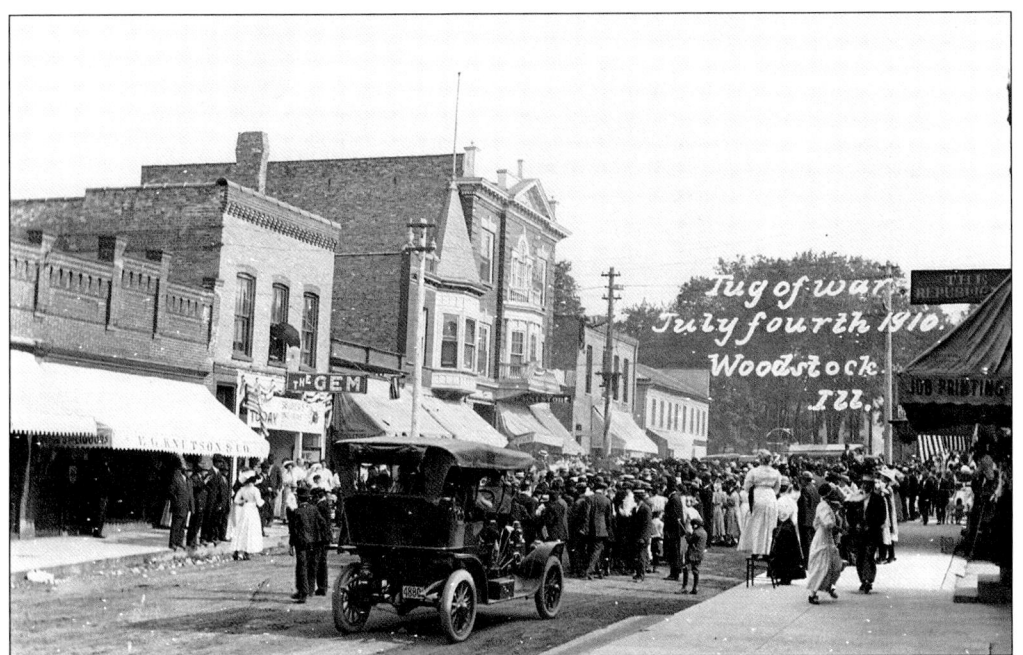

Movie theaters provided a new source of entertainment for Woodstock residents. One of the first theaters was the Gem, seen in the background of this 1910 photograph. It was one of several nickelodeon theaters operating in town for a few short years. (Courtesy of Woodstock Public Library.)

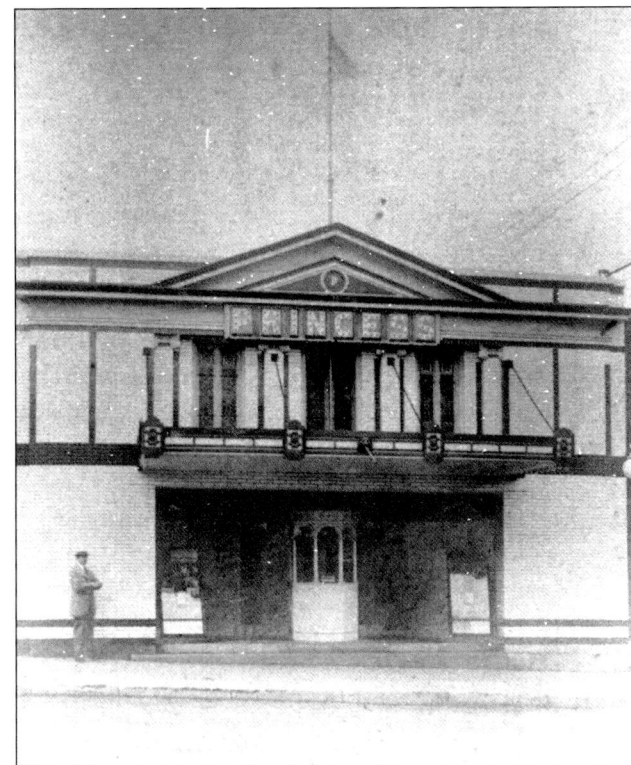

Across the street from the Gem, the Princess Theater had white-enameled terra-cotta brick walls with green trim. It provided more seating, better ventilation, and more exits than the other theaters. (Courtesy of McHenry County Historical Society.)

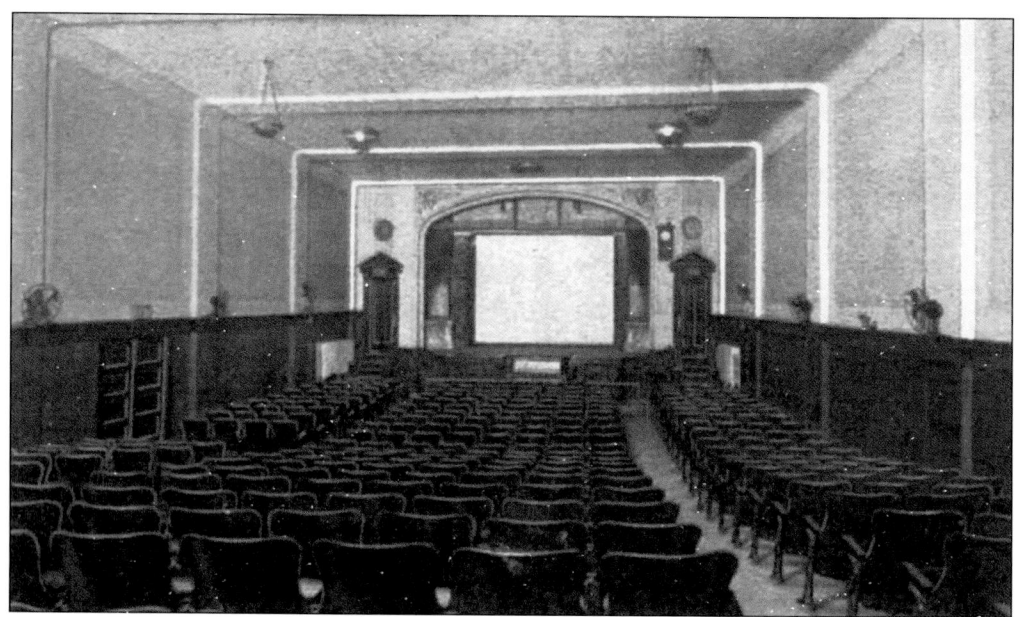

The Princess had sloped floors and permanent seats, while wicker lounge chairs were provided in the balcony for the more affluent patrons. In 1920, the Beverly Theater opened just up the street. It too had a white terra-cotta front. The Beverly building was recently returned to theater use when the Woodstock Theater expanded. (Courtesy of McHenry County Historical Society.)

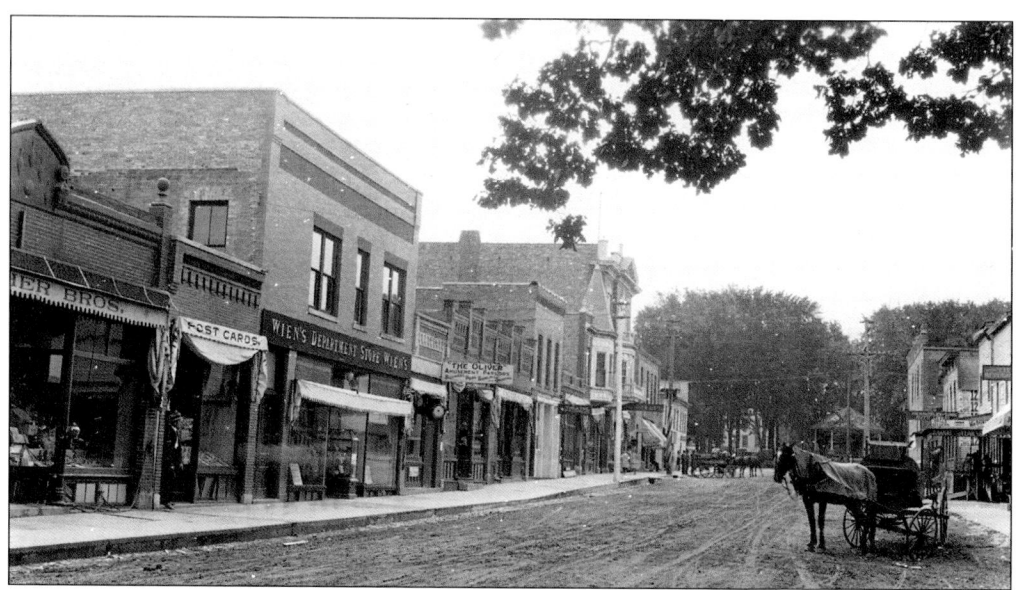

At one time or another during the early 1900s, several bowling alleys stood on Main Street. The bowling pins on the pediment of the building in the foreground are evidence of the structure's original use. Lanes were located on the second floor of the Wien's building, and in this photograph, the Oliver Amusement Parlor sign advertises billiards, pool, bowling, and shooting. When the three-story Waverly House opened in 1900, it contained a bowling alley in the basement, which extended out under the sidewalk. (Courtesy of McHenry County Historical Society.)

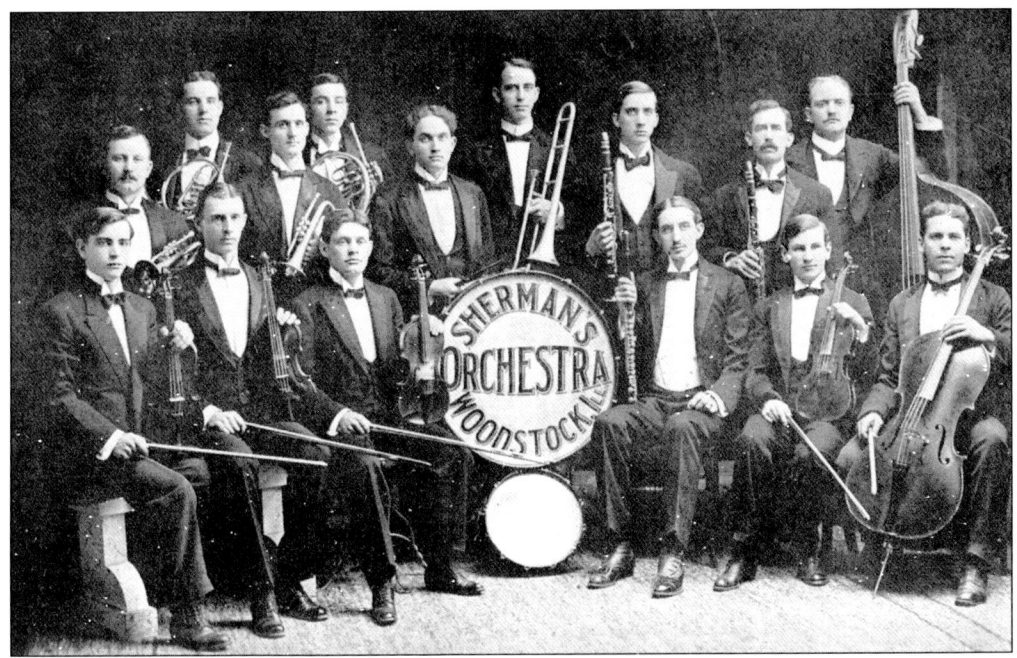

A local band formed in 1869 and played on the Fourth of July. After the Spring City Band was formed in 1885, a temporary platform was built for its April 1886 performance in the park. Sherman's Orchestra was one of many instrumental groups providing music at public occasions and private parties. (Courtesy of McHenry County Historical Society.)

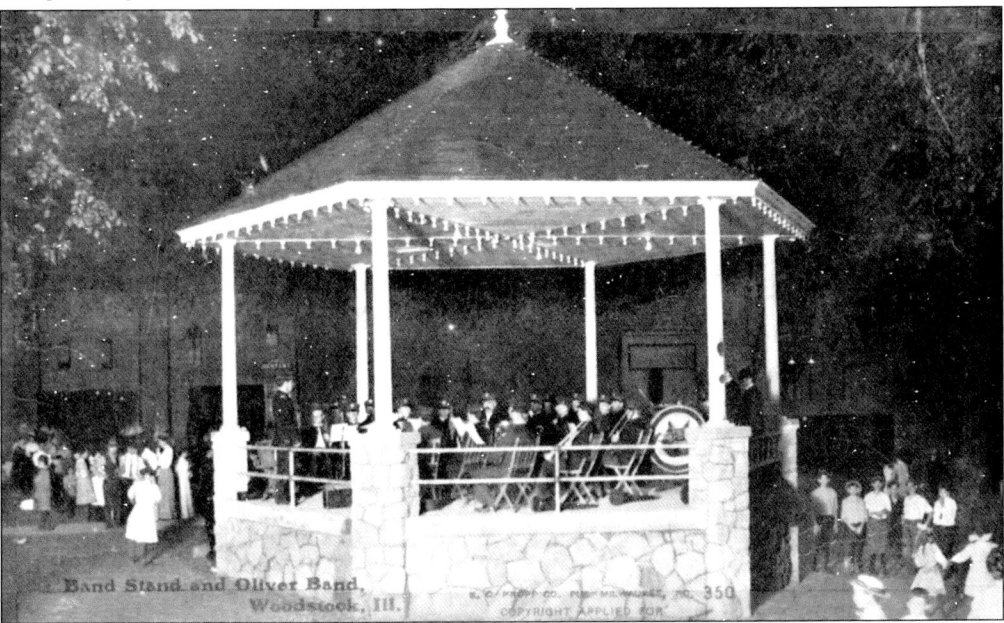

The Oliver Typewriter Band performed summer concerts in the park for many years. In August 1909, a new bandstand was dedicated. The lit structure was an impressive site when approaching the square from Main Street. At least some of the members of the Oliver Typewriter Band were not company employees; two members were hired to play during the winter months, when they were not working for the Ringling Circus. (Courtesy of McHenry County Historical Society.)

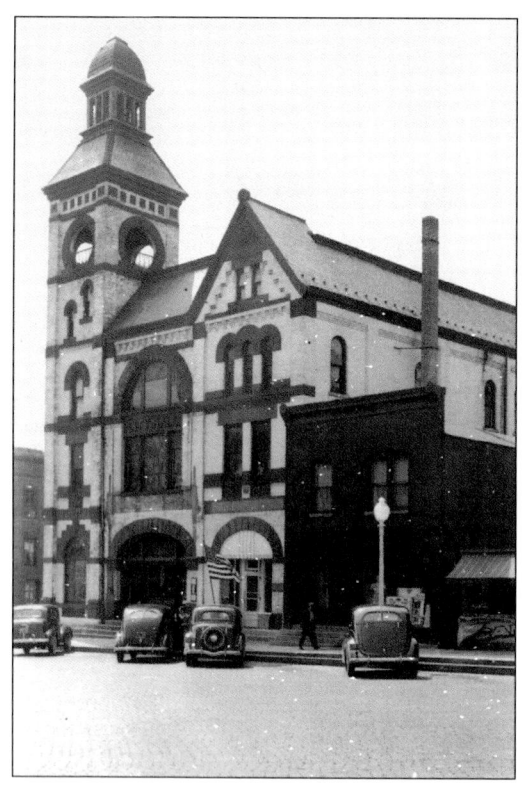

The Woodstock City Hall was constructed in 1889–1890 as a multipurpose building with offices, a council room, public library, police department, and fire department on the first floor, an opera house above, and jail cells in the basement. The building was designed by Elgin architect Smith Hoag, and construction was overseen by Woodstock contractor Simon Brink. An addition was constructed on the south side of the building in 1938 to provide space for the fire department, with city council chambers situated above. (Courtesy of McHenry County Historical Society.)

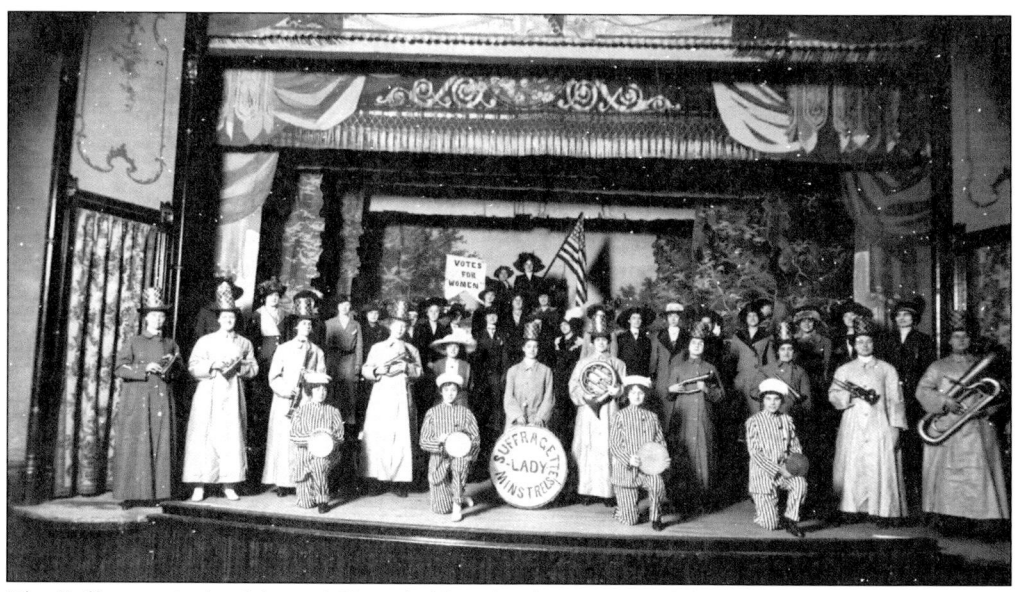

The Suffragette Ladies Minstrel Show, held under the auspices of the Woodstock Rebekah Lodge, appeared at the Woodstock Opera House in the fall of 1912. Around 60 Woodstock ladies performed such musical numbers as "The Ladies Coontown Brass Band" and "The Minstrel Boys and Taxi Girls." Seats were priced from 25¢ to 50¢. (Courtesy of McHenry County Historical Society.)

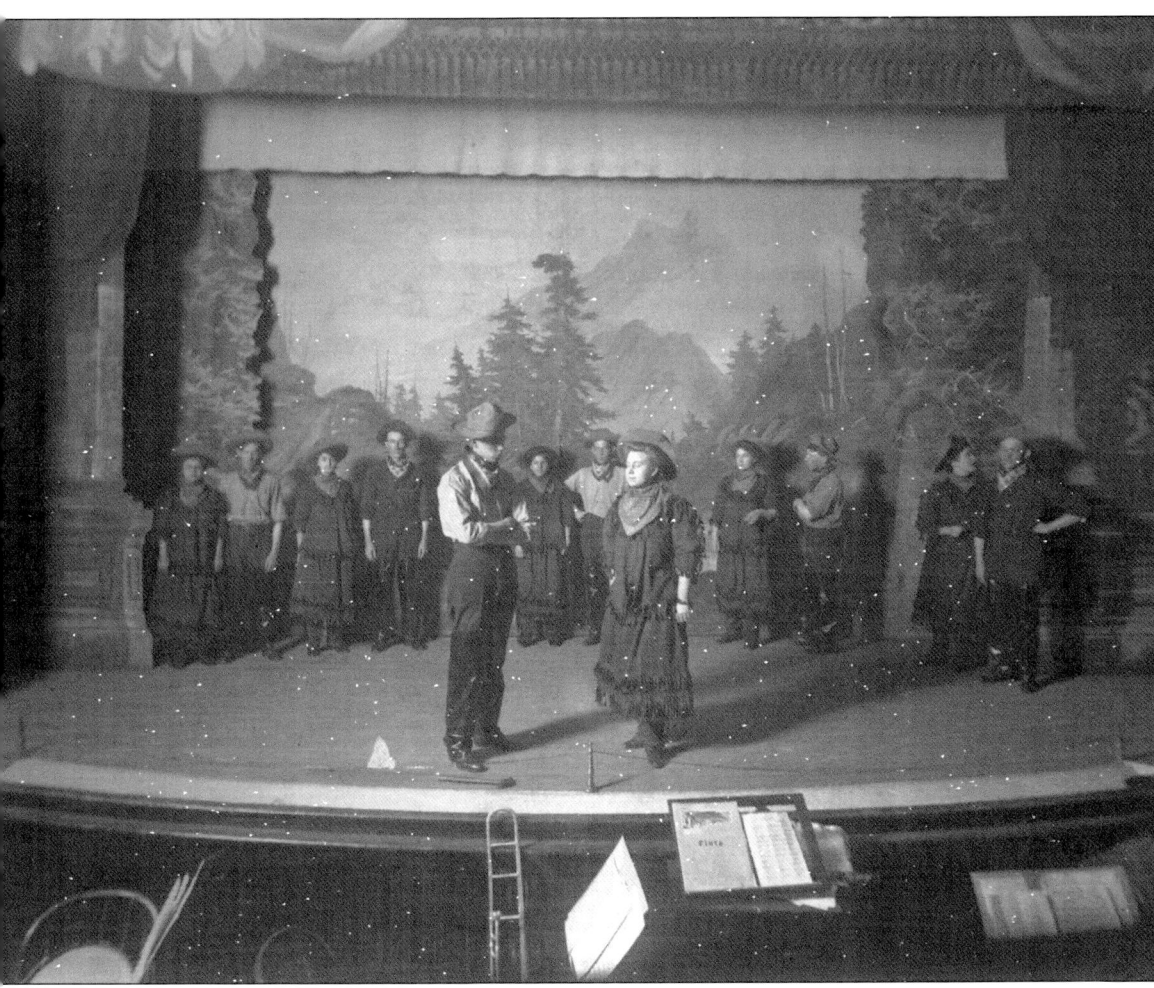

The Woodstock Opera House hosted performers ranging from local students and theater companies to nationally known celebrities. It served as an auditorium for political rallies and school graduations and was even rented out as a temporary movie theater when the Miller Theater was under construction. Before the opera house was completed in city hall, the third-floor hall of the Murphy Block on Benton Street was used for theatrical performances, variety shows, lectures, and dances and was referred to as the opera house. (Courtesy of McHenry County Historical Society.)

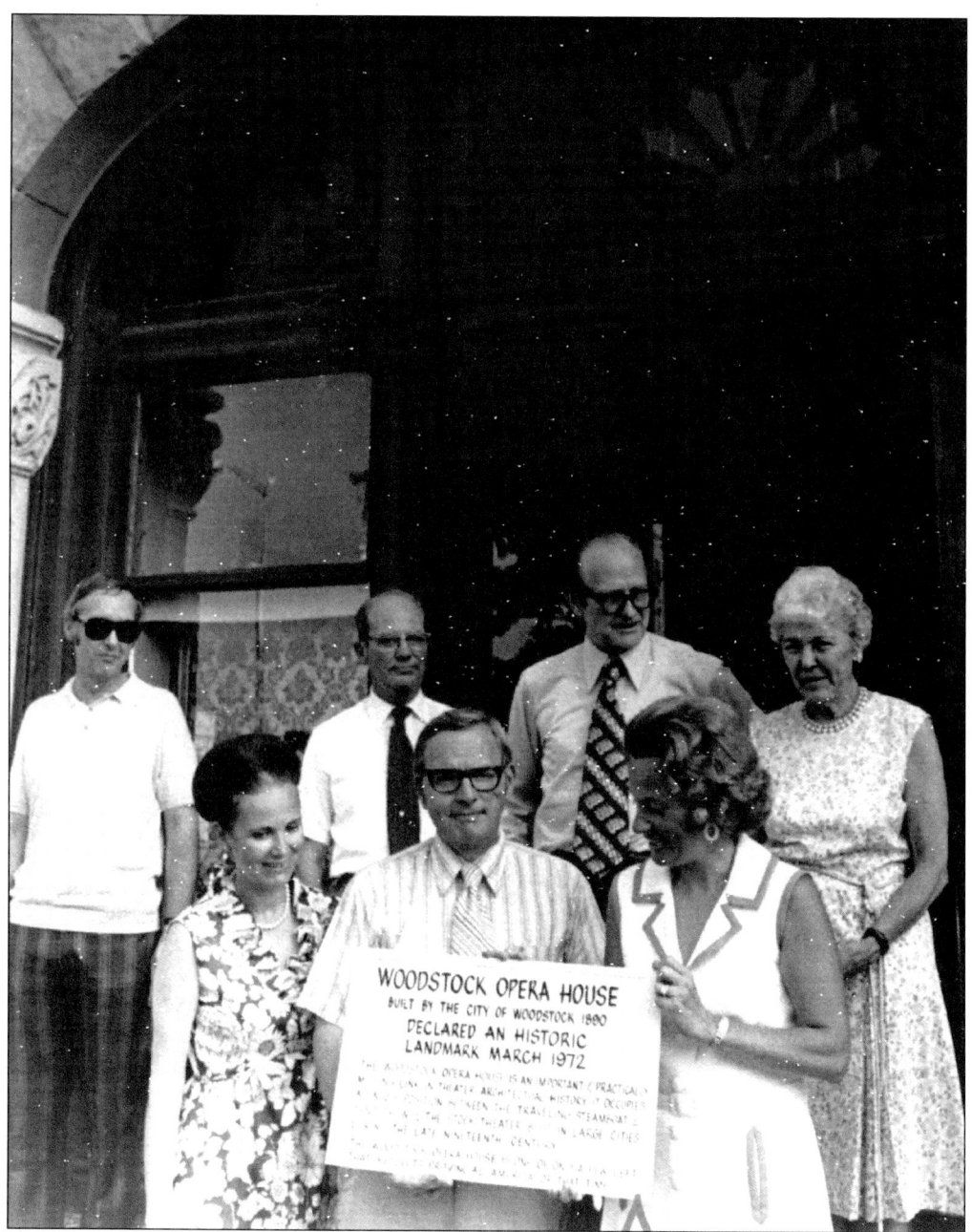

The Woodstock Opera House was listed on the National Register of Historic Places in 1972. At the ceremony, Margery Sharpe, chairwoman of the landmark committee, presented Gov. Richard B. Ogilvie with ashtrays containing photographs of the opera house and the courthouse. Pictured here, from left to right, are the following: (first row) Dorothy Ogilvie, Governor Ogilvie, and Margery Sharpe; (second row) Andrew Kuby Jr., Don Still, John Strohm, and Dorothy McEachren. (Courtesy of McHenry County Historical Society.)

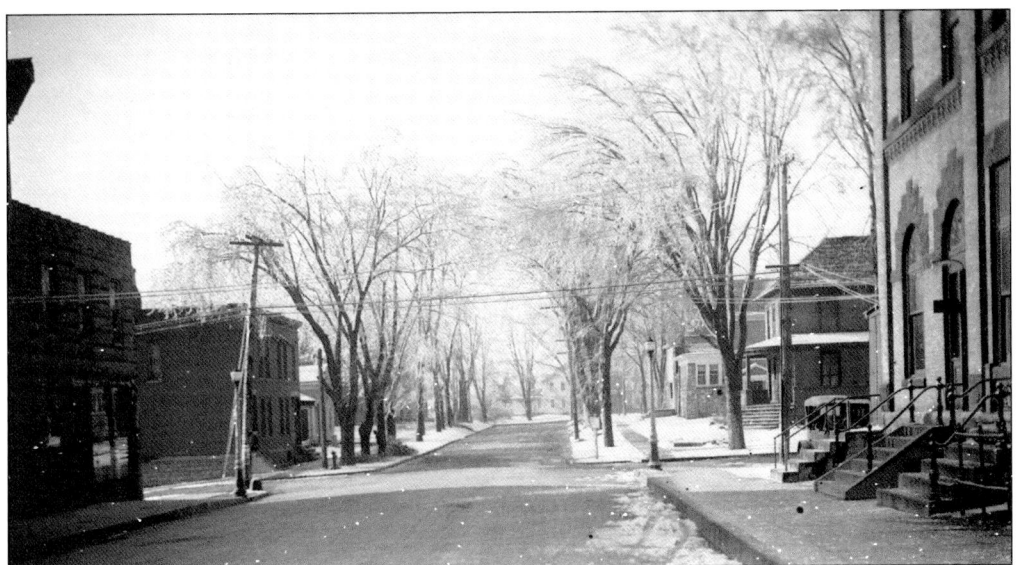

In days of little commercial or organized recreation, an ice and snowstorm was especially welcomed by Woodstock's youth. The city would close South Street and allow children to sled down the hill. One day in the early 1890s, a set of bobsleds were fastened together. Ed Hanaford steered the smaller sled in front. The sleds sped down from the top of the hill on South Street and, with a little help at Dean Street, rounded the corner, heading for the square where they went around the southeast corner to East Judd Street, then down and across the railroad tracks. (Courtesy of McHenry County Historical Society.)

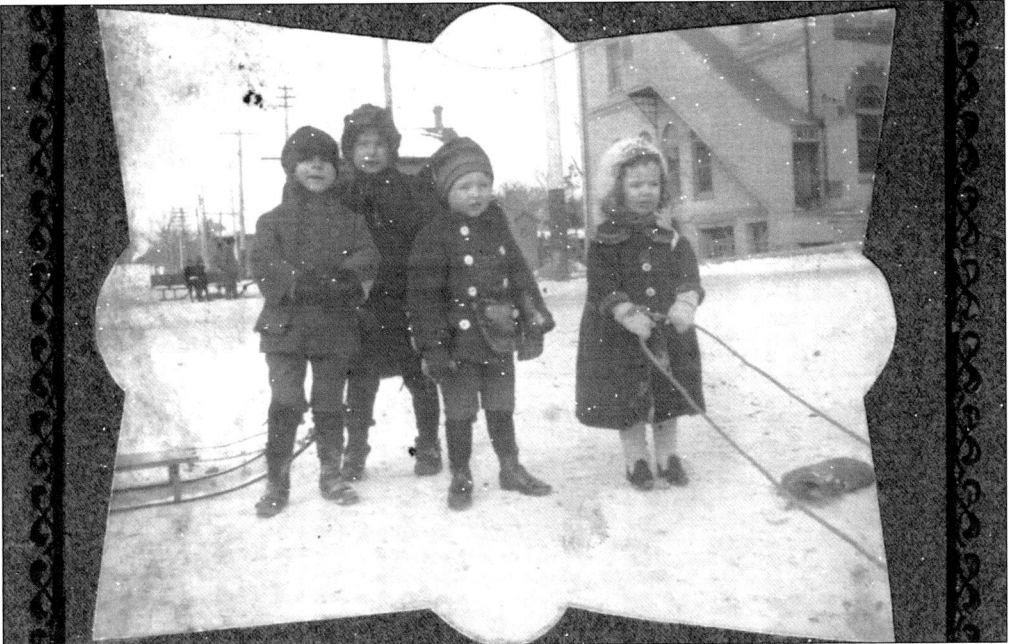

Though an extended bobsled ride might have been too much for the children in this photograph, the bobsled run was experienced by many that day. Shown near city hall in 1906 are, from left to right, Otis and Anna Bente, Armour Wright, and Helen Windmueller. (Courtesy of McHenry County Historical Society.)

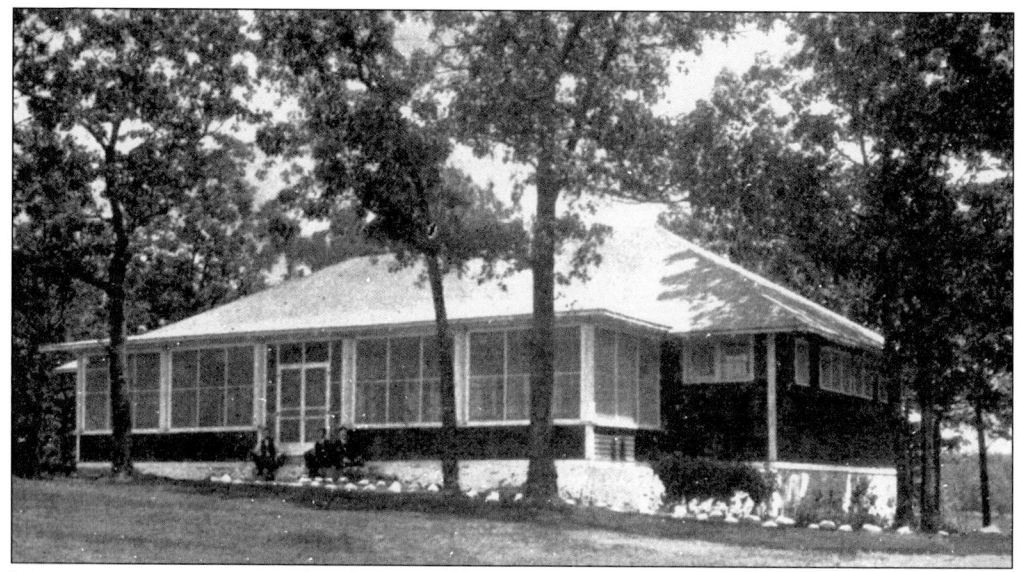

Numerous sites were considered for a golf club, but Woodstock businessmen settled on the cheapest. The original 36 acres were purchased at a cost of $50 per acre in 1915. Many of the professionals and businessmen of the city spent long hours digging rocks out of the fairways and moving dirt to form the greens. During the first year, a farmer rented the land. Club members sometimes had to play around the cattle. For a while, a dead horse rotting in a hollow caused golfers to avoid the No. 7 green. (Courtesy of McHenry County Historical Society.)

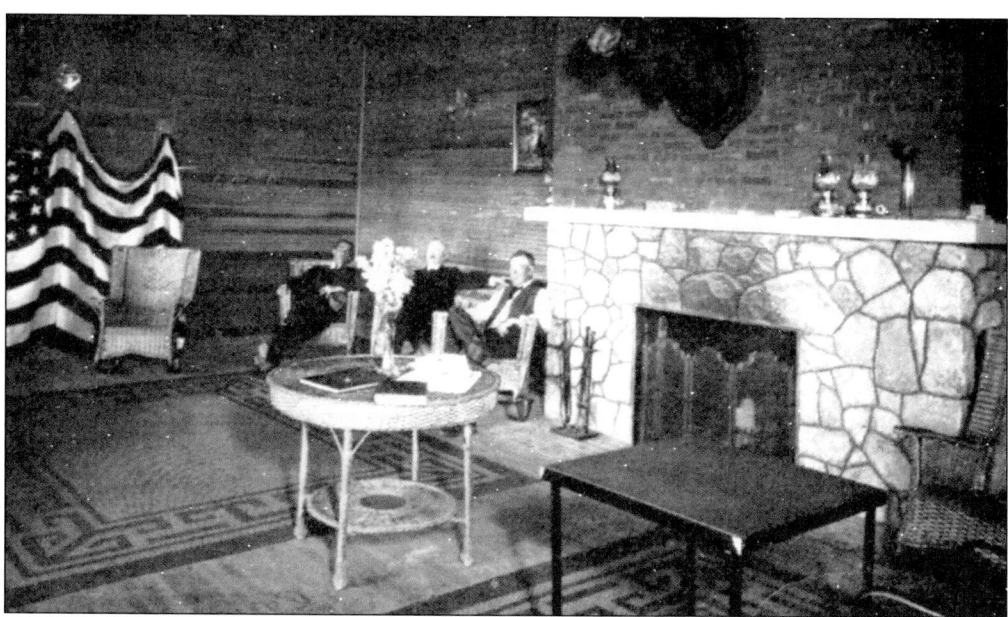

In 1921, the club reorganized as a corporation instead of the original stock company. From 1923 to 1935, it was called the Glen Crest Country Club. Although activities declined during the Depression, the newly named Woodstock Country Club survived because it had not overspent. (Courtesy of McHenry County Historical Society.)

High school provided a few brave girls with the opportunity to play organized sports. The girls of the 1908–1909 basketball team played several games against area teams. Note the shoes on the girl in the front. Erma Seiler, the sister of Illinois standout football player Otto Seiler, served as captain. Players are listed as Ada Johnson, Bessie Barnes, and the Doten girls. The team won five out of nine games that season.

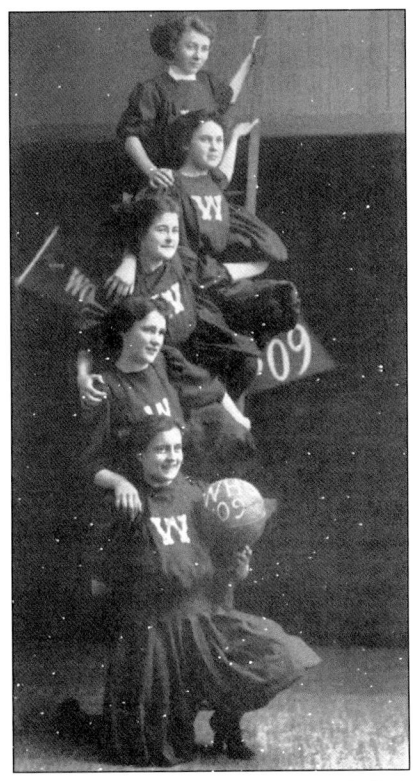

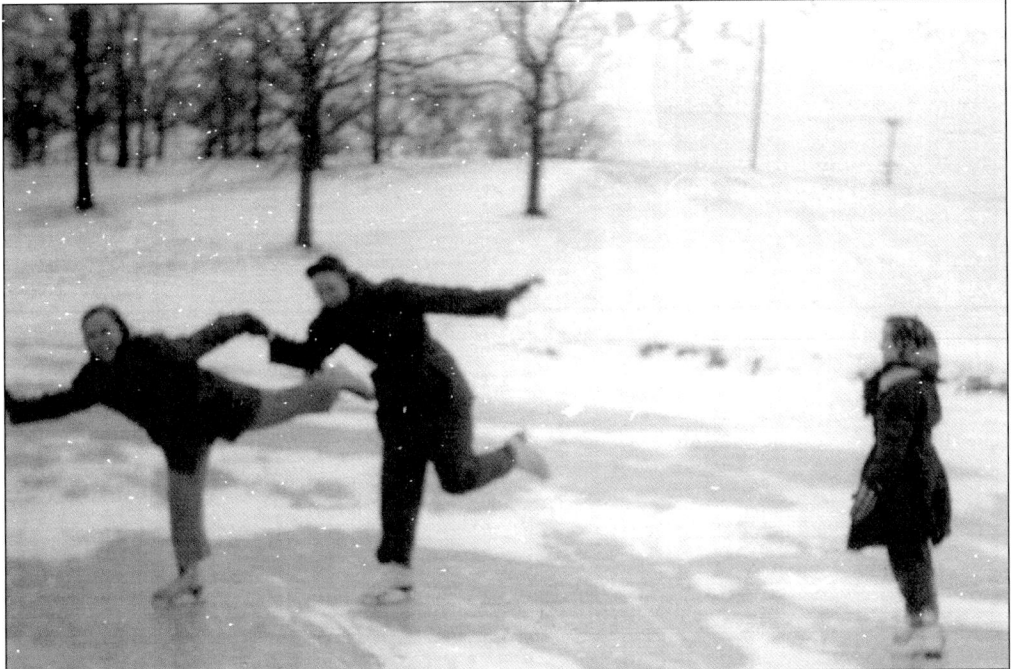

The school yard was always a place for students to play jump rope and other traditional games at recess. An outing at the skating pond gave these two young teachers a chance to demonstrate their skating skills for their Westwood School students.

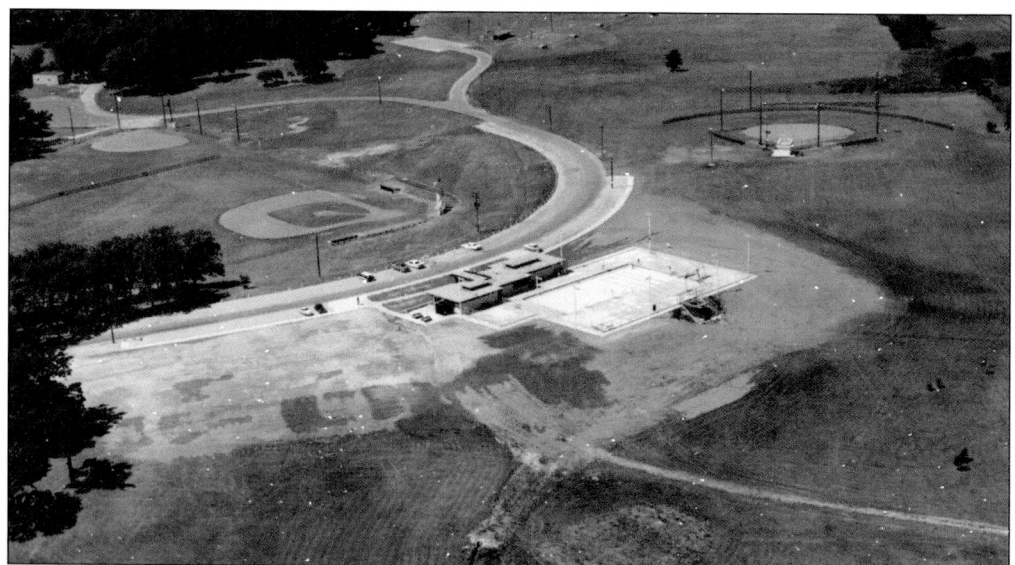

In the early 1940s, alderman Thore Emricson convinced the city council to establish a park where people could gather for activities. In 1945, the city purchased 80 acres between South and Jackson Streets from the Woodstock Sportsman's League. A professional engineering firm was hired to lay out the park. The league's clubhouse and baseball diamond were retained, though the diamond was so greatly improved that the Chicago Cubs and the Chicago White Sox held tryouts there. Volunteers from the Autolite factory helped clear stones for the park. (Courtesy of McHenry County Historical Society, Don Peasley Collection.)

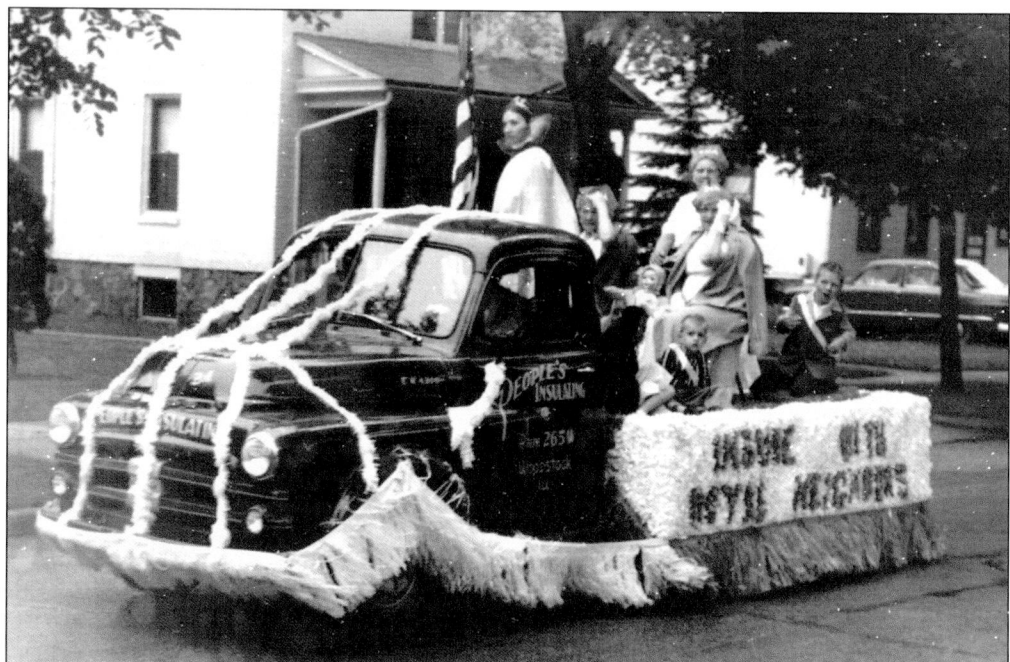

In 1952, Woodstock celebrated the centennial of its incorporation as a village. The parade, chaired by police chief Tiny Hansman, included floats, bands, drum and bugle corps, vintage cars, old and new fire trucks, and other decorated vehicles.

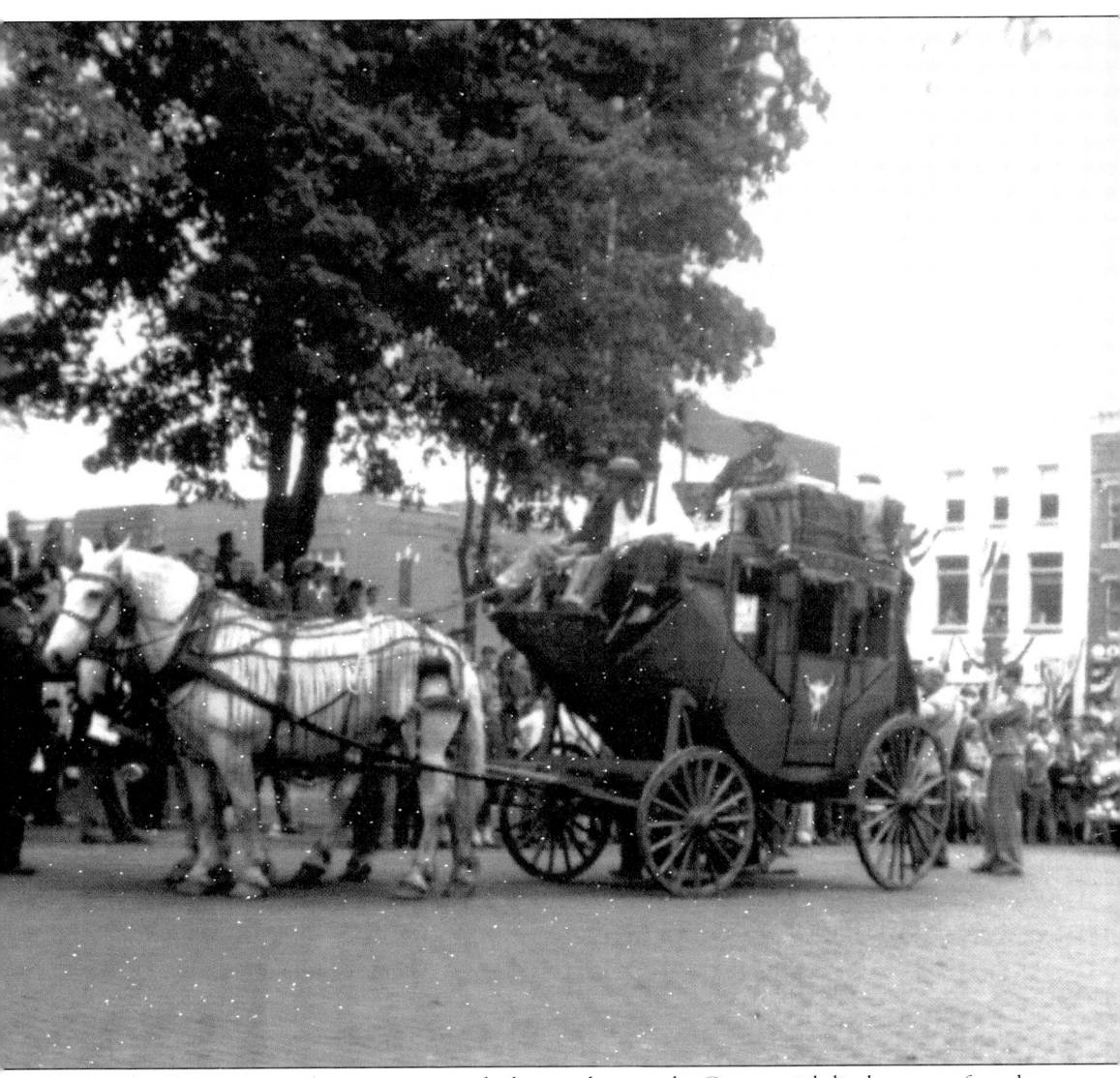

Gov. Adlai Stevenson rode on a stagecoach during the parade. Centennial displays were found in many store windows, and a historical pageant was presented at the high school. Among the many other events was a beard-judging contest.

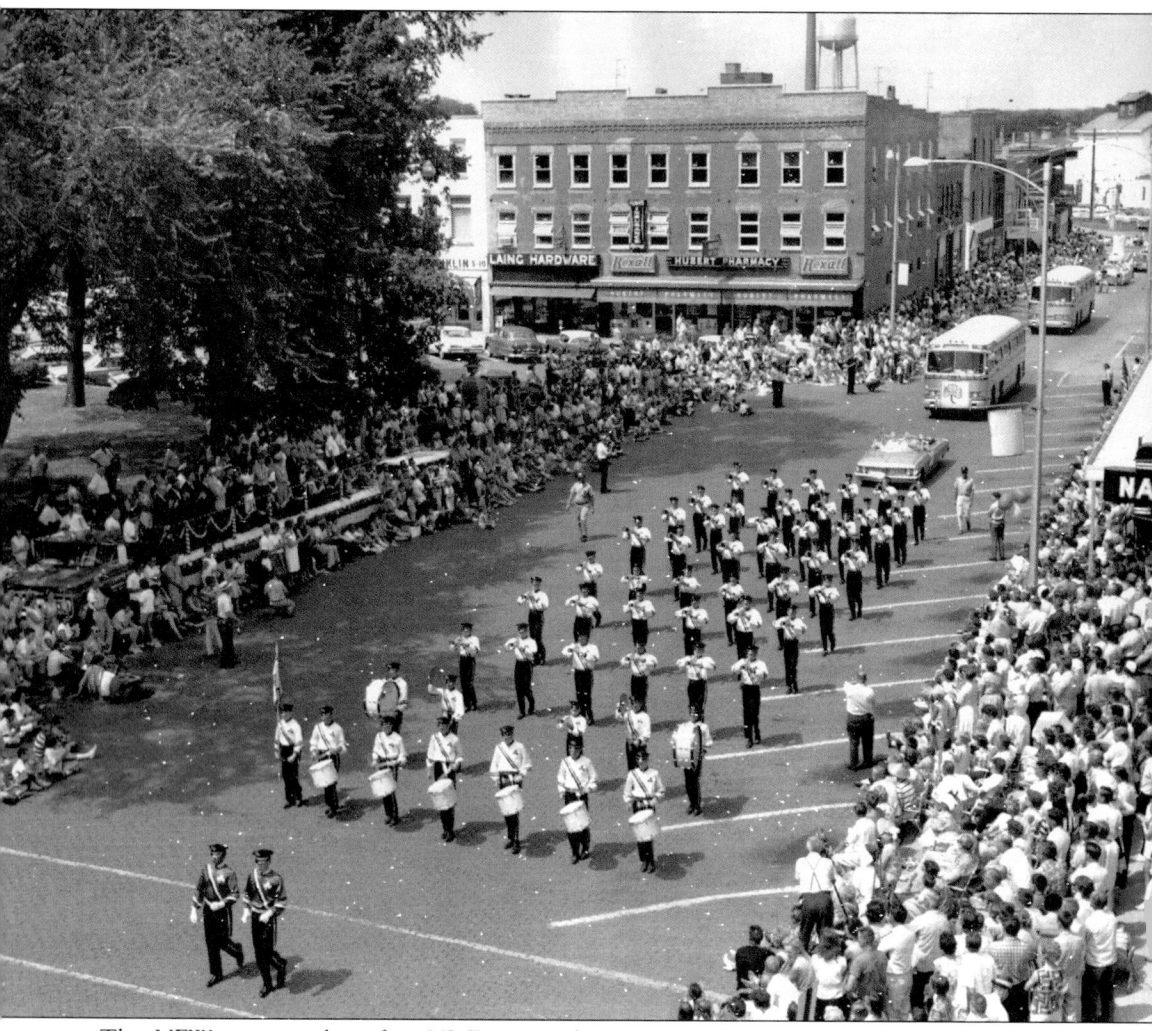

The VFW sponsored its first VJ Day parade in 1955, when some 20,000 people lined the two-and-one-half-mile route. Maynard Wilkerson chaired the 1955 parade and those that followed for several years. Drum and bugle corps, invited from around the country, competed at the high school in the evening. (Courtesy of McHenry County Historical Society, Don Peasley Collection.)

Nine
SOME SIGNS OF THE TIMES

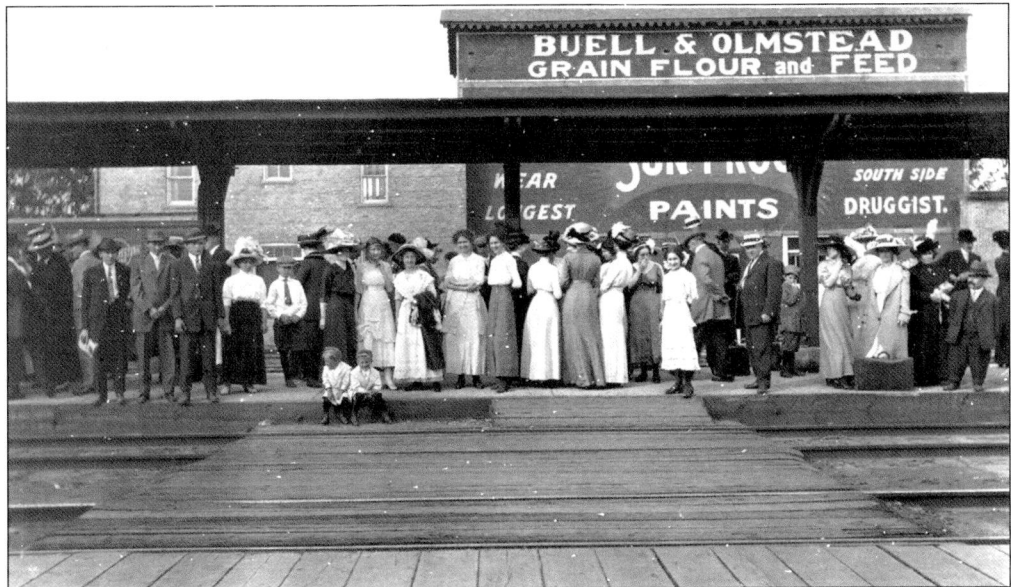

One of the first things passengers saw when they stepped off the train and onto the platform at the Woodstock depot was the Buell and Olmstead sign. The Buell and Olmstead feed store and grain mill was located on Clay Street, on the north side of the tracks. The mill started out as F. W. Buell Flour and Feed. Adelbert Olmstead later acquired an interest in the business and became the manager. (Courtesy of McHenry County Historical Society.)

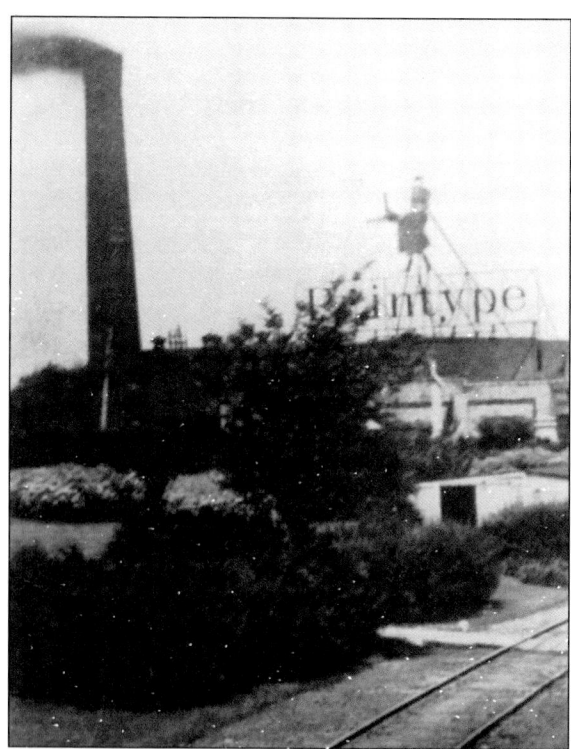

The Oliver Printype sign was a unique feature on the Woodstock horizon. The company also grew a large bed of flowers spelling out the name "Oliver," among its other attractive landscaping features. (Courtesy of McHenry County Historical Society.)

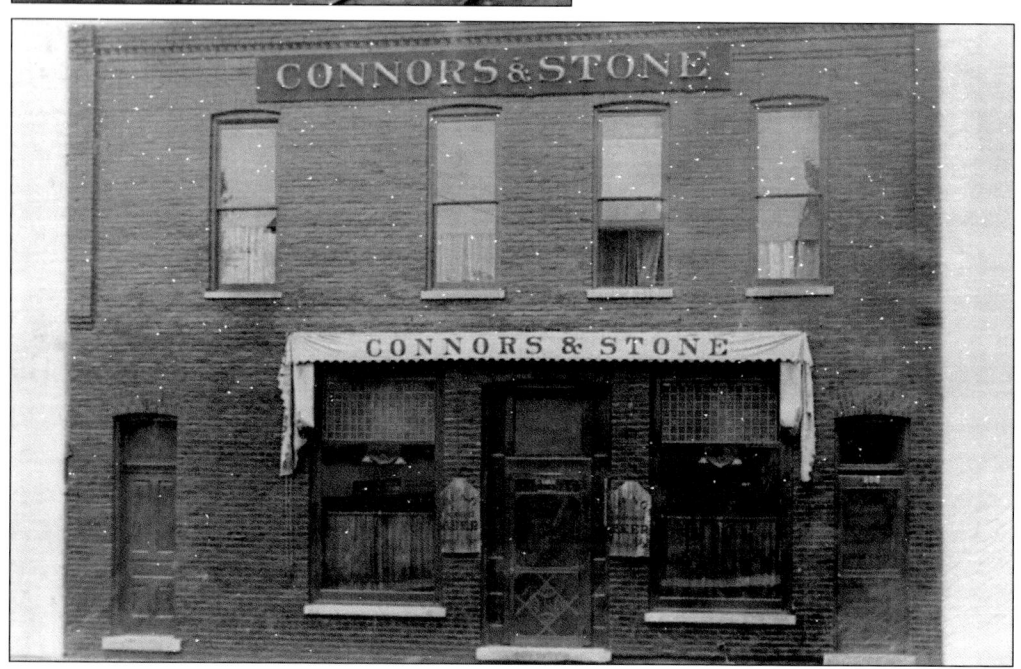

H. J. Herdklotz relocated his business from a Benton Street basement to this building on Main Street. The H. J. Herdklotz Crystal Palace tavern opened with new fixtures, cigars, and liquors a few months after the 1892 fire that destroyed most of Main Street. Due to failing health, Herdklotz sold the business to Joseph Connors and Charles Stone in 1901. (Courtesy of McHenry County Historical Society.)

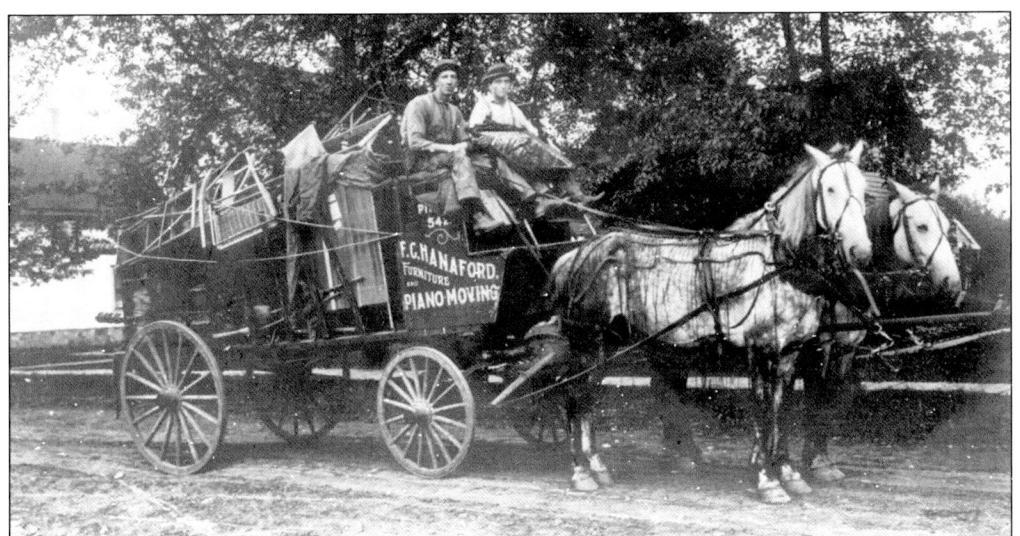

Frank E. Hanaford enlisted in Company A of the 15th Illinois Volunteer Infantry in 1861. He was captured and taken to the Andersonville prison, where he was assigned to remove the bodies of those who had died during the night. Moved to other locations, he ended up near Thomasville, Georgia, nearly 100 miles from Union lines. He and four other prisoners, all members of the 15th, escaped. With almost no supplies, they traveled 21 days, mostly at night, foraging food along the way before finally reaching Union troops. Hanaford was actively involved in teaming work, which his son Frank C. took over upon his retirement. (Courtesy of McHenry County Historical Society.)

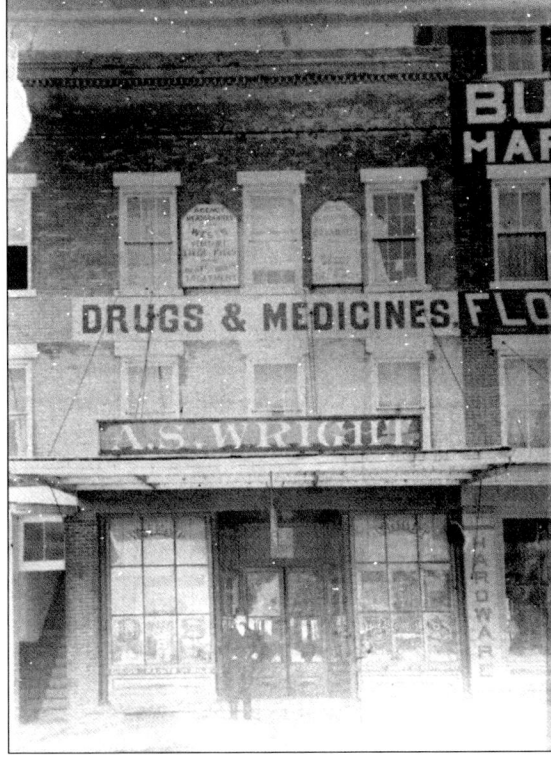

Adelbert S. Wright was orphaned in Onandaga County, New York, at age 9 and enlisted in the 22nd New York Cavalry at age 15. After the Civil War, he came to Woodstock to work for W. P. Adams, who had previously been his employer in New York. After Adams's death, Wright acquired the business and for 70 years operated "the Old Red Front Drug Store," as it was known. (Courtesy of McHenry County Historical Society.)

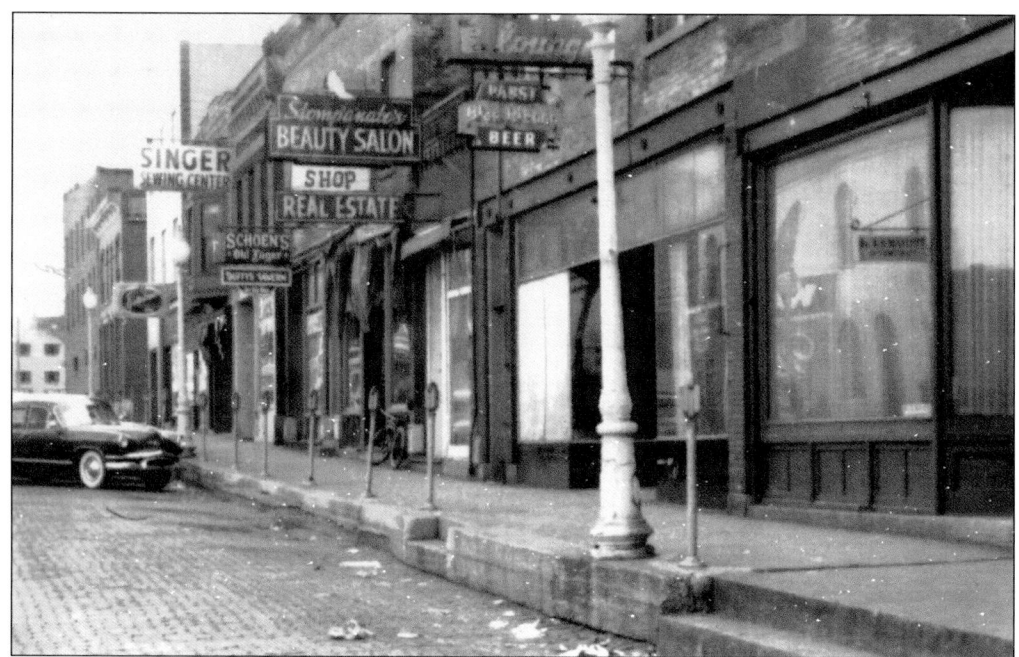

Benton Street was lined with signs in the 1950s. The 15-foot-wide Stompanato's Beauty Salon and Real Estate office was a bowling alley in 1912. In 1929, John Stompanato leased the building for a barbershop, and his daughter later ran the beauty shop. By 1975, Stompanato's was one of several taverns located along North Benton Street. (Courtesy of Woodstock Public Library.)

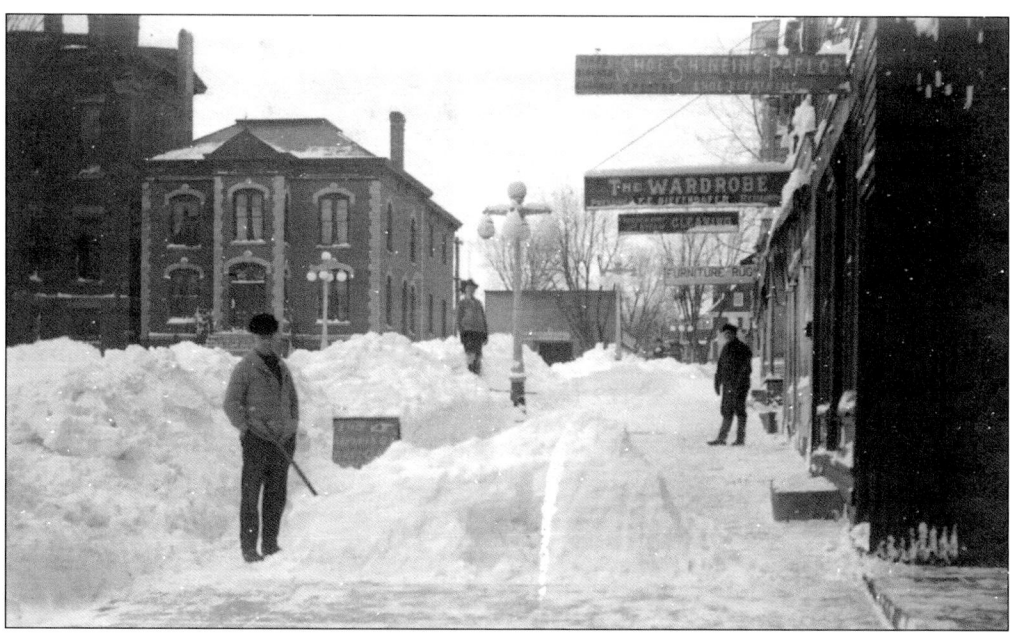

F. F. Diffendafer's steam and dry cleaning, pressing, and tailoring business, the Wardrobe, occupied the old McGee building as well as the new building erected in its place. Stuck in the snow in front of the Wardrobe, a sign advertises shoe repair. (Courtesy of McHenry County Historical Society.)

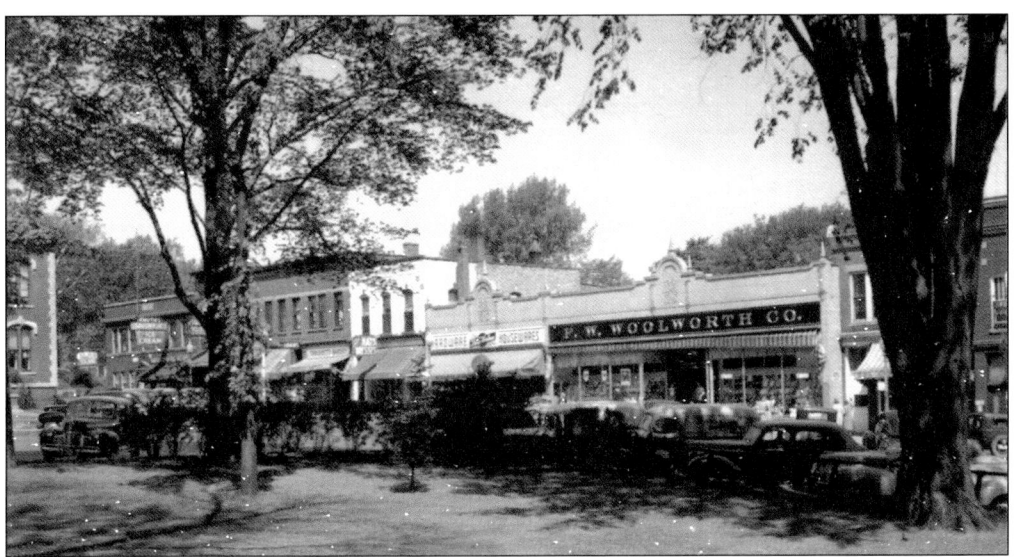

This F. W. Woolworth store displays the trademark gold lettering across its front. It was constructed by local contractor Henry Ohlrich in 1928, and its decorative terra-cotta facade was produced at American Terra Cotta near Crystal Lake. The western third of the building was first occupied by the A&P Tea Company in the 1930s and by True Value Hardware in the 1940s and early 1950s. (Courtesy of McHenry County Historical Society.)

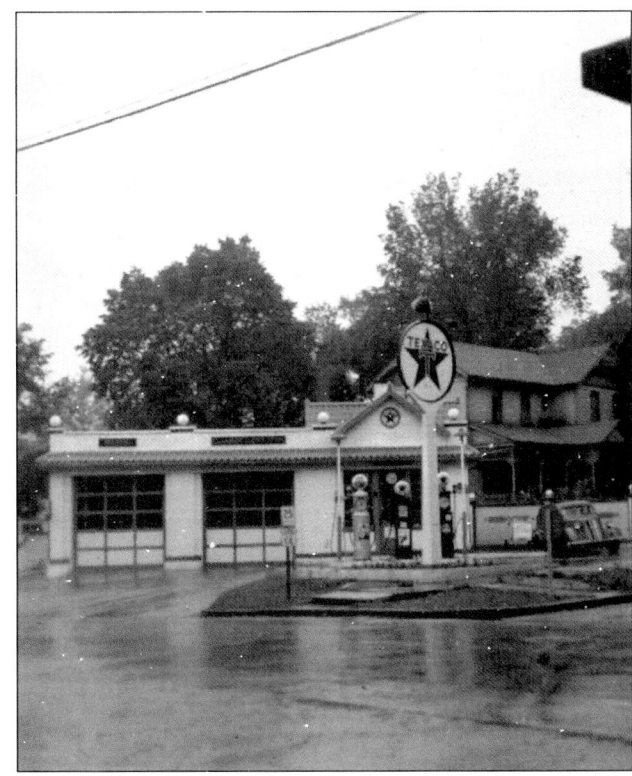

Before the U.S. 14 bypass was constructed around the west side of Woodstock, the highway wove through town using Washington, Throop, and South Streets and Lake Avenue. Numerous gasoline stations were located along this route. Like most stations of its time, Texaco offered automobile repairs and full-service fuel pumps.

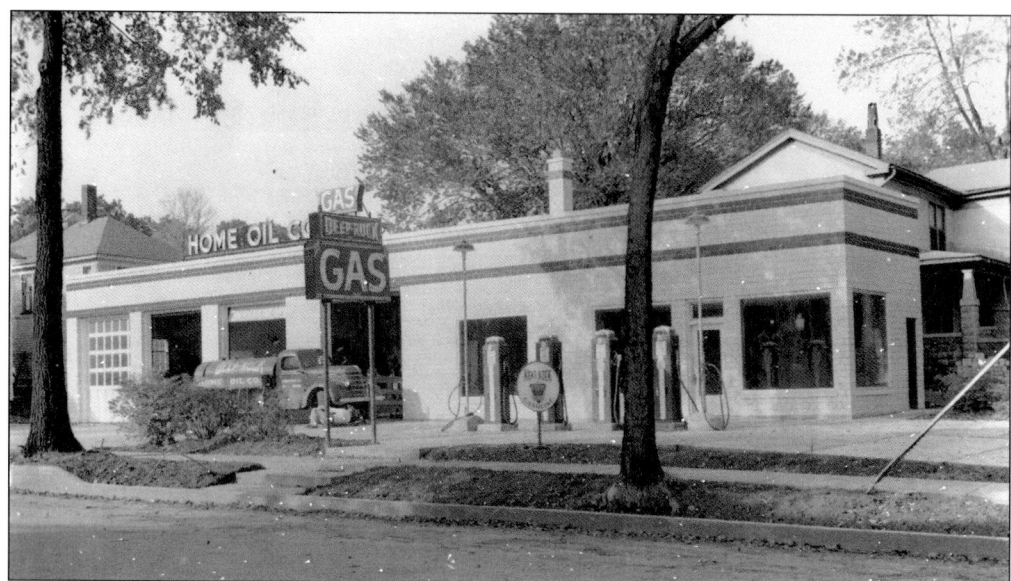

In 1915, G. W. Frame and E. L. Hanaford organized the Independent Oil Company on the old mill property east of the railroad tracks. They became local distributors of Deep Rock oil and gasoline products. In 1919, they moved to Calhoun Street, next to the city hall and Woodstock Opera House. Two years later, they moved to the southwest corner of Throop and West Judd Streets and erected one of the first drive-in gas stations in the area. Frame bought out Hanaford's interest in 1928. (Courtesy of McHenry County Historical Society.)

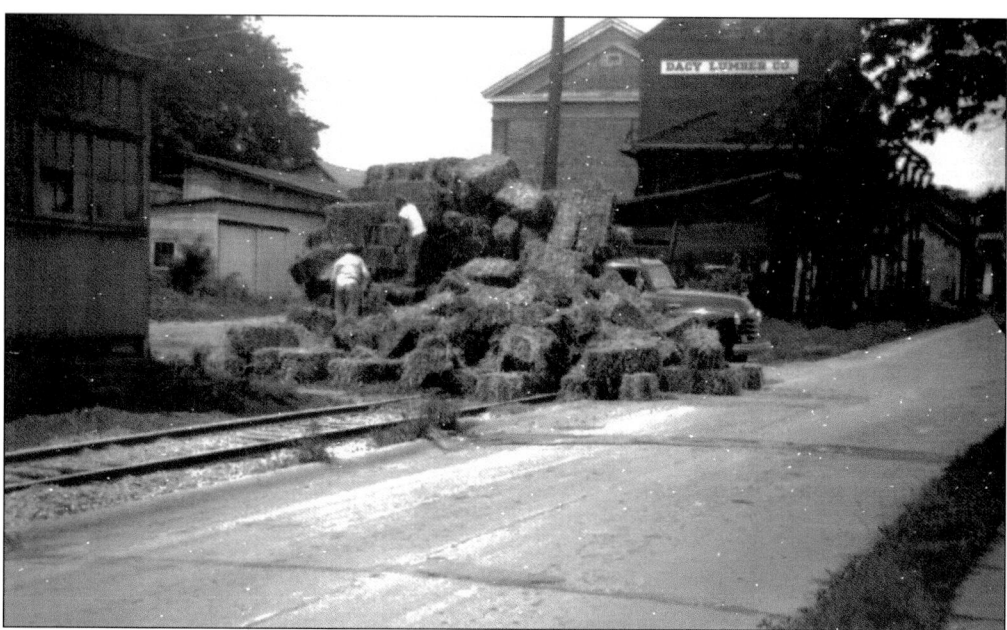

The Dacy Lumber Company was located in the block bounded by Church, Jefferson, East Judd, and Madison Streets. It narrowly escaped fire when the Hall and Eckert Lumber Company burned to its south. The railroad track running along the street extended to the Woodstock Typewriter factory. The narrow street in the foreground is Route 120, and the former Presbyterian church, which had been used by the lumberyard for many years, is the brick structure in the background.

The Dacy electric store may have been damaged by fire in 1957, but signs still proclaimed the many products available inside. Dacy repaired the building, restocked, and remained in business selling appliances and electronics until 1979. (Courtesy of McHenry County Historical Society, Don Peasley Collection.)

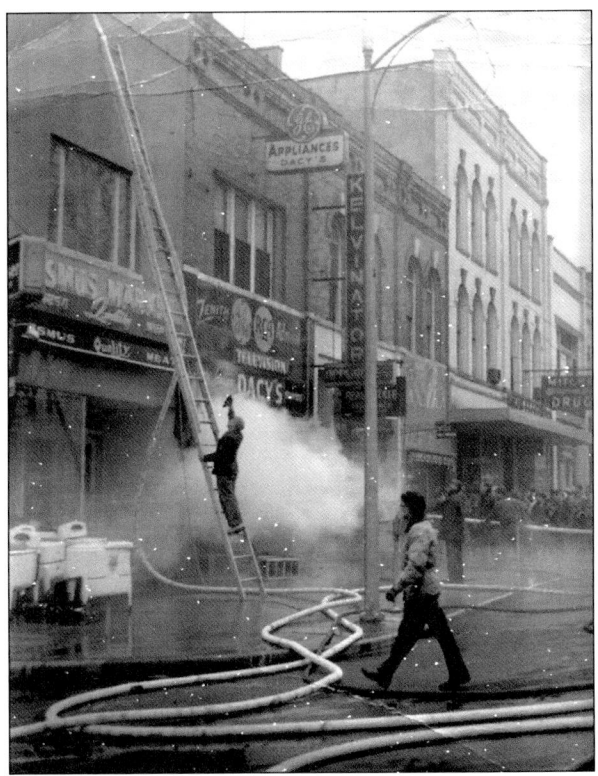

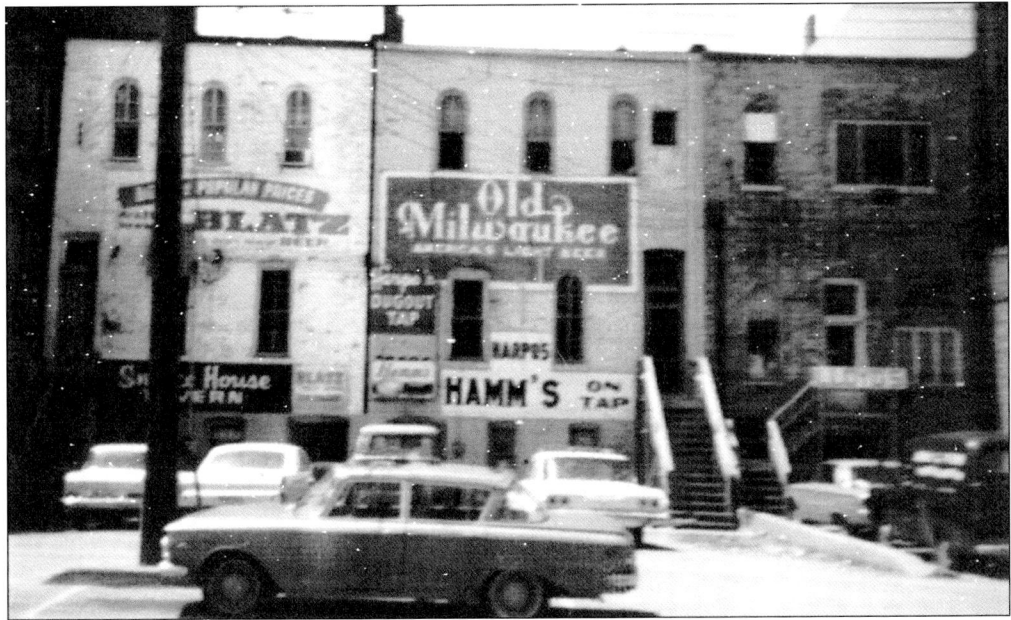

The Smoke House Tavern and the Dugout Tap both advertised prominently on the Jefferson Street sides of their buildings, which fronted on the square. Originally, several buildings had outside stairs leading from street level on the square to businesses in the basements. Most of these stairwells have been eliminated, but the stairs that led to the Smoke House and the Dugout remain.

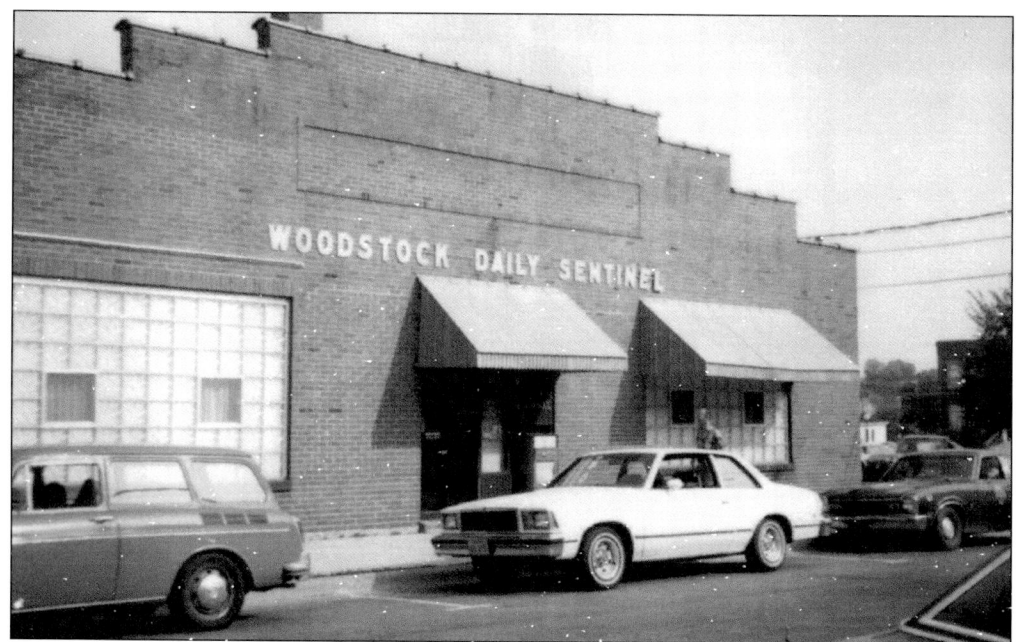

The first issue of the *Woodstock Sentinel* was published on July 17, 1856, from the Phoenix Block on Van Buren Street, but the newspaper soon moved to the third floor of the Hoy Block, where a large sign with the word "Sentinel" projected above the roof. The *Sentinel* became a daily newspaper in 1921. In 1953, it moved to the former Bakkow machinery shop building on Jefferson Street.

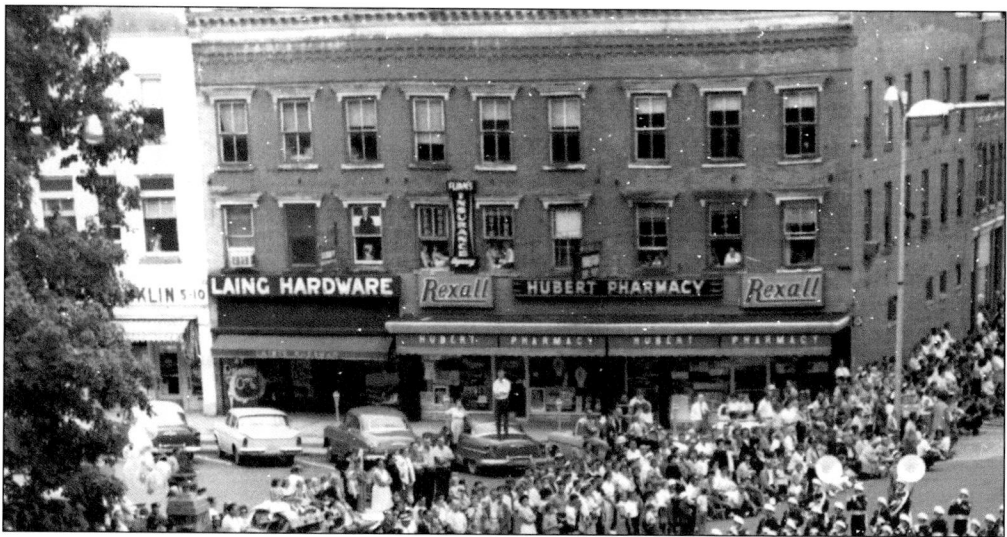

John Laing opened Laing Hardware in 1952 in the space vacated by Bohn's Hardware. Next door was the Hubert Pharmacy, which had started in 1944. As the signs indicate, Hubert's was a Rexall store. The business included a soda fountain and, in 1956, advertised air-conditioning. (Courtesy of McHenry County Historical Society, Don Peasley Collection.)

Ten
Caring for Young and Old

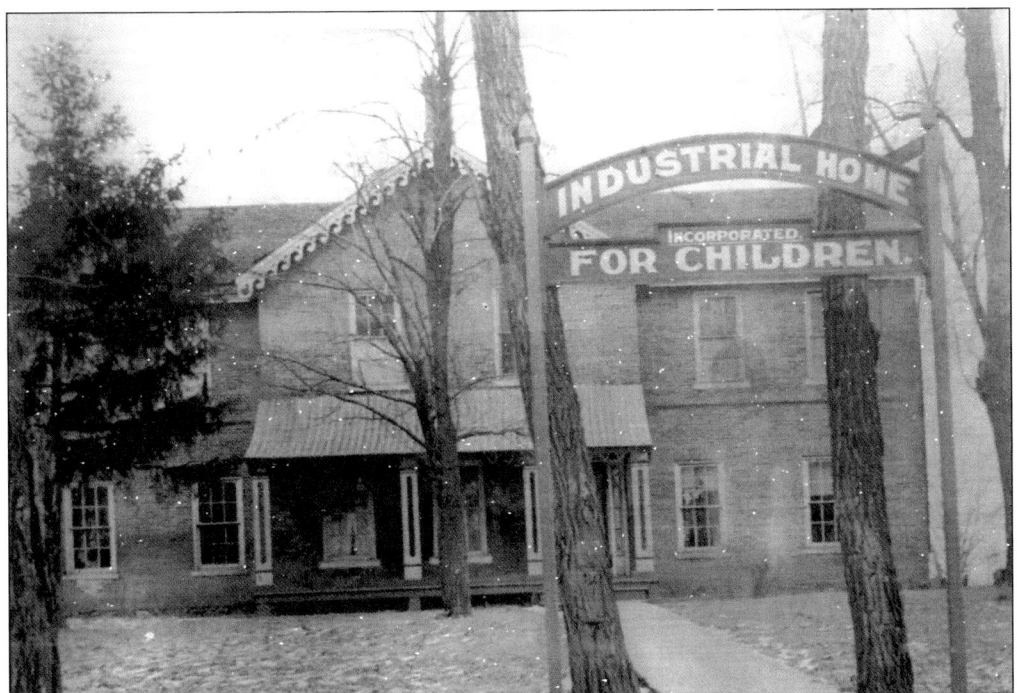

In 1886, Rev. Thomas B. Arnold, a printer and publisher, took two young boys living out of garbage cans into his Chicago home. Soon more children joined them and the Arnold family grew to 18. In 1888, Roxy Stevens of Woodstock offered her farm to Reverend Arnold, and the Chicago Industrial Home for Children was established there in 1889. Arnold served as superintendent of the home until 1898, when Rev. John D. Kelsey assumed this role. The home functioned like an adoption agency, providing temporary shelter until the children could be placed in permanent adoptive homes. (Courtesy of Woodstock Christian Life Services.)

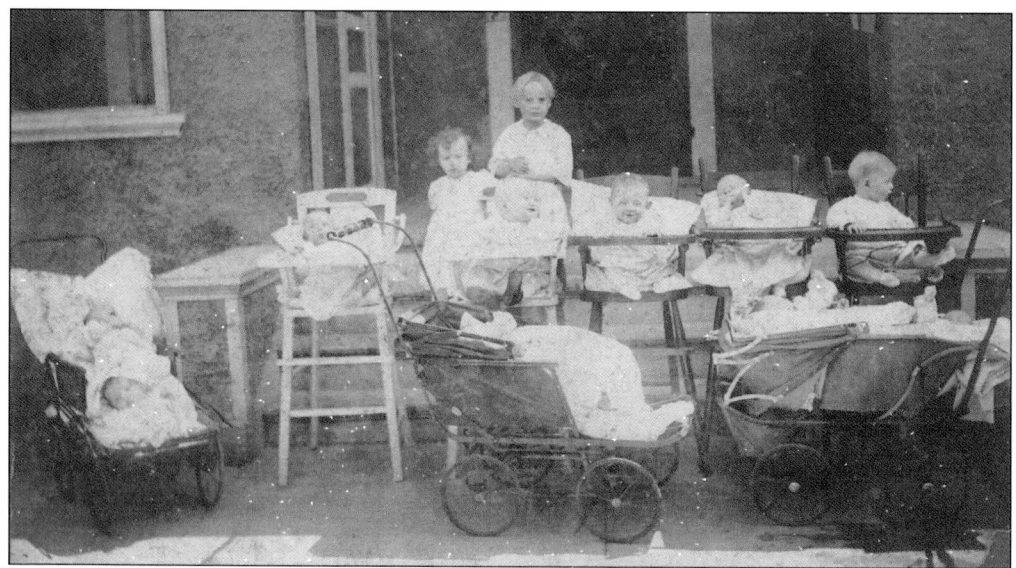

The *Chicago Tribune* printed a story in 1903 that included a photograph of a five-year-old boy named Timothy propped up in a bed, with the headline "5-year-Old Drunkard and Cigaret Fiend." The article went on to describe the boy, the conditions in which he suffered, and his alternating violent temper and listlessness. The children above are outside for some fresh air. (Courtesy of Woodstock Christian Life Services.)

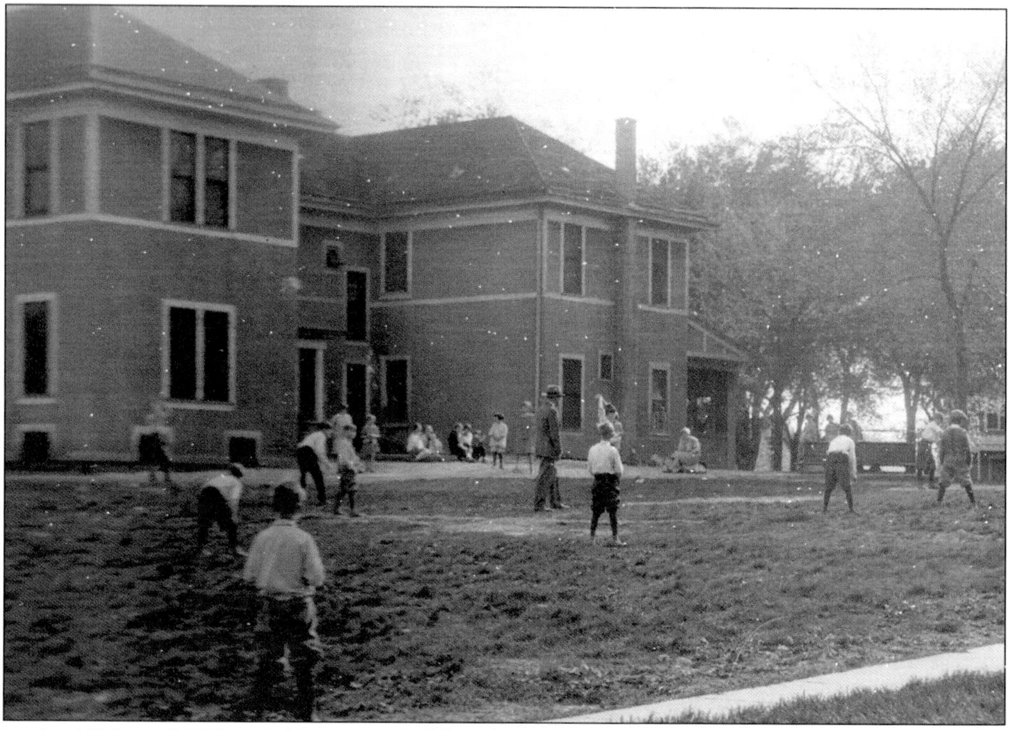

In the 1920s and 1930s, children were held at the Industrial Home for Children until foster care could be found. From the 1930s on, most children were placed in the home by the courts and continued to live there as wards. (Courtesy of Woodstock Christian Life Services.)

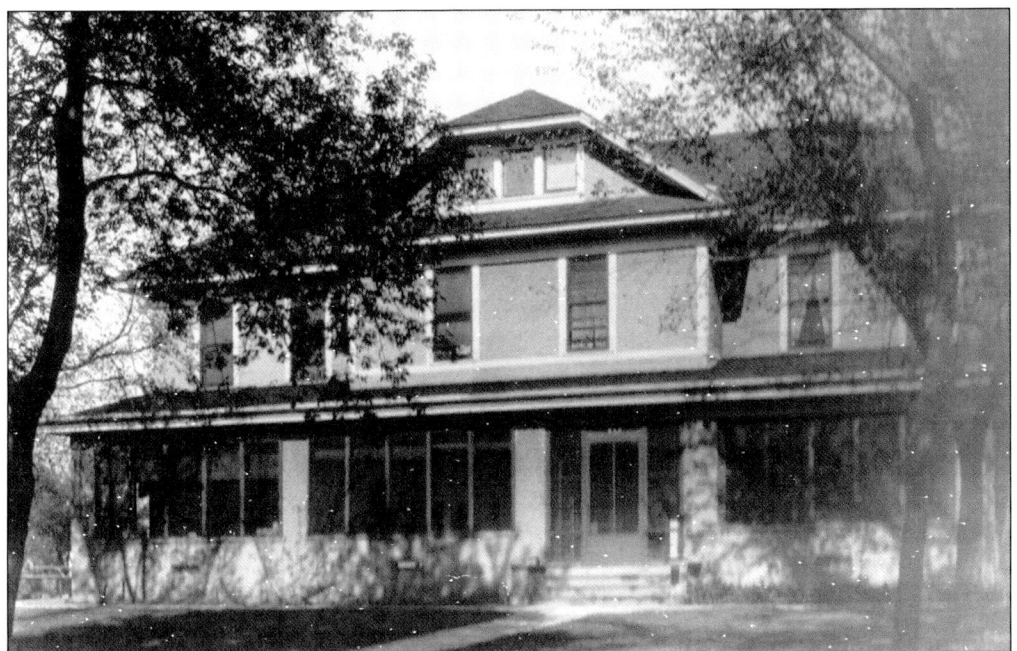

Charitable donations were critical to the operation of the children's home. The Industrial Home for Children was one of the institutions the Chicago Federated Charities gave funds to. In 1924, W. P. Tuttle donated money to build an annex. (Courtesy of Woodstock Christian Life Services.)

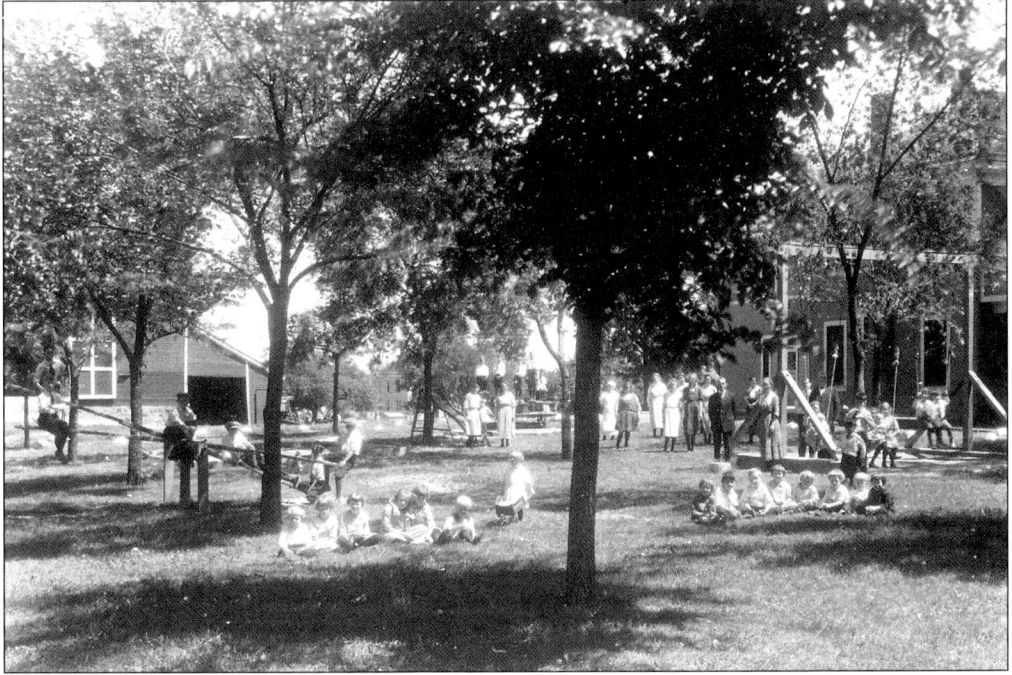

Before W. S. McConnell died, he requested that his friends give the money they would have spent on funeral flowers to the Industrial Home for Children instead. In his memory, the playgrounds were equipped with swings and slides. (Courtesy of Woodstock Christian Life Services.)

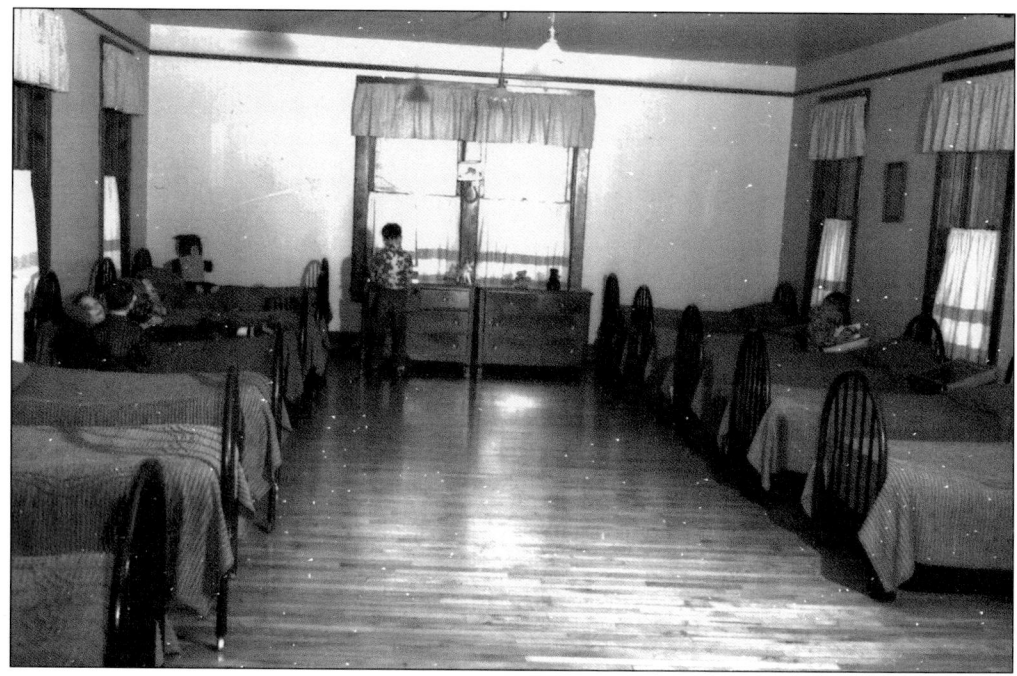

In 1942, there were 42 children residing in the huge gray stucco house surrounded by spreading elm trees and gardens. The girls' quarters had apple green bedspreads, while the boys' rooms were painted sky blue. (Courtesy of Woodstock Christian Life Services.)

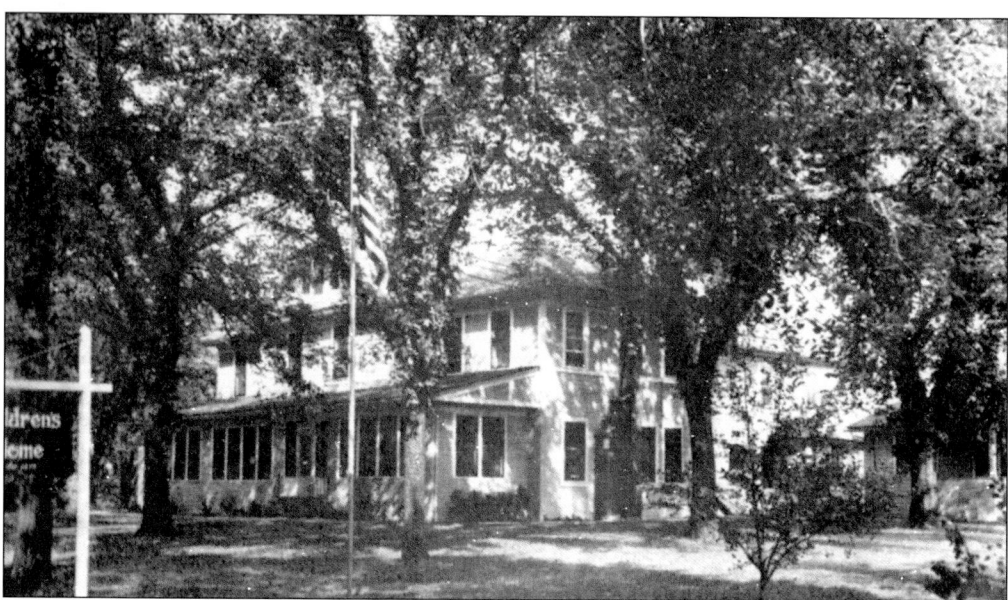

The name of the institution changed to the Woodstock Children's Home in 1950, as most of the children living there were from McHenry County. In 1956, Woodstock resident Nellie Harrison left enough funds in her will to purchase the Todd School athletic field and Grace Hall. Following renovations, Grace Hall was renamed Harrison House and was opened as a coeducational unit for high school–aged youth. Before Harrison House, older children were transferred to other institutions.

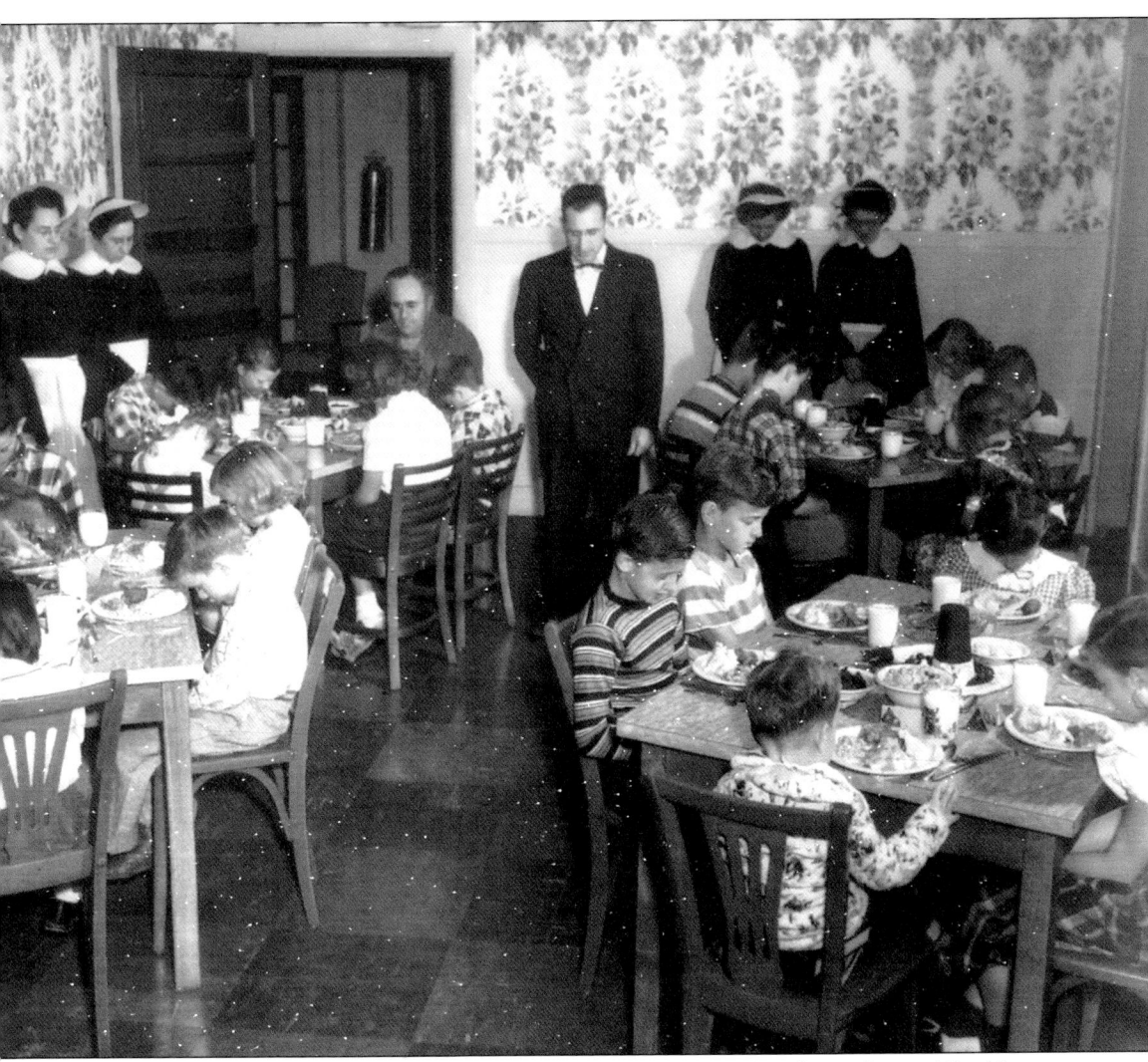

In December 1936, the children heard what sounded like a canary. Employee Oscar Allred later heard the noise and discovered a small gray mouse. He captured it in a jar, but it escaped when he attempted to transfer it to a wire cage. Superintendent Herbert Gensch was summoned, and the two men chased the mouse around; Gensch caught it, but the mouse ran up his shirt sleeve. From there, it dropped down in his shirt and crawled around at his belt line. The mouse was finally captured. The children named it Mickey until later determining that it was actually female. Minnie, as the mouse was then called, was invited to sing on the radio. Her appearance on newsreels caused protests from the Free Methodist Church, with which the children's home was affiliated, so Minnie was turned over to the Woodstock Civic Club. She earned $500 from her appearance on the *National Barn Dance* show and at least $500 from other appearances. This money was turned over to the children's home. Minnie died approximately two years after her discovery. (Courtesy of Woodstock Christian Life Services.)

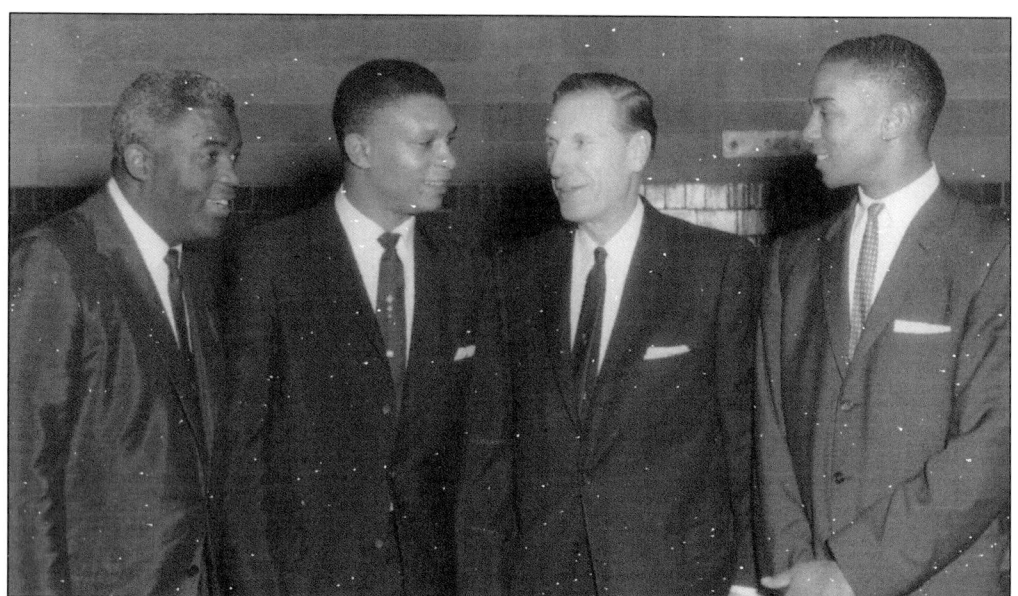

In the 1960s, the Woodstock Children's Home was licensed by the Illinois Department of Children and Family Services. Two-thirds of the financial support for the home came from child care sources; the remainder was raised through donations. Various fund-raisers were held, including the event attended by Jackie Robinson (far left), George Baker, and Ernie Banks (far right) shown above. High school coach Tony Roskie appears second from the right. (Courtesy of Woodstock Christian Life Services.)

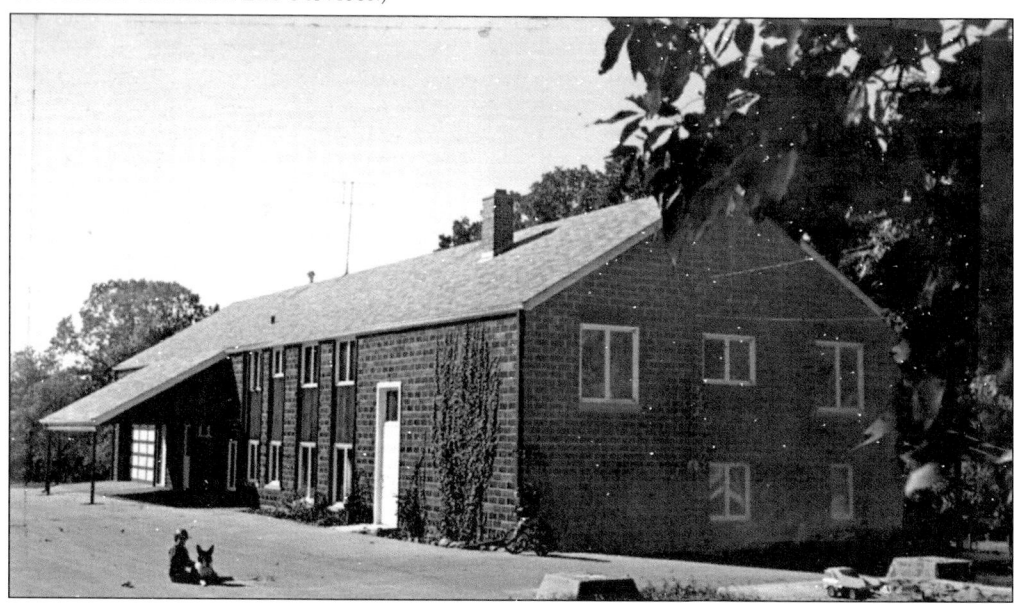

The facilities of the 1960s included the main building, Harrison House, an administration building, and a staff house. Any child between the ages of 6 and 16 who was mentally and physically well, and not habitually delinquent, could be admitted. In 1966, the Graham property on Kishwaukee Valley Road was acquired and remodeled into a modified home-style arrangement known as Kishwaukee Cottage. The institution closed in 1980. (Courtesy of Woodstock Christian Life Services.)

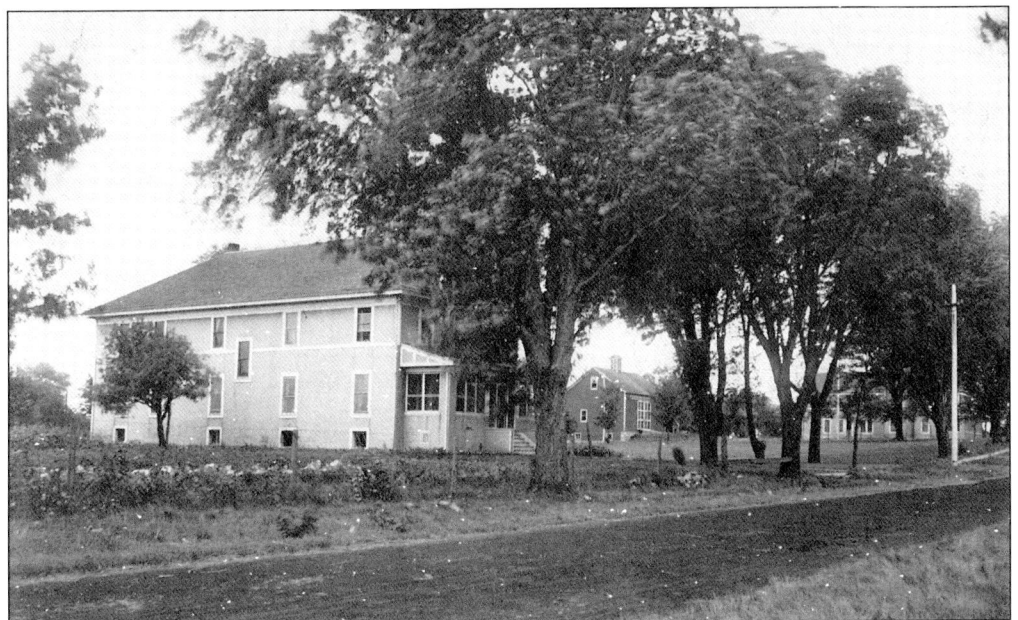

In 1903, Chicago Industrial Home for Children superintendent John D. Kelsey became interested in the care of the aged and founded the Old People's Rest Home on the 15-acre James Allen property, north of the children's home. Kelsey subdivided the property into 40 lots, platted as "J. D. Kelsey's Addition to Woodstock." Income from the development helped to finance the new facility. (Courtesy of Woodstock Christian Life Services.)

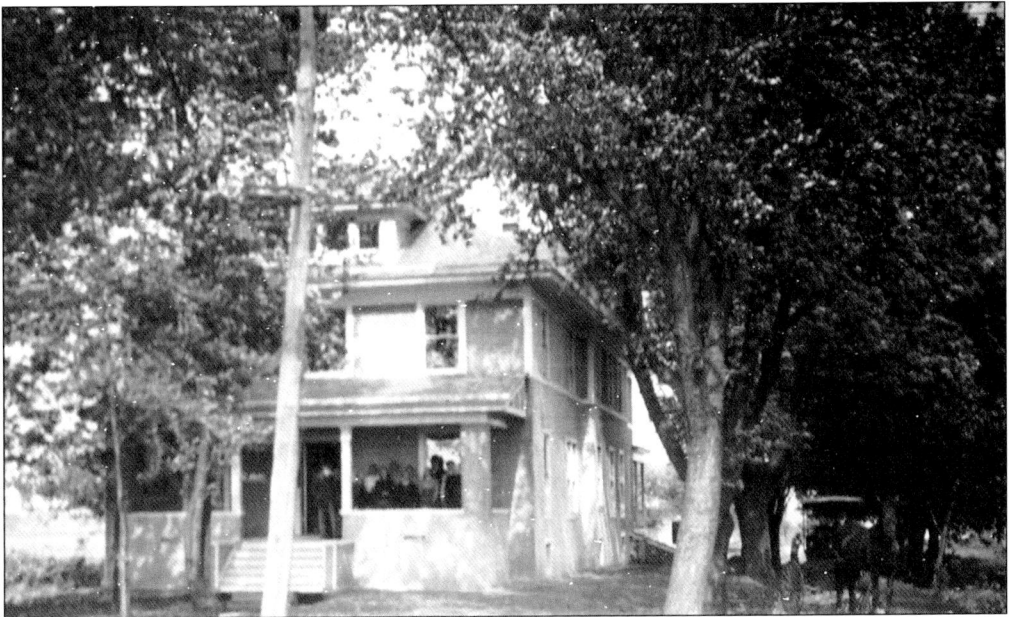

Kelsey's goal was to provide a Christian home for the aged and infirm of both sexes. The atmosphere of the home was to be cheerful and without the coldness of institutional life. Required upon entering the home was a payment of $500, an amount that would ensure good care during life without further expense. The original structure was named the Kelsey Building. Two additions were added in the 1920s. (Courtesy of Woodstock Christian Life Services.)

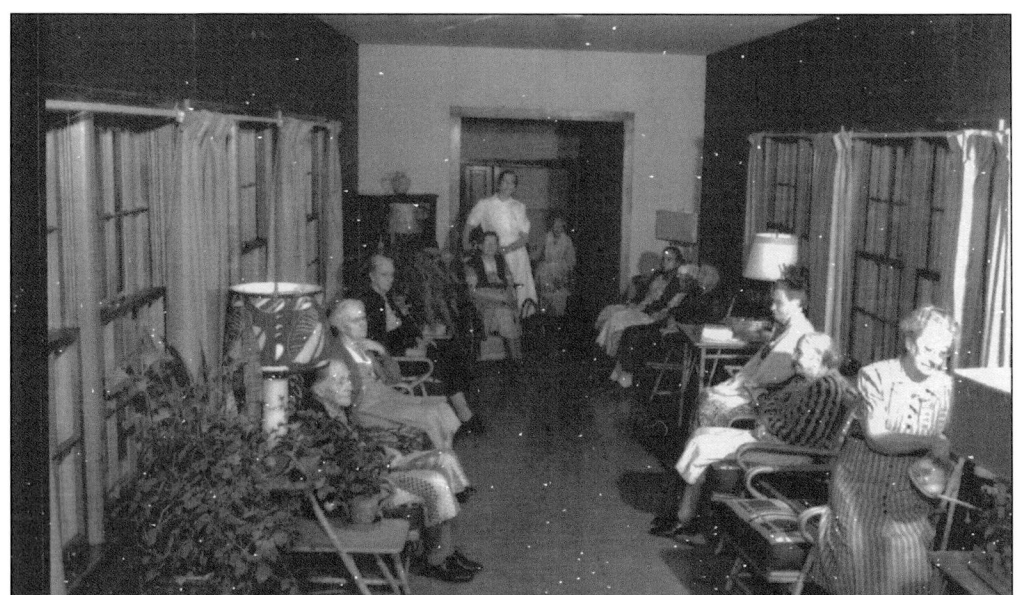

A three-story brick building, connected to the Kelsey Building by a solarium, was constructed in 1950. It increased the capacity of the home from 22 to 55 residents. Cottage units for couples were started in 1953, and quadruplex apartments were constructed in 1964. In 1973, a new wing with more skilled nursing care, a new dining room, and a guest room to accommodate overnight visitors replaced the Kelsey Building. The name was changed to Sunset Manor in 1959. (Courtesy of Woodstock Christian Life Services.)

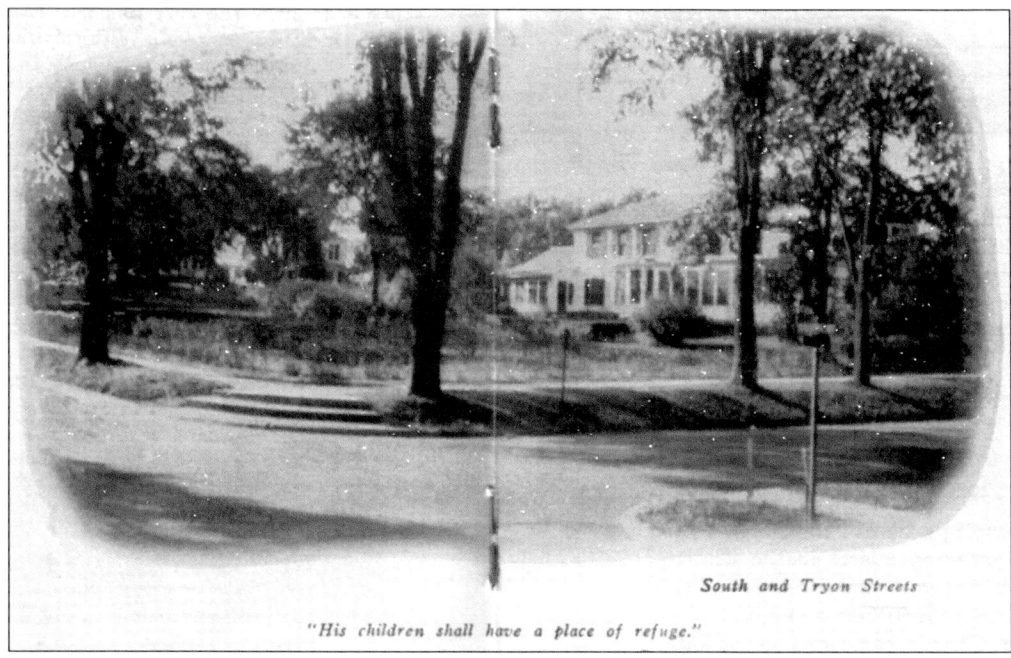

Home-based elderly housing also existed in Woodstock. Probably the best known, the Crosby Rest Home was located on Tryon Street between South and Calhoun Streets. Elizabeth Crosby bought the home in 1921. For those who only desired rest, quiet, and study, the annex was a block away from the main building. (Courtesy of McHenry County Historical Society.)

THE WOODSTOCK HOSPITAL
WOODSTOCK, ILLINOIS

Telephone 953   Open to the Public   Located one block north of the C. & N. W. R.R. on Clay St.

Modern Hospital accommodations at home, near relatives and friends. Away from the noise and confusion of the city.

Special attention given to Surgical and Obstetrical cases. No contagious or insane cases admitted.

Information regarding any case upon request

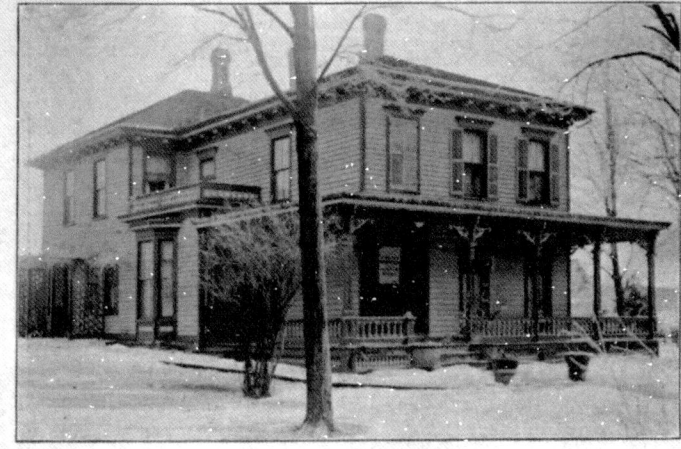

THE WOODSTOCK HOSPITAL

A Well Equipped Operating Room Adds Much to the Safety of the Patient

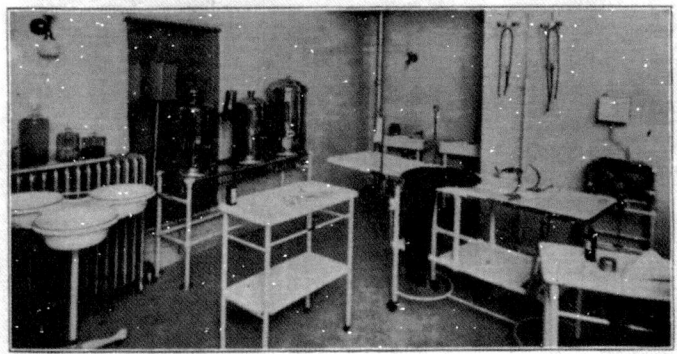

The Hospital is equipped with the most modern electro-therapeutical appliances including static, galvanic-faradic and high frequency currents, vibratory massage and the X-Ray. X-Ray diagnosis and skyographs made for the profession.

OPERATING ROOM

RATES, $15 Per Week and up. The fee of the attending physician or surgeon is distinct from the hospital fee.

Visitors Welcome. Visiting hours 1 to 5 and 7 to 9 P. M.

Woodstock's first hospital, standing on the west side of the 400 block of Clay Street, was founded by Dr. J. E. Guy in 1906. Privately owned, it was unavailable to people who could not pay, and admittance was refused to contagious or insane cases. Special attention to surgical and obstetrical cases was advertised. In 1912, Dr. Hyde West took over the hospital and continued to operate it as a private facility. The Woodstock Public Hospital Association was formed in 1914 to organize a public hospital. With doctors serving on the founding committee, this effort was more successful than previous attempts. The association acquired Dr. Hyde's private hospital, hired private nurses to run the facility, and opened the doors to the public.

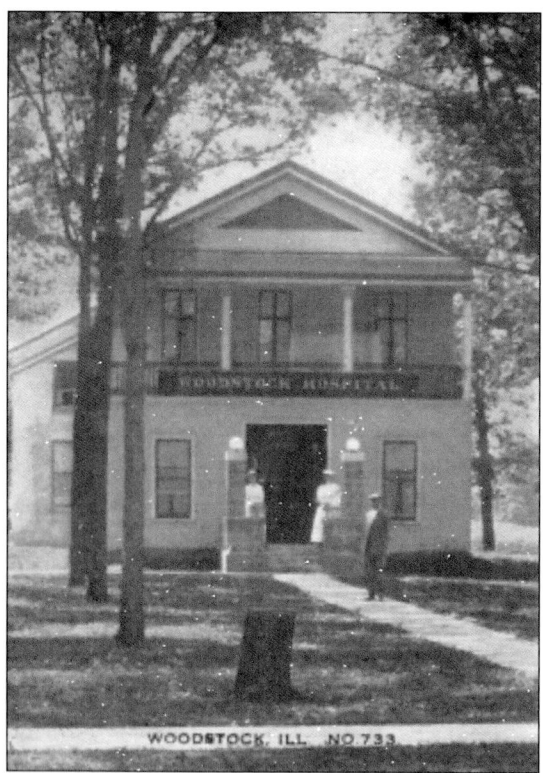

On January 4, 1915, the old homestead of the late judge Theodore Murphy on South Street was purchased and converted into a 15-bed hospital. In 1922, a 10-night stay cost a patient $30 in room charges, plus $10 for the operating room, $10 for anesthetic, $1.50 for dressings, and 50¢ for paper supplies.

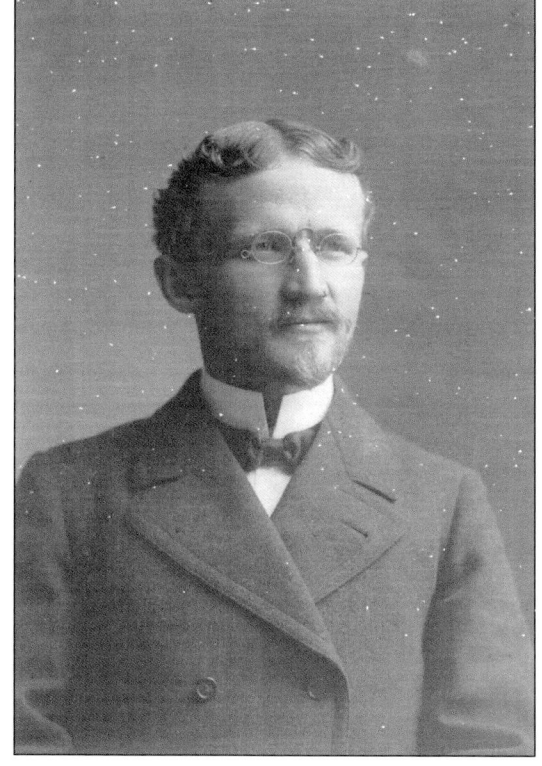

Dr. Emil Windmueller, an early supporter of a public hospital, served on the Woodstock Public Hospital Association Board of Directors. A graduate of Rush Medical College who moved to Woodstock in 1894, he reportedly delivered more babies in town than any other physician of his day. In 1922, while attempting to repair an X-ray machine, he received an electric shock that left him unconscious for several hours and perilously close to death. (Courtesy of McHenry County Historical Society.)

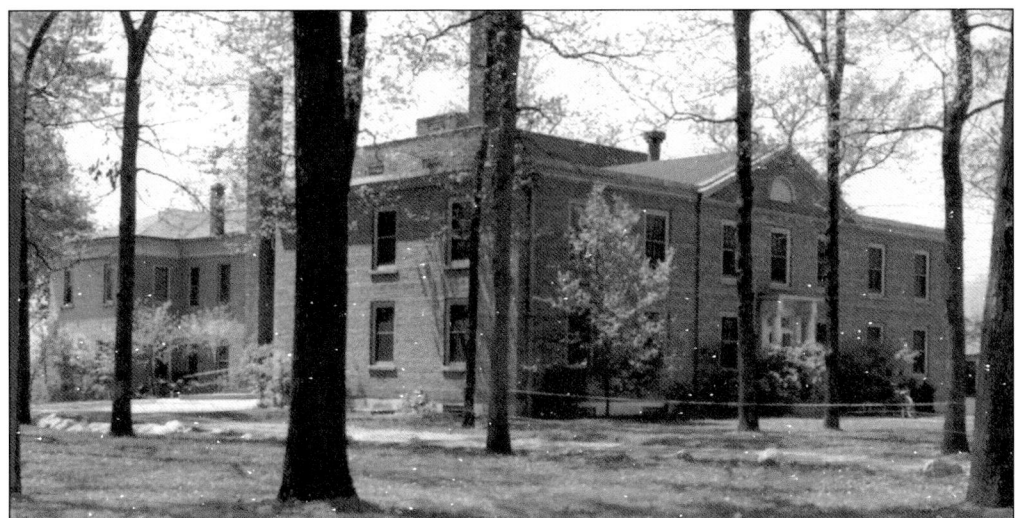

Several major additions were constructed on the South Street hospital. In 1937, Dr. Bentley Harrington and his wife, Julia, donated funds that allowed the construction of a 20-bed expansion. Following World War II, the name was changed to the Memorial Hospital of McHenry County to honor the men and women who had served in the armed forces. (Courtesy of McHenry County Historical Society.)

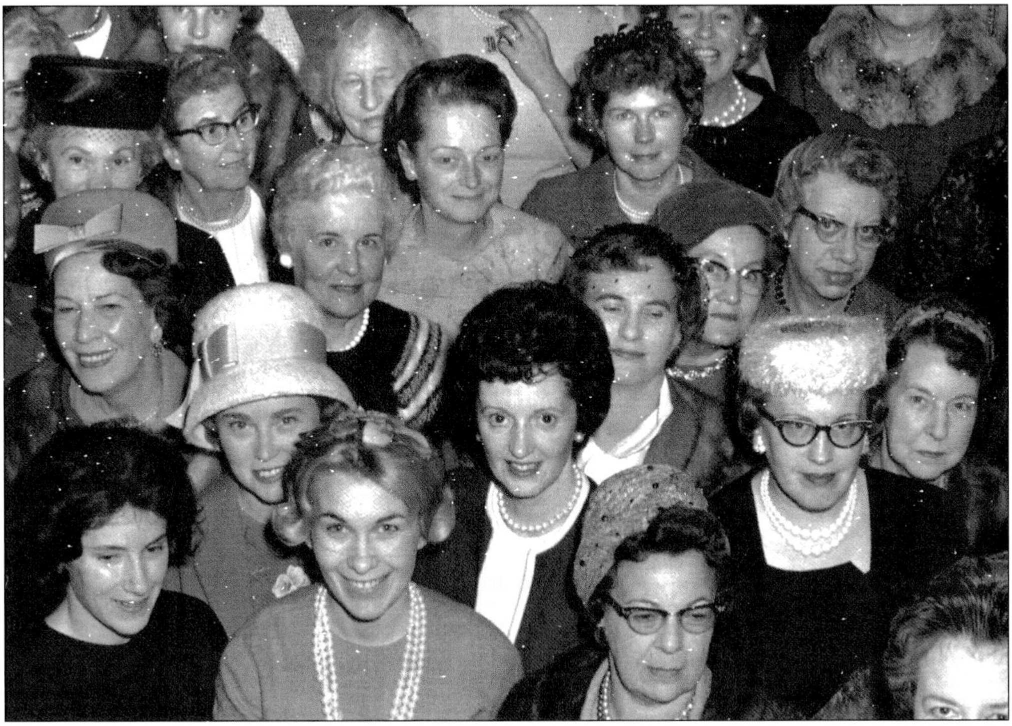

In 1940, the hospital purchased the adjoining Kellogg property and converted the residence into nursing quarters. The building eventually became the Women's Hospital Auxiliary Thrift Shop. The women's auxiliary was organized to make patient stays more comfortable and to provide both volunteer service and fund-raising support. Members are shown in this photograph. (Courtesy of McHenry County Historical Society.)

Discover Thousands of Local History Books Featuring Millions of Vintage Images

Arcadia Publishing, the leading local history publisher in the United States, is committed to making history accessible and meaningful through publishing books that celebrate and preserve the heritage of America's people and places.

Find more books like this at
www.arcadiapublishing.com

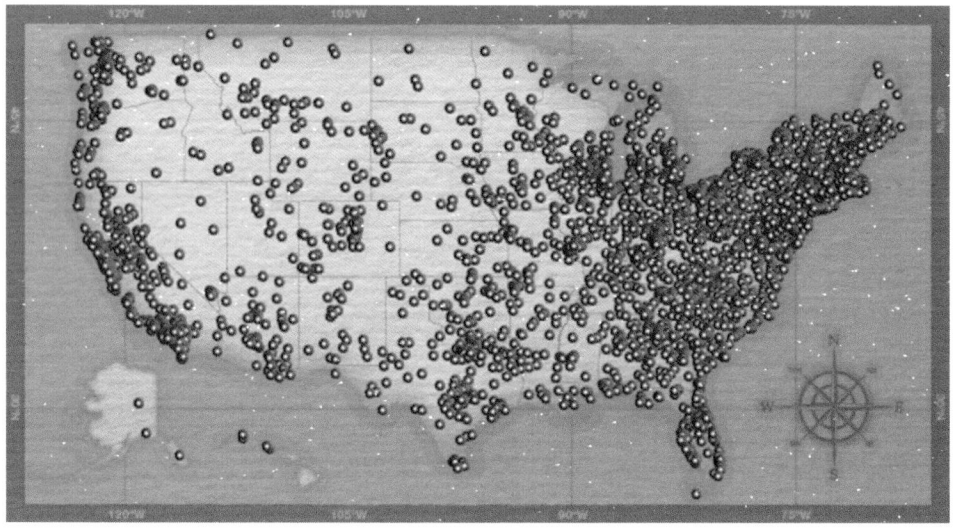

Search for your hometown history, your old stomping grounds, and even your favorite sports team.

Consistent with our mission to preserve history on a local level, this book was printed in South Carolina on American-made paper and manufactured entirely in the United States. Products carrying the accredited Forest Stewardship Council (FSC) label are printed on 100 percent FSC-certified paper.

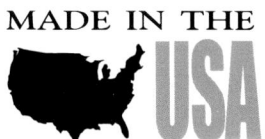